# THE MURDERER AND THE TAOISEACH

Harry McGee is a political correspondent with *The Irish Times* and previously worked for the *Irish Examiner*, the *Sunday Tribune*, RTÉ and the current affairs magazine *Magill*, which he edited. He has written and presented TV documentaries in English and Irish for RTÉ and TG4, and he produced the podcast series *GUBU* for *The Irish Times*. A native of Salthill, Galway, he is a graduate of the University of Galway and the King's Inns. *The Murderer and the Taoiseach* is his first book.

# THE MURDERER AND THE TAOISEACH

**Death, Politics and GUBU –
Revisiting the Notorious
Malcolm Macarthur Case**

# Harry McGee

HACHETTE
BOOKS
IRELAND

First published in 2023 by Hachette Books Ireland

Copyright © Harry McGee

A CIP catalogue record for this title is available from the British Library.

ISBN 978 1 39971 859 2

Typeset in 12.5/17pt Sabon LT Std by Jouve (UK), Milton Keynes
Printed and bound in Great Britain by Clays, Elcograf S.p.A.

Hachette Books Ireland policy is to use papers that are natural, renewable
and recyclable products and made from wood grown in sustainable forests.
The logging and manufacturing processes are expected to conform to
the environmental regulations of the country of origin.

Hachette Books Ireland
8 Castlecourt Centre
Castleknock
Dublin 15, Ireland

A division of Hachette UK Ltd
Carmelite House, 50 Victoria Embankment, EC4Y 0DZ

www.hachettebooksireland.ie

# Contents

To Fiona and our daughter Sadhbh.
*Agus i gcuimhne ar mo mháthair agus athair.*

# 1

# THE MAN WITH THE BLUE
# HOLD-ALL BAG

"I did not wish anybody to know that I was in Ireland."
Malcolm Macarthur

The man with the blue hold-all bag arrived in the coastal town of Dún Laoghaire, Dublin, on a pristine summer's day in 1982. He was tall and slim, with dark curly hair and a bronzed complexion. The date of his arrival – 8 July – marked the beginning of a long dry spell that would last until mid-August, making it a rare and memorable rain-free summer in Ireland.

The skies had cleared of recent showers. By mid-afternoon, the mercury rose to 22 degrees in this busy ferry port, with its two distinctive parallel piers jutting into Dublin Bay. Dún Laoghaire was thronged with visitors for whom the weather provided an opportunity to sail, stroll, queue for ice creams or sip pints of beer under Harp Lager umbrellas at seafront bars.

The bathing areas were full of people swimming, sunbathing, or watching the nearby passenger ferries glide slowly in and out of port. The grassy verges of the seafront promenade were lined with deckchairs. Boys wearing satchels and brandishing evening newspapers slalomed the deckchairs, their cries of "Herald, Press" competing with the squawking seagulls swooping overhead. The headlines in both papers told of a no-confidence vote challenging the fragile minority of the Fianna Fáil government of Taoiseach Charles J Haughey. His administration had been tottering since its formation the previous February. Relying on the support of independent TDs, it had been lucky to survive until the summer.

Summertime pop music seeped from transistor radios through open shop doors onto the town's main shopping drag of George's Street. The Bagatelle hit 'Summer in Dublin' was barely off the airwaves and perfectly captured that July's sweltering mood, even referencing a bus trip to Dún Laoghaire.

The striking dark-haired man who slipped into the town that day did not arrive on a bus but on one of the ferries that periodically docked in the southside port. Head bent low, he mingled in the crowd that streamed from the terminal building, their bags bulging with duty-free loot. In their wake followed a snake-like line of cars and trucks. Boys from the nearby council estates raced down to meet the ferries as they docked. There was money to be made in "tacking" – carrying the bags of older passengers from the building to the train station or the bus stop – for a tip of 20p or so.

The man, who was in his mid-thirties, continued on foot up the hill towards the town centre and on along George's

Street until he came to a guesthouse at number 79. It was an Edwardian building set back from the road. The décor of the guesthouse itself was also of another vintage, faded and a little dowdy, with busy wallpaper, well-trodden carpets and shared bathrooms. It was cheap and that suited the man. He was met at the reception by the owner, an elderly woman called Alice Hughes. He registered under a false name, John Eustace.

It was an ordinary transaction, except in one respect. Most of those who lodged with Ms Hughes stayed for a single night. They were passengers who'd either disembarked from late-night ferries or were catching early ferries the following morning. With a minimum of conversation, the man, who was crisply spoken, paid in cash for two weeks' lodging in advance. She did not think twice about it. The man was mannerly and seemed ordinary enough.

The events that would follow over the next two long, hot weeks of summer, however, were far from ordinary. Forty years later, their ripples still pulse in the water.

From this inauspicious boarding house, the man with the blue hold-all bag would launch an audacious and outrageous plan to get rich quick. By any rational judgement, the plan was delusional. What he himself would come to see as a "cold-hearted operation" was also marked by incompetence, alongside detachment from reason.

Fitting, perhaps, to a man for whom fiction and reality were, it would transpire, readily interchangeable. From esteemed Cambridge academic to man of limitless independent means, the personae of Malcolm Daniel Macarthur – once familiar of the Dublin bohemian scene – were built on lies and deception.

3

The reality that Macarthur did not dare face was that this once-rich son of a land-owning Meath family was secretly on his uppers, a significant inheritance all but squandered. Now, in the long, hot Dublin summer of 1982, he began a desperate venture to restore his fortune and prevent his mask of deception from slipping.

The events that followed would lead to the loss of two innocent young lives in brutal circumstances, and on to a series of incredible fallouts that would shake the summer out of its peaceful somnolence. The debacle would end up – literally – at the doorstep of the government of Ireland's controversial leader, Charles J Haughey, dragging him into an international scandal caused by a man he had never met and did not know.

The only phrase that fully captures this is the unfortunate one coined by the taoiseach himself at the time: "Grotesque, unbelievable, bizarre and unprecedented."

Or shortened to its infamous acronym: GUBU.

# 2

# THE FLANEUR

"To them, Malcolm, with his polished behaviour, cultured
accent, academic ways and plenty of money, must have
seemed like Prince Charming to Alice in Wonderland."
Bartley Dunne, pub owner

Just as he did on that hot Dún Laoghaire day in 1982,
Malcolm Macarthur seems to have spent his whole life
appearing out of nowhere.

It was in February 1974 when he first walked into Bartley
Dunne's pub in Dublin city centre, heart of the city's
bohemian scene. The pub had probably the most eclectic
clientele in Dublin, yet even so, the new customer stood
out. The male fashion trends of the time were flared jeans,
acrylic pullovers and long hair. Bucking the trend, Macarthur
looked like he had walked straight out of *Murder on the
Orient Express*. His favoured wardrobe consisted of tweeds,

bow ties, silk cravats, polished brogues and raffish polka-dot pocket squares.

He knew nobody in Bartley Dunne's save for one customer, Victor Melia, a Trinity College mathematics lecturer whom he had bumped into in Cambridge the previous year. He had arranged to meet Melia there without knowing very much about the bar or its reputation. Very quickly, it would become a familiar haunt to Macarthur.

Dublin at that time was a city on its knees. There were large areas of dereliction and poverty, especially in the densely populated flats and tenements of the inner city, where a heroin epidemic was on the cusp of taking hold. Modern container technology and a new port closer to the sea had turned the north quays and south quays into a zombie zone. For much of its run from Liberty Hall to Dublin Bay, the Liffey was flanked by shuttered warehouses, the ghosts of a docklands that had once employed thousands of people. Close to the city centre, much of Temple Bar had fallen into dilapidation. The city generally had a shabby and run-down feel.

For all its air of melancholy neglect, beyond the frayed facades there was always merriment to be found. A vibrant traditional music scene revolved around pubs like O'Donoghue's on Merrion Row and The Cobblestone in Smithfield. When punk rock and New Wave came along in the late 1970s, a host of raw and exciting young bands arrived, including The Boomtown Rats, The Blades and U2. Punks with calf-high Doc Martens, safety pin piercings, and flaming mohawks paraded around the Central Bank on Dawson Street and the Dandelion Market at Stephen's Green.

Emily O'Reilly, a journalist who would cover the Macarthur

saga less than a decade later, recalls of that time in the city: "No matter how poor it was, there was always craic to be had. There was this lovely, wonderful journalistic, literary and political culture . . . around pubs like Toners, and Doheny and Nesbitts. Dublin, no matter how bleak and dreary, always had a very rich seam of interesting life being lived in the pubs and the bars."

Bartley Dunne's was tucked away on Stephen's Street, near the main southside shopping drag of Grafton Street. It was named after Bartley Dunne Sr who opened it in 1948. Now it was run by his suave trilby-wearing son, also Bartley, along with his brother Gerard. In a country where homosexuality was still illegal and heavily stigmatised, the pub, though of a mixed clientele, was one of a few haunts known for its open door to gay people – a bar where anyone and everyone was welcome, the more alternative the better.

The owners had tried to recreate a Left Bank Parisian bistro on the south side of the Liffey. The staff dressed formally: the bar staff in aprons, the waiters in stiff tunics. The music was a never-ending loop of French chansons, especially from Edith Piaf.

Malcolm Macarthur was 28 years old in 1974. His aura was unmistakably aristocratic, with his cut-glass accent and superior affectations – aloof, distant, not given to small talk. Many assumed he was titled, an Anglo-Irish lord or baronet of some kind. It was also generally believed he held a post-graduate degree from Cambridge University.

Although he was not titled, he was a wealthy young man. An only child, after his father died in 1971 Malcolm inherited the proceeds from the sale of his substantial family estate, Breemount in County Meath, with its grand Georgian mansion. His parents had separated nine years earlier and his mother no longer lived on the estate.

Macarthur lived in Breemount until 1974, when he moved into a spacious top-floor flat at 47 Fitzwilliam Square, an elegant three-storey ivy-clad Georgian townhouse in Dublin city. The flat had two bedrooms and was furnished with some period pieces.

Fitzwilliam Square was one of the best-preserved Georgian squares in the city, surrounding a pleasant, gated wooded park that was accessible only by residents. There were a small number of families living there, but most of the houses were set out in offices or flats, ranging from grand apartments, to cramped garrets with poor plumbing.

Macarthur used his inheritance to live the life of a flaneur, having successfully created an impression even among those close to him of being of high academic standing. His own mother, Irene, was convinced he had attended King's College Cambridge for three years and was now a member of the staff, interviewing prospective students and lecturing on political economics. Others believed he had a doctorate in quantum physics. None of it was true.

Macarthur's one degree was in fact obtained in economics at the age of 21 from the University of California, Davis. Now in his late 20s, Macarthur spent a lot of time visiting Cambridge's libraries, and researching matters that were of interest to him. But despite the impression he gave, he had no formal connection with any educational establishment, no thesis to complete, no postgraduate research to do. His inheritance allowed him time and space to become something of an autodidact who could speak with authority on a wide range of subjects including philosophy, astronomy and economics. He always seemed to be working on drafts of academic books which he planned to publish sometime in the future. To all who knew him, he looked every part the professor that he was not.

While Macarthur's appearance was extravagant, his personality was reserved to the point of introversion. He would not speak to people unless they addressed him first, and he only engaged if the topic of conversation interested him. He seems to have had an unusual combination of two seemingly conflicting tendencies. On the one hand, he often socially appeared withdrawn and cold to the point of rudeness; while on the other, he was deeply attracted by Dublin's artsy social life.

"I'm quite sure that when he went to live in Dublin in 1974, he had extreme difficulty in making friends," recalled his mother, Irene Macarthur. "One must remember he had no school pals, really, in this country, like one would have had if they'd been sent to a boarding school. He was also an only child and had no cousins in Ireland."

Despite his solitary, diffident nature, Macarthur threw himself into the bohemian Dublin scene. Bartley Dunne, the pub's owner, said he was a regular customer in his bar during the mid-1970s. He recalled Macarthur splashing the cash, especially on young women. "He was a man of expensive tastes," he said. "He would consort always with female company and in his early days coming here, he sometimes took a girl off to England for a weekend. On one occasion he took two girls over with him, ordinary Dublin girls with city accents," said Dunne.

"To them, Malcolm – with his polished behaviour, cultured accent, academic ways and plenty of money – must have seemed like Prince Charming to Alice in Wonderland."

Macarthur had a few short-term liaisons with young women, but none developed into anything serious. His mother Irene believed he was involved at one point with a married "titled lady", but also felt he was too shy and too inexperienced to be a womaniser.

His friend Victor Melia, the mathematics lecturer he'd meet in those early days in Bartleys, was a gay man in his 60s, and fulfilled the role of "point man" for most of the bar's clientele: he was a walking telephone directory and kept the names, addresses and numbers of his wide circle of acquaintances in a pocket notebook. Macarthur was straight but shared a passion with Melia for astronomy, which they discussed when they met.

Over time, as he got to know other clientele in the pub, Macarthur began to get invitations to house parties and soirées. Some were spontaneous affairs, arranged on the spur of the moment to extend a night's drinking. Others were elaborate, catered affairs in swish houses. Macarthur was not a big consumer of alcohol and, lacking in social confidence, he tended to hang around the periphery, saying little. When he did attempt conversation, it didn't always come off.

One such exchange occurred with a female acquaintance at a party one night. Out of the blue, he proposed marriage to her, saying they should have a son. They would raise him to the age of seven and then abandon him, just as he had been abandoned at that age. She didn't know whether he was joking but came away with a distinctly uncomfortable feeling.

His odd nature was not lost on those around him. "I think the best way you could describe him is as a loner who did not seek out company and was not inclined to idle conversation," said Bartley Dunne. "You got the impression talking to him that he really didn't want to listen, that he only replied as a means of ending the conversation. There was something eccentric about his whole manner, even the way he walked."

During that year, Macarthur was regularly seen on the Trinity campus in Dublin city centre, or sitting by himself in bars, bookshops or cafés, his head buried in a book. The impression he gave to the world was of a loner, a poser, an outsider and a flaneur.

1974 was also the year Malcolm Macarthur met with his future partner and mother of his son. On the face of it, Brenda Little was everything that he was not. A young working-class woman from Finglas in north Dublin, unlike the solitary Macarthur, Brenda was one of nine children, seven boys and two girls. Her father, William, was an army man who had retired early because of the onset of arthritis, and the children had a strict upbringing. Unlike the distant Macarthur, Little was garrulous and full of empathy.

Now 22 years old, Brenda had finished with formal education when she left secondary school. After this she had gone to London with a school friend for an adventure. She worked in a number of casual jobs; the longest-lasting was a stint at hand-painting pottery. She returned to Dublin in 1971, aged 19, and tried a variety of jobs to make ends meet. One position was in the office of a contracting company on

Richmond Road in Drumcondra. She moved on to a part-time job as a hairdresser on Wicklow Street. She also sold raffle tickets in between jobs to make ends meet. Her interests were far removed from the succession of short-lived humdrum jobs she flitted between. In her spare time, she began going to art-house movies, which could only be seen in film clubs which used venues like schools and parochial halls. She was also developing a nascent interest in opera.

Attractive and fashionable, Little socialised in Dublin's most bohemian bars and hung around with an eclectic mix of poets, musicians, actors, artists and people from the gay scene. She belonged to a set that was regularly invited to openings and to fashionable parties in the well-to-do southern suburbs.

One of her closest friends was Paddy Connolly, a well-known Dublin barrister and man about town. He was 45 when he met Little by chance in 1972 on the streets of the capital. She was selling raffle tickets in aid of a residential home for underprivileged children in Oldtown in north County Dublin. Connolly stopped in his tracks. He was from Oldtown and was also a trustee of the charity.

Intrigued, he struck up a conversation with the young woman. He was utterly charmed by her. Before he left, he bought tickets worth £5. It was an extravagant gesture, the equivalent of €100 in today's money. He gave her his number and arranged to meet up with her again.

That singular coincidence marked the beginning of an unwavering platonic friendship between Paddy Connolly and Brenda Little that was to last a lifetime and survive extraordinary vicissitudes.

The pair began to meet regularly. They shared an interest in opera and film. They joined the Dublin Film Society. It showed arthouse and foreign-language films, including some that would have been considered risqué or avant garde. Because it was a members-only club, the society could show films without them being scrutinised by the notoriously conservative film censors.

Almost 25 years Little's senior, Connolly relished her company despite the age difference. She was direct and unpretentious in conversation. In her dealings with people, she judged everybody according to their own lights. Little's honesty was one of the qualities Paddy most liked about her. She had no hesitation pointing out barristerial pretentiousness on his part – his own brother, Tony, conferred him with the nickname 'Lord Dalkey', alluding to both his upper crust accent and his expensive tastes.

Connolly and Little often met up in city centre bars such as The Bailey, Bartley Dunne's and the swanky Shelbourne Hotel. She also liked to go with her friends to Mooney's on Harry Street. Nowadays called Bruxelles, Mooney's was a neo-gothic pub known for its live music and as the place where Phil Lynott and Thin Lizzy first cut their teeth in the late 1960s.

It was there that Brenda first met Macarthur at a live music gig in the autumn of 1974. The force of her personality quickly cut through his air of distance and arrogance and the pair hit it off. Macarthur was smitten. He invited her to dinner and they started seeing each other. Within a few weeks they had moved in together.

Little soon introduced Macarthur to her friend Paddy

Connolly and gradually Connolly warmed to the younger man, with whom he found it difficult to connect in the beginning.

"The first predominant impression is one of shyness," Connolly later observed. "But also a person of considerable courtesy and what I would describe as impeccable manner.

"He was a little withdrawn and aloof. If you became engaged with him in an intellectual topic, he would open up to become a very good conversationalist and companion. The sort of man you would be interested to have at a dinner party or at a cocktail party in which intelligent conversation was appreciated."

In late 1974, Little and Macarthur moved to London and began to travel extensively, in England, Scotland and Europe. In early 1975, they moved back to Dublin and into the two-bedroomed flat on Fitzwilliam Square. Little was pregnant at this stage but neither agreed with marriage. A son, Colin, was born that autumn. He was not baptised. Although Macarthur had been brought up a Catholic, he was by now an atheist and a humanist.

The somewhat distant relationship Macarthur had with his mother had continued into adulthood and he only visited her twice during 1974 and 1975. At this stage, his parents had split up and Irene was now living about half a mile away at an apartment at her friend Norman Potterton's grand house, Freffans.

Irene knew nothing of her son's partner's pregnancy, and hadn't even met Brenda Little in person by the time Malcolm arrived at her home, unannounced, in December 1975 with two-month-old baby Colin. Irene was astonished to find out that the baby was her son's. When she asked if it was a boy or a girl, Macarthur replied matter-of-factly: "It is a boy, of course."

It was some time yet before Irene and Brenda did finally meet, and her first impression of her son's partner had more than a shade of the dowager duchess about it. "She is totally opposite socially to everything Malcolm stands for," she said.

Whatever the differences in social background, the relationship between Macarthur and Little was described by those who knew them as very close. Macarthur was very involved with Colin's upbringing. He and Brenda spent much of their time at home with him. It resulted in a marked change in their lifestyles: Malcolm and Brenda pulled back almost completely from the pub and party scene. Over the next six years, Macarthur rarely visited Bartley Dunne's and, when he did, it was only to buy a bottle of expensive wine from its cellars.

On one such visit, at a time when Colin was approaching school-going age, the pub owner, Dunne, struck up a conversation about the boy's education. Macarthur told him he was educating Colin privately.

Dunne, who himself had teenage children, queried that choice. "I asked him if it was not unfair to the boy, being deprived of the company of other children at a normal school. He said the child would get a very good upbringing."

Macarthur himself had been educated privately at home until he was eight, as had his parents. With his wide breadth of reading and study, he considered himself better equipped than anyone else to teach his son. Perhaps borne from his own experience of his school years, he also had a dislike of formal structured education.

In 1976, the couple and their child stayed for almost six months in Florence and Milan and spent time on the Riviera. According to accounts of friends and relatives, Macarthur and Little were devoted to their son. "That child was their project," Irene Macarthur recalled. "When they travelled abroad, which they did extensively, they would use separate modes of transport, one going by plane and the other by boat, in case anything would happen and the child would be left parentless."

It would become apparent in time that Macarthur, the doting parent, did not extend empathy or thought to the devastation he would wreak so grievously on two other sets of parents, less than a decade later.

# 3

## FALL FROM FORTUNE

"For the past two years my finances have been diminishing.
This is something I could not cope with." Malcolm Macarthur

By the late 1970s, Macarthur's inheritance was dwindling. Investments he'd made in the previous years had all been disastrous and he was burning through hundreds of pounds each month. With mounting debts, he began to borrow money from his mother.

He told Irene that he was experiencing delays in accessing money from his inheritance which he had invested in banks in France and Belgium. "There seemed to be this shortage of money," she said. "I understood that he invested money in some French bank. He said to me that he was only little fry and, therefore, he would have to wait. I would assume it was something to do with the socialist government over there. He would have to wait until the bigger people were paid. If there was any truth in that I just can't answer."

It was a cockamamie story, but she seemed to buy it.

"It was always, 'I'm only borrowing it off you and I'll be giving it back to you when I get my own money,'" she added.

Irene's own mother, Queenie Murray, had long since moved to Dublin from County Meath where the Murray family had, for centuries, owned large swathes of land amounting to over 1,000 acres. She now lived in a large house on Iona Drive in Glasnevin. When she died in 1981, she left a considerable inheritance, the residue of the once vast Murray estates, to Irene. She left the Glasnevin house to Macarthur. However, it was left to him in trust, as a means of minimising inheritance tax. He, Brenda and Colin moved in there in early 1980 and lived there until he cajoled his mother into selling it in 1981. To do this, his mother had to agree to break up the trust set up by Queenie for him. Malcolm received £10,000 from the proceeds of the sale.

Again, it was a considerable sum, the equivalent of over €100,000 in today's terms, but the money was much needed. As he waited for funds from the house sale to be drawn down, he badgered Irene for more money. She would resist at first but invariably relent.

By this time, Brenda's old friend Paddy Connolly was a senior counsel. He was unaware of the couple's precarious financial situation, having always assumed Macarthur to be a very wealthy man. Connolly had recently bought a penthouse apartment in Pilot View, an upmarket gated development in the well-to-do coastal Dublin suburb of Dalkey. The lease on his flat, Sleepy Hollow, at 4 Seaview Terrace in Donnybrook, still had at least another year to run and he decided to retain it. It was a well-appointed basement flat in a grand Georgian terrace in Dublin 4. The Victorian novelist Anthony Trollope had lived in the house next door soon after the terrace was built in the 1850s.

When Connolly moved to his new southside home in Dalkey, he told the couple they and their child could stay in the flat in Donnybrook. It was to be a temporary arrangement. Brenda had told him they were thinking of moving abroad and he suggested they take his flat in the meantime. Typically generous, he insisted they pay no rent. It would otherwise have lain empty, he told them.

Brenda Little had a flair for design and helped fit-out Connolly's impressive new coastal apartment, which extended over the top floor of the block and had a balcony with splendid views over Bulloch Harbour.

She, Malcolm and six-year-old Colin remained in the Donnybrook flat for nine months, rent-free. During the spring of 1982, Little began to make plans to move to Tenerife with a view to staying there for an extended period of time. She knew that her partner had periodic financial problems, but he assuaged her concerns with blandishments that his money was tied up in investments in Zurich or Liège. Still, she was conscious that they needed to budget over the medium-term. One of the reasons she chose the Canary island of Tenerife was because of the reasonable cost of living, as well as the weather, which would be helpful for their son's childhood eczema.

As far as Irene Macarthur was concerned, the sale of the house in Glasnevin had sorted her son's financial difficulties.

"The last money I gave him was in December 1981. It had to do with the sale of our house. There was no question of looking for more money because he was going out to Tenerife and I understood he would be collecting some money from the French bank.

"There was no question of him coming back [from Tenerife], and he never asked me for money. If he had asked me for money I would have given it to him. He knew that very well."

What neither she nor Brenda Little knew was how desperate Macarthur's financial situation really was. He was now down to the dregs of a once substantial inheritance and he was quickly running out of options.

If Macarthur were to settle anywhere in Tenerife the natural place would have been the capital, Santa Cruz. Situated to the north of the island, it still had vestiges of its colonial past. There was a British club where tennis, bowls and croquet were played. The biggest draw for an ex-pat was the British Library in Santa Cruz, which housed the biggest collection of English-language books in the non-English-speaking world. Such a place would have provided ample grazing pasture for the bookish Macarthur.

Instead, though, the family booked a cheap package holiday in the resort of Los Cristianos, where Brenda had holidayed previously. It was located in the sparse, treeless volcanic landscape of the south of the island, about 80 kilometres from Santa Cruz. Once a fishing village, the 1970s had put paid to that. Dozens of multi-storey hotels and apartments had been built along the seafront. Along with nearby Playa de las Américas, Los Cristianos had essentially become an industrial estate for mass tourism, serviced by a new airport, Tenerife South, operating since 1978.

The family's one-bed apartment in Torres del Sol was part of a large development built in the 1970s. The complex was dominated by two 15-storey towers, painted in inescapable brown and yellow. The apartments themselves were compact, sparse, and functional. There were two swimming pools, and it was close to the beach.

The landscape of the south was arid, and so was its cultural life, which was dominated by pubs and restaurants serving English breakfasts, and fish and chips. If sunbathing was not your thing, there was very little else to do.

Macarthur, Little and Colin stayed in apartment B705 throughout June and into July of 1982. While Brenda and Colin happily mingled with other holidaymakers on the sun-saturated beaches, Macarthur spent most of his time either in the apartment or walking up and down the seafront. He was constantly fretting about money.

Occasionally he would pick up British newspapers that could be bought in the town, often a few days after publication. That summer there were regular reports of armed hold-ups of banks and post offices carried out by the Provisional IRA in Ireland. All had been successful.

The news stories planted an idea in Macarthur's head. He began to formulate a fantastical plan to restore his fortunes. He conceived it as a means of getting easy money, quickly. He would need to return to Ireland, procure a lethal weapon, and stage a hold-up.

Early on the morning of 6 July 1982, Macarthur left the holiday apartment in Torres del Sol for the airport. He paid the rent for the apartment in advance and left Brenda Little enough money for two months. He told her he was going to Ostend in Belgium to encash investments he had made. He said he'd return in two or three weeks.

Instead – and unbeknownst to Little – Macarthur boarded a plane that took him to London. He then took a train to the ferry port of Holyhead, and on the morning of 8 July, he docked in Dún Laoghaire. It was less than two months since he'd left Dublin. He was armed with a plan that would free him from his interminable money worries. He had come from wealth and from privilege. This gambit would restore him financially, allowing him to keep the status to which he was entitled. If it was to work, however, he would need to invent himself again: this time as a ruthless bank-robber.

For that, he would need to get his hands on a gun.

# 4

# A BEARD, A FISHERMAN'S HAT, AND A CROSSBOW

"He looked a bit weird." John Monks, news vendor, Dún Laoghaire

Amongst the first to notice the new visitor to Dún Laoghaire was young newspaper seller John Monks. From Roscrea in north Tipperary, the 22-year-old had drifted into Dún Laoghaire the previous year and had worked at various casual jobs around the town, including as a night porter at the Royal Marine Hotel.

By day Monks worked at a newspaper stand on George's Street, just down the road from the lodgings that Macarthur had booked into for two weeks. Over a number of days, Monks observed the man who visited his stand daily. He was someone he had not seen before around the area, and there was something off about him. His dress style alone made him stand out. It was mid-summer with almost continuous sunshine. Yet the stranger's garb was a beige military jumper with patches on the shoulders and sleeves, a fisherman's hat with a distinctive orange feather, and thick reading glasses.

"I know 80 per cent of people in Dún Laoghaire, and you spot strangers," Monks recalled. "When I first saw him, he was in the process of growing a beard. He looked a bit weird."

Another quirk was that he pulled his glasses "up on his brow" to read the papers.

"I thought he might have been on the run or living rough. He certainly looked like that. He never talked much, only to say hello, and then he'd try to read the papers with those glasses.

"Every evening he picked up the *Evening Press* and checked through the small ads. When he didn't see what he wanted, he put it down and got the *Herald*."

What Monks was observing was Macarthur scanning the papers for guns for sale. He would only buy the *Evening Press* if there was something in it of interest, but he always got a copy of *The Irish Times* and *Evening Herald*. However, getting his hands on a gun was proving difficult for the would-be bank robber. He was unsure as to how to proceed. Macarthur's whole life had been lived on an elevated plane. He lacked an iota of knowledge about the criminal or paramilitary worlds. While he continued to pursue finding a gun, he was also brewing other plans – to create a proxy one.

On 9 July, the day after his arrival, Macarthur had taken a bus into Dublin city centre where he headed to Garnetts and Keegan's, a fishing tackle and shooting shop on Parliament Street. There he purchased, for the not inconsiderable sum of £22, a 'pistol crossbow' – a small crossbow with an internalised cocking mechanism that can be held in one hand, designed for target practice or for shooting small game.

Over the next few days, Macarthur bought more equipment: a square-head shovel in Murdochs, a hardware store in Dún Laoghaire; and a lump hammer, which he purchased in Lenehans on Capel Street in Dublin city centre.

Back at his guesthouse in Dún Laoghaire, Macarthur cut part of the barrel off the crossbow and used a soft, pliable filler material to fashion it into the shape of a realistic-looking gun. Once the filler hardened and he painted it black, it looked pistol-like. He even added a sight.

His surgery meant the crossbow was no longer a weapon, merely a replica, but it did now look like a real pistol. Studying it carefully, Macarthur was not satisfied it looked real enough. It was, to all intents and purposes, a glorified toy gun. He turned his sights again to finding a real one.

On the afternoon of Friday, 16 July, he left the guesthouse with the hammer and mock firearm stowed in his blue holdall bag. He also brought the shovel he'd purchased, wrapped tightly in black plastic to carry in his other hand, having first taped the shovel's sharp cutting edge.

Now sporting a short beard, and wearing his signature disguise of military jumper, fisherman's hat, and glasses, Macarthur travelled on two buses to the village of Swords in north Dublin. He then walked over two miles to the Balheary Clay Pigeon Shooting Club. The club's grounds were in a rural area, on a protected green corridor directly north of Dublin Airport. The club had a modest clubhouse and a shooting area surrounded by grassy banks. The predominant sounds when the shoots were in session were of the clay traps being released, the two rapid discharges from the shotguns and – every few minutes – overhead jets rumbling in and out of the nearby airport.

The club's shoot would not begin until the following morning. Arriving a day early gave Macarthur time to reconnoitre the site. That night, he slept in the open. A newspaper report, published months later, claimed he placed sausages on his square shovel and cooked them over an open fire. An embellishment, perhaps.

Macarthur arrived back at the shooting grounds in the early afternoon on Saturday, 17 July. Dr William Irwin, a club member, said he stuck out like a sore thumb.

"He actually spent most of the afternoon sitting on a seat [at the edge of the grounds]," Irwin said. "He would occasionally wander into the clubhouse and look at the scores and results and then come out again.

"He took my notice because of his unusual stance and his dress and the fact that he was carrying a form of handbag that appeared to have a long object."

Des Foley was another member of the club. A tall, broad-shouldered man who had starred for Dublin in both football and hurling, Foley was also a former TD who was politically close to Taoiseach Charles Haughey. Foley had taken part in one of the competitions that day and was packing up for the evening.

While he shuttled back and forth from the clubhouse collecting equipment, Foley left his gun lying against the bonnet of his car in the car park. Macarthur sidled close to the car, but Foley returned before he had a chance to swipe it. Macarthur then tried to strike up a conversation with him.

But Foley didn't like the cut of this stranger's jib and stood his ground near the bonnet of his car, staring at him. The conversation soon dried up and Macarthur sloped away, leaving a distinct impression on Foley and others who saw him.

Later that evening, Macarthur travelled eight miles, likely on foot, to the village of Ashbourne in County Meath, just across the Dublin county border.

Another clay pigeon club was holding a similar event the next day, Sunday, at Archerstown on the outskirts of the village. Macarthur stayed that night in the Ashbourne House Hotel. He left the following morning after breakfast without paying the bill.

He arrived at the meet in the same odd get-up and repeated the routine from the previous day, loping around the grounds without engaging with anybody. As on Saturday, after a fruitless and futile afternoon, he left the meeting empty-handed and boarded a bus back to Dublin and on to his Dún Laoghaire lodgings.

On the afternoon of Tuesday, 20 July, as was his well-established ritual by now, Macarthur walked from the guesthouse to the nearby newsstand operated by John Monks on George's Street. He leafed through the classified adverts in the *Evening Press* and there he finally found the ad he was looking for: a shotgun for sale in Edenderry, County Offaly, that would suit his purposes ideally.

He bought the paper and made a call from a nearby phone box. It was answered by a young woman. Macarthur said he was interested in buying the gun advertised. "It's for you, Dónal," the young woman called out to her brother.

A young man, Dónal Dunne, came to the phone and told

Macarthur that the gun was a Japanese-made Miroku shotgun.

Dunne gave Macarthur instructions on how to get to the house. Macarthur told him he would travel up on the Thursday evening, 22 July. His plan was finally coming to fruition. Now he just needed a car to make the journey.

# 5

# BONFIRE OF THE VANITIES

"The difficulties of the present are temporary and something to be overcome." Charles J Haughey, 23 July 1982

**21 July 1982, Galway**

The counting of votes was still going on at the Temperance Hall in Loughrea, County Galway, when Charlie Haughey's driver nosed the black state Mercedes out of the car park.

As they travelled east from the town, they counted the string of bonfires that blazed along the side of the road. This was a rural tradition, whereby victories were celebrated by setting bonfires. The villages and towns of east Galway were alight with them: Kilrickle, Cappataggle, Aughrim and Ballinasloe.

Haughey was in jubilant form. He had spent most of the previous week in the Galway East constituency canvassing in a by-election caused by the death of one of his own Fianna

Fáil TDs, Johnny Callanan. After a bitter and heated campaign, the party's candidate, 30-year-old Noel Treacy, had triumphed, being elected on the first count.

After months of political trials and tribulations, it looked like things were finally turning Haughey's way. In a moment of undisguised relief, he shook his fists in victory when told by his tallymen that Treacy was certain to win.

The political stakes could not have been higher for Haughey going into that by-election. The demise of his predecessor, Jack Lynch, seemed to be repeating itself with Haughey. Lynch had lost two by-elections in his native county of Cork three years previously, in 1979. At that moment Lynch knew his time as taoiseach was at an end; that one morning he would come out on deck to see a plank being readied on the starboard side. Lynch decided he would preclude such a showdown by stepping down early.

Haughey had already lost one by-election in 1982 in Dublin West. If he lost a second, he too would be a goner. Noel Treacy's victory in Galway East had steadied the ship and ensured Haughey's survival.

Charles James Haughey was at the pinnacle of his political career in 1982. At 57, he was, indubitably, the most colourful and controversial Irish politician of the late 20th century. He was a natural politician: full of charisma, with a formidable presence. He had been an exceptional minister in the justice and finance portfolios earlier in his career.

From the time of his boyhood in a poor household in north Dublin, Haughey was marked out for greatness. His academic brilliance, his leadership qualities, as well as his over-vaulting ambition, were apparent from an early age.

His flaw, however, was a major one. He wasn't trusted. Naturally secretive, a plotter, Haughey was regarded by many as lacking integrity. There were good reasons for people's suspicions – from the unexplained source of Haughey's vast wealth to his cloak and dagger tactics on the political pitch.

There was no half-way house with Haughey. He provoked responses that were visceral and tribal. He was either revered or reviled, depending on which side of the divide you were on. His detractors forgave nothing. His supporters forgave everything.

The nearest you can get to capturing the totality of Charles Haughey is John Randolph's famous put-down of the 19th-century US politician Henry Clay: "So brilliant. So corrupt. Like a rotting mackerel by moonlight, he shone and stank."

In Irish politics, 1981 and 1982 were marked by instability and churn, with three elections in the space of 18 months.

In July 1982, Haughey was determined that the mistakes leading to the loss of a by-election in Dublin West would not be repeated in Galway East. All of the party's representatives were ordered to go to the constituency for the last week of the campaign. Haughey himself visited every hamlet and village from Tuam in the north, to Eyrecourt and Peterswell in the south. He shook thousands of hands, slapped countless backs, bought pints for strangers in rural 'spit on the floor' pubs. He clambered up on the backs of lorries, or on tractor trailers, to make speeches outside rural churches and community halls.

"Give us that old Fianna Fáil loyalty in Galway," he implored a large crowd outside the church in Glenamaddy. Again and again, he summoned up de Valera's visit to East Galway 50 years beforehand to establish what became a Fianna Fáil heartland.

On the Sunday before polling, Haughey travelled by helicopter to Tuam in north Galway and promised that the imperilled state-run sugar factory in the town would be safeguarded into the future. On the same day, the Connacht football final was being played in Tuam Stadium. That game was a big occasion in the west of Ireland, as it involved the traditional kingpins of the province, Galway and Mayo.

Haughey's rival, Fine Gael leader Garret FitzGerald, arrived early into the town with a large campaign team. He shook hands with spectators as they went into the stadium. Fine Gael were pulling out all the stops. The party chartered a single-engine plane that flew over the stadium, trailing a banner proclaiming: "Better to Back Burke", referring to Ulick Burke, the Fine Gael candidate.

Not to be outdone, Haughey succeeded in getting on the pitch along with the candidate, Noel Treacy. He walked diagonally across the grass, waving to the crowd in the courtly manner of a British royal. He then positioned himself strategically in the front row of the stand, flanked by Bishop Eamonn Casey, another prominent public personality destined to end his career in disgrace. (Eleven years later, in 1993, Annie Murphy – with whom Casey had had an affair in the 1970s – would go public on the existence of their child.) Meanwhile, back in the stadium in Tuam in 1982, Fine Gael's Garret FitzGerald had to content himself with sitting a few seats back behind Haughey and Casey.

At times, the campaign had been like a faction fight from the

19th century. There were physical clashes between supporters outside churches and in the main streets of villages. There were also allegations of dirty tricks made by both sides. The outcome had national relevance. In the end, Fianna Fáil prevailed. The hard graft had paid off. Haughey survived to fight another day.

For Haughey, that was all that mattered.

As he returned to his north Dublin mansion that Wednesday evening, 21 July, he was wholly oblivious to the coming storm. At that very moment, a man whom he did not know, whom he had never met, and whom he never would meet, was preparing to set out on a murderous spree that would make all Haughey's other difficulties seem as threatening as sprat swimming near a pier.

But in those glorious few days after Fianna Fáil's by-election victory, the headwinds of the previous months had stilled. On Friday, 23 July, Haughey attended a formal dinner in the Burlington Hotel in Dublin to celebrate his 25th anniversary as a TD. It was a glitzy affair. Just before the speeches, nine waiters walked in procession into the centre of the room, each carrying a baked Alaska, the classic 1980s dessert of ice-cream-centred meringue, doused with brandy and flambéed at the last moment. As the desserts burst into flames, the crowd ooohed and aaahed.

The atmosphere was celebratory. Haughey still glowed with the by-election victory when he addressed the Fianna Fáil faithful. Looking back over his quarter of a century in politics, he said: "There has been constant activity, one event following another, one battle following the next . . . The difficulties of the present are temporary and something to be overcome."

Little did he know what was barrelling down the track.

# 6

## THE FIRST MURDER

"I wanted this venture to succeed." Malcolm Macarthur

**Thursday 22 July, 1982. Phoenix Park, Dublin**
The glorious weather followed the pattern of the previous fortnight, with high heat and brilliant sunshine. It was still hot by the time a young nurse, Bridie Gargan, finished her shift at St James's Hospital in the late afternoon and headed for home.

Bridie was originally from County Meath and now lived in a flat in the Dublin suburb of Castleknock. One of a family of 11 children, her parents, Vincent and Brigid, ran a farm in the townland of The Riggins near Dunshaughlin. That bright evening, her father was saving the hay.

Bridie was 27 years of age, with short-cropped hair. She was well regarded by colleagues as a conscientious medic, with a warm, quiet, open personality. She had done well academically since she began training as a nurse a decade earlier, winning a gold medal for her performance in coronary care studies in the Richmond Hospital. Now she was three months away from qualifying as a midwife, her ultimate ambition.

She always looked forward to Fridays, when she headed back to the home place in County Meath as soon as she had finished work, to spend the weekend. She loved being home. A multi-instrumentalist, she enjoyed playing music with friends at traditional sessions at the nearby pub Swan's of Curragha, a converted forge. Bridie's other big interest was politics. She was secretary of the local Fianna Fáil branch, or *cumann*, in Curragha, the local branch of Ireland's biggest political party of the era. Her father, Vincent, was a senior officer with the party in County Meath and his passion for politics was shared by his children, especially Bridie and her sister Mary. Bridie followed current affairs avidly and loved debating politics with her family and friends.

On that Thursday evening, Bridie's journey back to her Castleknock flat took her past the Guinness brewery on St James Street, northwards across the River Liffey, and three miles along Chesterfield Avenue. It is the main road that dissects Dublin's Phoenix Park which, at 1,700 acres, is one of the largest enclosed city parks in the world.

It's likely that at some point, as Bridie drove through the park on that sultry late afternoon, she passed a man walking along the parallel joggers' path, sporting a tweed fisherman's hat, a heavy jumper, and a blue hold-all bag.

In the still-baking heat of early evening, the young nurse decided to take advantage of the fine weather in the lush and serene park surroundings. She drove past the roundabout in the centre of the park – with its extravagant monument depicting a phoenix – and continued towards Castleknock. However, about 300 metres further along, Bridie turned left off the main road and drove slowly down a lane that served as a service road to the back entrance of Deerfield, the lavish estate in the park which is the residence of the US ambassador to Ireland.

She did a U-turn on the narrow laneway and parked her silver Renault 5 on a grass verge, its bonnet facing out to the main road about 30 metres away. It was close to a defined path popular with joggers that ran parallel to Chesterfield Avenue for the entire length of the park. The grassy path was lined on either side by beech, chestnut and oak trees, all of which were dripping with greenery in the height of the summer.

Bridie walked a few paces to the longer grass at the edge of the path, so that she was not in the shade of a magnificent beech tree. In a quiet spot in the meadow, away from the crowds, she lay on her stomach, removing her top to expose her back to the sunshine.

After a long day's work, Bridie relaxed into the sweltering heat of the evening.

Earlier that afternoon, the man with the blue hold-all took a bus from Dún Laoghaire to Eden Quay near O'Connell Street in Dublin. He stood out from the crowd, in their light summer clothes, dressed as he was in a heavy military-style pullover and tweed fisherman's cap pulled tight over his forehead.

He stopped at Eden Quay to observe an art installation in

the middle of the river – a pontoon made to look like an island, with a large wooden pyramid at its centre. Inside the pyramid were mementos from the famous Theatre Royal, which had closed 20 years beforehand.

After lingering for 15 minutes or so there, he began walking along the north quays towards the Phoenix Park, some two miles upriver. It was hard going in the heat. Besides his heavy clothing, he was also carrying the shovel wrapped in the polythene, and the blue bag, which contained a lump hammer, rope, tape and the imitation gun that he had fashioned from the pistol crossbow.

At Parkgate Street, just before the park, he stopped at a shop to buy an orange and a bottle of water. He then joined the trickle of people walking uphill towards the park's front gates.

It wasn't Malcolm Macarthur's first time in the park that July. On 8 July, the day he had surreptitiously crept back into Ireland from Tenerife, he had gone there for a walk.

Later today, he was due to go to Edenderry, to meet Dónal Dunne and acquire the shotgun he had advertised for sale in the *Evening Press* two days previously. Edenderry was 60 miles away and it was now 4pm. He needed to get his hands on a car quickly if he was to make it on time.

Macarthur walked along the grassy joggers' patch, which ran parallel to Chesterfield Avenue. He stayed on the left side, passing the large obelisk of the Wellington Monument and the cricket grounds. Herds of deer grazed in the meadow grass nearby.

Macarthur came across a car parked in a field of long grass. At the side of the car, a mother was laying out a picnic for her young children. She looked up and to her surprise she saw a man crawling through the grass towards the front of the car. Startled, she cried out and her husband, who was lying nearby, quickly rose to his feet. On seeing him, the stranger sloped off through the grass back towards the joggers' path.

He stopped to take a rest at the Phoenix Monument roundabout, near the centre of the park. It was close to the gated entrance to the president's residence, Áras an Uachtaráin, the white porticos of which were – reputedly – the inspiration for the White House.

He had now walked over three miles since getting off the bus in Dublin. It had taken an hour, in temperatures close to 25 degrees Celsius. He was sweating profusely. Several people noticed the strangely attired man as he sat there in the middle of the roundabout, eating an orange and taking swigs out of his bottle of water.

Revived, he left the Phoenix Monument and continued his journey along the joggers' path towards Castleknock. Thirty or so metres away, on the main road that ran parallel to the path, the occasional car rumbled by. He walked close to the back wall of the park's other sumptuous white mansion with extensive grounds.

As he approached the back gate of Deerfield, and the narrow service road that crossed the joggers' path, he spotted a silver Renault 5 parked nearby. The driver's door was open. He could see somebody lying on the grass close to the car, but at that stage could not tell if it was a man or a woman.

He passed the car and then doubled back, hiding behind trees.

Unbeknownst to Macarthur, he was being watched. Inside the walls of the grounds of the residence, gardener Paddy Byrne had just finished hacking back some bushes near the rear wall. It was the end of his working day. He began walking towards his cottage, inside the back gate of Deerfield.

"I started moving back along the wall to my own house. I noticed the young woman sunbathing on the grass and noticed a man standing in the trees. I did not take too much notice. I kept walking along slowly."

It was then that he noticed something a little odd. The man was creeping from tree to tree like a pantomime villain. "I was near my own house when I saw him sneaking in behind where the car was parked and hiding behind a tree, looking around. And then I said to myself, this fellow is up to something."

He noticed the man's heavy clothing, so out of kilter with the hot day. He stopped and watched the man approach the woman lying on the grass near her car.

Out of his sightline, though, was the imitation pistol Macarthur produced.

Bridie Gargan couldn't at first take in what she saw: a man standing over her pointing what looked like a gun directly at her. "Is this for real?" she asked, sitting up and covering herself. She remained calm as he ordered her into her car, asking him if she could first put back on her top. The bearded man agreed and then bundled her into the back seat of the car. Her panic set in when he told her that he was going to tie her up. As Bridie started to struggle, her assailant reacted explosively, pulling a lump hammer from his bag.

Paddy Byrne had stopped to watch the couple get into the car. A few seconds later he noticed the car was shaking and knew there was something suspicious happening. He thought at first it might have been a row between a couple. However, from his vantage point, Byrne could access a good view of the inside of the car through its back window. What he saw next shocked him to the core.

"I could see him hitting her on the head with his fists and belting her. I could see he had her head held in his hand. Whatever way the sun caught the light, I could see her hair and all."

The act was conducted with remarkable speed and cold aggression. As soon as he realised what was unfolding, Paddy leaped over the wall and ran towards the car. He was a big, strong man but was not used to running at such speed. "By the time I got to the car I was out of breath. I shouted, 'What the fuck is going on here?'"

It was a two-door car. The man had lifted the driver's seat forward and had initially attacked the woman from the front. When he saw Byrne arriving, he squeezed himself into the back seat and tried to cover his victim's head with a newspaper that had been left lying there, before continuing his attack.

"There he was sitting sidewards in the back seat, and he had a paper around her and he had a lump hammer in his fist. I did not see it until I got near him, that he was hitting her with the lump hammer."

Macarthur jumped out of the car with the imitation gun in his hand and, with the look of a man possessed, pointed it straight at Byrne. "He said to me, 'If you don't get fucking back, I'll put a bullet through your head. Back off. Back off.'"

Everything slowed down for Byrne. A man was pointing a gun at him telling him if he didn't back off, he'd kill him. There may have been hundreds of people in the park, but the world was oblivious to this terrifying tableau involving only three people: a victim, a witness and a killer wielding a lump hammer and a gun.

Movement came from the car and the men looked to see the young nurse as she struggled to get up. Byrne recoiled. "There was a big, massive red stain around the side of the face and on her blouse," he recalled.

With the momentary distraction, Byrne seized his opportunity and grabbed the barrel of the gun, grappling with Macarthur for control of the weapon. Byrne was a bigger and stronger man. "We tumbled to the ground. My hands were sweaty with the tension and heat and I could feel that I was losing my grip on the gun."

Macarthur managed to regain control of it and again pointed it at Byrne, repeating his threat to put a bullet in his head.

"If it had been a real gun, and he had made a more successful attempt to block my escape, I may have shot him," Macarthur later said.

Afraid for his life, Byrne retreated, and while going backwards he stumbled and fell into a drain behind him that ran beside the joggers' path.

Seeing his chance, Macarthur jumped into the car, where the keys had been left in the ignition. He started it and sped off along the joggers' path. The young nurse lay supine in the back seat, grievously injured, bludgeoned to the point of death.

Byrne watched as the car raced along the dirt track towards the front of Deerfield, then turned right, leaving a fog of dust in its wake. Byrne ran out onto the main road, Chesterfield Avenue, and desperately tried to flag down a car.

# 7

# THE ATTACKER FLEES

"You see a lot of strange things in this pub but that was something else." Customer of Fingal House pub, Dublin

The Renault 5, with Malcolm Macarthur at its wheel, veered off the joggers' path, across a grassy patch, and then joined a road that ran south across the wide expanse of the park. He passed the man-made hillock on which stood the enormous white Papal Cross, where Pope John Paul II had said Mass to a million people only three years before.

Meanwhile, a park employee driving along Chesterfield Avenue spotted a furiously signalling Paddy Byrne and stopped. They soon alerted a security guard, William Carolan, at the front gate of Deerfield and yelled at him to ring the gardaí.

As Byrne and his colleague began driving around the park in search of the getaway car, Macarthur was making good his escape. Stuck in a low gear, he continued as fast as he could go towards the Islandbridge exit to the south. Its stone arches were narrow and could only accommodate one car at a time. A queue of cars had formed at the gate. By now, he was panicking. He tried an overtaking manoeuvre but found himself stranded in the lane for oncoming traffic. A Waverley ambulance travelling to St James's Hospital happened to arrive at the gate around the same time. One of the ambulance crew spotted the sticker for St James's Hospital on Bridie's car and, in a bitter twist of fate, on seeing a bloodied girl in the back, took the respectable-looking man to be a doctor responding to a medical emergency.

At that moment, Bridie Gargan, though badly injured, was still conscious. She managed to raise a hand to the window, leaving behind a smear of blood on the pane. Several motorists stuck in the queue spotted that poignant silent plea for help from a dying woman. But seeing the presence of the ambulance, they assumed all was in hand.

The ambulance driver signalled to Macarthur to follow and began flashing its blue lights. It gave him an escort through the evening traffic to the back entrance of St James's Hospital, where the young nurse had been working that very afternoon.

As soon as the Renault 5 reached the gates, however, to the ambulance driver's surprise, Macarthur did a U-turn and exited the grounds. He turned left and drove along the South Circular Road, speeding through Rialto village. He then stopped and took a sharp turn left into a laneway and abandoned the car along with his victim, who lay dying across the back seat.

Macarthur fled the car in a panic, grabbing his blue hold-all bag but leaving behind the lump hammer. He ran blindly back to the South Circular Road and continued towards town. As he passed Dolphin's Barn he tried, unsuccessfully, to hail down a bus. He was out of breath and slowed to a walk. Noticing that his beige pullover was soaked in blood, he dived into another laneway, took it off and threw it over a high wall. He shoved his fisherman's hat underneath some builder's rubble further down the laneway.

Back on the South Circular Road, he began jogging again, sure that the gardaí were going to pounce on him at any moment. He had to get off the streets. It was then that he saw what looked like a house with its door open. As he approached, he could see a stand inside the door. It was stacked with travel brochures.

Rita Brennan was finishing up for the day at Odyssey Travel in Rialto, when a man entered just before closing time, at 5.50pm. He was panting and sweating profusely, as if he had been running. Bearded and dressed in a white shirt and dark trousers, he was carrying a blue hold-all bag.

He said he was looking for information on a Magic Bus Tour, a strange request as the once-popular tours to a mystery destination in Ireland were all but obsolete by then.

The man asked for a glass of water and gulped it down. He requested another and then a third. He told Rita he had been running in the Phoenix Park and had forgotten to bring his salt tablets. It struck her as unusual that he should go running in an ordinary pair of trousers and shirt, but she kept her thoughts to herself.

It quickly became obvious that the bearded man, who seemed ill-at-ease and a bit hyper, had no interest in the Magic

Bus Tour. He ordered her to call a taxi for him, saying he needed to go to Blackrock, which was about 10 kilometres to the south.

She pointed to the street outside and said there were numerous buses passing in that direction from outside the door that could take him there just as easily. He insisted on her calling a taxi for him. With his crisp accent, she had an impression of someone who was used to ordering servants around. Sensing his unease, she agreed, but as she went to the telephone, the man ran out the door and jumped onto a bus that had just that moment pulled up. Rita Brennan could see that it was headed in the wrong direction and went to alert him, but it had pulled away from the kerb by the time she got to the door.

It was an odd encounter, but Rita didn't think too much more about it as she shut up shop and headed for home. As she went about her busy weekend, she was completely unaware of the breaking news of a vicious attacker on the loose.

At 6.25pm the same evening, soon after a dismayed ambulance driver had reported to gardaí the strange incident he'd just been party to, a teenage boy coming home from work took a shortcut. He spotted a car parked in the middle of the laneway with the driver's door open. As he neared the vehicle, he saw the red smears on the window and then spotted the bloodied figure in the back seat, a young woman lying unconscious. The teenager ran to the nearest house to contact emergency services.

It took a while for Macarthur to realise the bus he'd taken was going in the wrong direction, but he remained on the northbound number 19 until it reached its terminus at Finglas, a working-class suburb in the north-west of the city. His partner, Brenda Little, was from there and over the years he had been an infrequent visitor to her home in east Finglas.

There was a strip of shops behind the bus stop, including a grocer's, two take-aways and a bookmaker's. Macarthur went into the grocer's and bought a pack of disposable razor blades. He then entered the nearby Fingal House pub, a neighbourhood establishment with a local clientele, mostly men who had stopped in for a pint on the way home from work.

He stood for a while getting his bearings before walking towards the toilets. Bloodstains on his shirt were noticed by customers. "It was a girl pointed him out to me," said one customer later. "I was sitting at the door and she came and said, 'That guy's shirt is full of blood, just gone by there.' I could see blood on his shirt all right. I though he was probably in a fight somewhere, and that was that."

Macarthur went to the toilets and, using all three razors from the packet he'd bought, set about cutting off his beard. With no cream, soap, or even a mirror, he had to shave blind with dry blades, a process that took a long time and left many nicks.

While he was shaving, several customers came in, one of whom asked what he was doing.

"I went in to have a hit and a miss," the man later said. "He was standing at the urinal with his shirt tucked in and blood on it. He was hacking away at his beard.

"You know, it really caught me because he just looked at me and said something like, 'What are you looking at?' and I said, 'Nothing.'

"I stood with my back to him and I just couldn't go. I had to walk by him again. He was really going at it. You see a lot of strange things in this pub, but that was something else. It was scary."

Macarthur returned to the public bar, now clean-shaven but with visible nicks from the blade. He ordered a soda water and asked for change to call a taxi from the public phone.

The taxi came quickly, arriving at about 7pm, where Macarthur was awaiting it at the pub door. The driver was a young man in his 20s. Macarthur asked to be taken to town and then extended the run to Dún Laoghaire. The taxi dropped him off near where the mail boat departed from Carlisle Pier.

From there, Macarthur went directly to his lodging house on George's Street, not more than 500 metres away. He changed his shirt and headed out again. Under cover of darkness, Macarthur walked down along the long pier and threw the blood-stained shirt and his imitation pistol into the sea.

The following morning, he called Dónal Dunne, the man selling the gun, from a nearby phone box. He explained that his brother had been involved in a car accident the previous day, and he hadn't been able to make it to Edenderry as planned. He would go there at the weekend and rearrange a meeting, possibly on Saturday.

# 8

## MAN ON THE RUN

"It looks like the work of a madman." Chief Superintendent
Jim Brogan

Just after 5pm the previous evening, a phone call had come in
to Cabra Garda Station, situated north of the Phoenix Park,
putting an abrupt end to a quiet afternoon. The caller was
William Carolan, a security guard at Deerfield, the American
ambassador's residence in the park. In a state of near panic, he
recounted how a gardener at the residence, Paddy Byrne, had
just witnessed a brutal attack. A man had bludgeoned a young
woman around the head with a lump hammer. He had then
driven off in her car with the badly injured woman in the back
seat. A park employee had been driving on the main road of
the Phoenix Park when he saw Byrne frantically trying to hail
down a car. Both had driven to the security post, alerted

Carolan, and then gone in pursuit of the killer. They were still out searching for the assailant.

The desk sergeant immediately contacted the radio of the garda car for the area. Its driver, Sergeant Larry Nugent, arrived on the scene within minutes. At 5.25pm Paddy Byrne arrived back, along with Paddy Moore, the man whose car he had flagged down. They reported they had not been able to find the Renault 5 getaway car.

Byrne then described what he witnessed – the crazed attack and his attempts to wrest the pistol from the perpetrator. He gave a good description of the suspect: the fisherman's hat, the neat beard, the dark hair, the sallow skin and his 'posh accent'. He also noted the attacker's "mad, mad eyes".

Byrne took Sergeant Nugent to the spot where the attack had taken place. Nugent noticed there was a long object wrapped tightly in black plastic. He cordoned off the area to preserve the scene.

At about 6.30pm, a 'three nine' call, cop slang for a 999 call, was received at garda headquarters. A teenage boy had rung to say he had come across an abandoned Renault 5 in a laneway off the South Circular Road with an unconscious woman in the back seat. A Garda Murtagh from Kilmainham was the first garda to arrive. He saw, to his horror, that the young woman's face and clothes were extensively bloodied. An ambulance arrived shortly afterwards to take the victim to hospital, where she was immediately placed on life support.

The senior officer in Cabra Garda Station, Chief Superintendent (CS) Jim Brogan, was fully briefed on what had occurred. He had no doubt in his mind about the gravity of the attack that had just taken place. "It looks like the work of a madman," he later told a reporter.

Within an hour of being alerted to the attack in the park, CS Brogan had contacted Detective Superintendent (DSI) John Courtney, at Garda Headquarters. Courtney was from Annascaul in west Kerry, and a 35-year veteran in the force. Tall, with impassive features and side-swept grey hair, Courtney cut an imposing figure. He had a gruff manner and a reputation for being as hard as granite with suspects, but also with his own detectives.

Courtney had joined the force as a 19-year-old in 1947 and was now the head of the investigations unit of the technical unit. In practice, he was the head of the force's murder squad.

A controversial policeman during his career, he had a reputation as an investigator who was tough, dogged and incredibly thorough, but whose interrogators were sometimes accused of using excessive methods to extract confessions from suspects. Courtney had taken charge of many major cases by then, including the investigation of the IRA murder of Lord Mountbatten and three others in a bomb attack on Mountbatten's boat in Mullaghmore, County Sligo, on 27 August 1979.

By 7.45pm that evening, a full investigation was underway. Teams of detectives were already in the Phoenix Park, in Rialto and at Richmond Hospital where the critically ill woman had been transferred. An incident room was set up at Kevin Street Garda Station the next morning.

One of those called in immediately was Tony Hickey, a detective sergeant with the murder squad. Hickey, who was from Killarney, County Kerry, had joined the force in 1965. He had gained a reputation for tenacity and for having a flair for dealing with criminals and for solving crime.

Hickey was on a fast and steady rise through the ranks. Within two years of joining as a 19-year-old, he was out of uniform and in plain clothes – or in garda parlance, a 'buckshee' detective. Now 37, he was a detective of ten years' standing, much of it spent in the tough environment of 'D District', Dublin's north inner city, where bank and post office robberies were regular occurrences throughout the 1970s and early '80s.

John O'Mahony was another detective who, like Hickey, would rise to the rank of assistant commissioner. Fresh-faced and with curly black hair, the Corkman was only 25 when he was called in to work on the Bridie Gargan case, having been appointed a detective only a few months previously.

O'Mahony's working life had begun in the vice squad, which included policing the street prostitution around the Grand Canal and Fitzwilliam Square, often at night. Now he was assigned to the Central Detective Unit (CDU), involved with investigating serious crime. His partner in the CDU was another novice detective, Frank Hand, then only 24.

Both Hand and O'Mahony had been in the west of Ireland on Thursday, 22 July at a funeral for a colleague who had been shot dead by paramilitaries. As they drove back into Dublin, they noticed a significant amount of garda activity around the Phoenix Park.

"We knew there was something happening," said O'Mahony, "but we said we'd find out sooner or later."

In the event, they were to find out sooner than they expected. Early the following day, Friday, 23 July, Detectives O'Mahony and Hand were summoned into the incident room in Kevin Street Garda Station. They were about to become involved with their first murder case.

Over 30 detectives assembled in the small, stuffy room in the ancient building to hear CS Brogan set out the facts of the case. He put particular emphasis on the frenzied nature of the attack. He told them that although the nurse was still alive, there was little hope she would survive, and they were to treat it as murder.

Investigations in those days were a completely manual affair. The person who performed the function of recording every small detail was an officer called the 'book man'. Every screed of paper, every statement, every piece of information or intel, and every order, went through him, as did every assignment of detectives to particular tasks.

Others were given responsibility for conducting searches or house-to-house questionnaires, taking statements from witnesses, accruing physical evidence, and finding out where such items had originated.

Already, there were several leads to follow. A detective based in Kevin Street, Cahal Murphy, had the foresight to go to St James's Hospital soon after the admission of the victim, who was now known to be Bridie Gargan, a nurse working at the hospital. She had lost so much blood that transfusions were urgently required. He obtained a small sample of blood before she went into the operating theatre, a move that ensured there would be no evidential contamination if it came to the question of identity at a later criminal trial.

Gardaí were able to get a clean set of fingerprints from the plastic around the shovel that was left behind at the crime scene. They quickly ascertained they could not establish a match with any known suspect.

As to the shovel, while gardaí deduced that the killer planned to bury their victim, it was also clear that they were not used to manual labour, having picked the wrong shape of shovel, a square-headed one. "That was completely impractical, because the shovel he had wouldn't dig a grave in a fortnight," Hickey observed.

Over the course of the weekend, gardaí released photographs of both the shovel and the lump hammer. On Saturday, a description of Bridie Gargan's attacker was distributed to all garda stations in Ireland. It read:

*20/25 yrs. 5ft 10 ins. Good strong build, athletic looking. Dark brown hair, brushed back, wavy at front, slight parting in centre and well groomed. Well-trimmed beard. Pale complexion. Good white even teeth, brown eyes, well spoken. Wore white open necked shirt, dark coloured trousers, dark leather shoes and FISHERMAN'S TWEED HAT.*

The description omitted any reference to the beige military jumper. Courtney and senior officers were conscious that in a high-profile case like this, time-wasting cranks and fantasists would come forward with information that, on the face of it, seemed credible. By keeping the existence of the jumper in reserve, they had a good means of testing those accounts.

## The Murderer and the Taoiseach

The same Saturday, 24 July, the shocking news of an apparently random vicious attack in the Phoenix Park the previous Thursday hit newsstands. Just as Malcolm Macarthur was preparing for another journey from Dublin city centre to County Offaly, to meet a man about a gun.

# 9

## POINT-BLANK

"I was trying to think of a way of getting this gun without paying for it and I was playing for time." Malcolm Macarthur

**Saturday, 24 July 1982**

Traffic was light on the sun-saturated south quays of the River Liffey as the 6.30pm bus bound for Edenderry headed out from Busáras. It was half-full, mainly of shoppers or Dublin-based workers going back to their home place for the night. Right at the back sat Malcolm Macarthur, wearing a tweed jacket, a soft peaked cap and thick horn-rimmed glasses.

It took an hour and a half for the bus to reach its destination. It stopped in the town's square and the remaining passengers stepped out into the calm summer's evening, including the distinctively dressed man carrying a blue hold-all.

There was a popular satirical news programme on RTÉ television around that time, *Hall's Pictorial Weekly*. Every week its opening sequence featured general shots of a small Irish town. The towns changed but the details and ambience rarely did: a Massey tractor trundling down the main street; old farmers with flat hats weaving by on black Nelly bicycles; kids waving at the camera; elderly women with headscarves deep in conversation; a delivery man in a brown coat unloading a van; people coming out of a bank or post office or grocery shop. The scene at Edenderry fit right in.

Taking a few minutes to find his bearings, Macarthur began to walk up the long Main Street until he arrived at the place known locally as The Harbour, a bucolic spot flanked by chestnut and plane trees, where barges are berthed. He surveyed the boats before walking further south as far as an arched bridge, where the spur met the canal proper. He strolled along the bank for a while.

"I forgot what I was there for, for the time being," Macarthur would later say. "I just enjoyed a walk along the canal bank."

It was two days since he had left Bridie Gargan for dead in a Dublin laneway. Now, with darkness starting to fall, he was in Edenderry to meet Dónal Dunne, the young man who had recently advertised a gun for sale.

Dónal Dunne was 27 years of age, strong and sinewy from working on the family farm. A single man, his big passions outside work were shooting, fishing and gun dogs. He was a leading member of the Edenderry Clay Pigeon Shooting Club. Six months earlier, he had bought the Miroku shotgun. It was a beautifully crafted gun, hand-finished, and expensive. It differed from conventional shotguns because its barrels were "up and over", placed vertically, one on top of the other, rather than side-by-side or horizontally. Dunne never got used to the gun and believed it had not improved his aim when it came to accuracy. Now he was keen to sell it on.

After Macarthur had finished his stroll along the canal, he headed back to Main Street. He stopped a man who was stepping into his car and asked where the Dunne family lived. The man said the farm was in Monasteroris, about a mile and a half outside the town. He was unsure of its exact location. Macarthur asked the man to give him a lift and he obliged, dropping Macarthur off on the Rhode Road, about a mile outside town.

By now it was dark. Macarthur called to the door of a nearby bungalow, and a young man in his early 20s answered. He pointed to lights at the end of a boreen. "That's the house down there, where those lights are," he said.

Macarthur walked half-way down the boreen, but then stopped in his tracks. It was now after 10pm. He abandoned his plan to procure the gun that night. He turned and retraced his steps to Edenderry, a two-mile journey.

He stayed the night at the harbour, sitting on a bench and pacing around when the temperature cooled in the early hours of the morning. He did not sleep.

On Sunday morning, Macarthur met a man who was passing on his way to check his cattle. He also had a brief conversation with a man who was out for an early walk.

A little further down the bank, two young men, who had arrived by motorbike, had camped for the night. One of them emerged from the tent and asked Macarthur what time it was. It was eight o'clock, he replied.

Macarthur had a razor and toothbrush with him in a plastic

bag. He used the canal water to shave and brush his teeth. He walked up to Main Street and waited for the shops to open. When they did so at nine, he bought *The Sunday Press*, a pint of milk, an apple and an orange. The newspaper headlines all told of the brutal attack of Bridie Gargan and the hunt for her assailant.

Macarthur returned to the canal bank, where he drank the milk and ate the fruit. He whiled away a few hours reading the newspaper.

Three people arrived into the harbour to take a barge for a trip down the canal. Macarthur watched as they prepared the vessel and set off from the berth.

In the rising heat of that Sunday morning, the stranger – with his soft cap and heavy tweed jacket – was noticed by passers-by. He was later described as a "bohemian" or a "vagabond". Those who had spoken to him – and all the conversations were brief and clipped – also discerned his ascendancy accent.

It was after 11am when Macarthur walked back up to the main square of the town and rang the Dunnes' home number from a telephone kiosk. Dónal answered the phone. Macarthur said he was in town and would like to meet him to see the gun. The young man agreed and said he would meet him outside the post office.

On the way, Dunne stopped by his brother Christy's house to tell him where he was headed. Christy later recalled, "I asked him did he want me to go with him. And he said, 'No, I will go on my own, but I may be calling in on my way back.'" That was the last time the brothers saw each other alive.

Dunne and Macarthur met outside the post office as

arranged. Dunne said the gun was in the boot. "We won't look at it here in the middle of the street," he said, and told Macarthur to hop into the car. They drove west down Main Street towards Tullamore.

At the end of Main Street, Dunne crossed a bridge over the Grand Canal and then turned his car left to drive southwards on the Rathangan Road. He drove about a mile before coming to a stop. In that short journey, the countryside changed from rolling fields to vast bog with big skies. The bog stretched all the way south to Kildare and west, as far as the eye could see, across County Offaly and into County Westmeath. With the ground baked and cracked by weeks of dry sunny weather, it gave the Bog of Allen the parched look of the Great Plains of North Dakota.

Dunne pulled the car into the side of the road and onto a patch of land that the Clay Pigeon Shooting Club used for target practice. It was close to the large, blocky Bord na Móna power station which dominated the flat landscape.

The gun was in a case as he took it from the boot. He removed it and ran through its operations with the prospective purchaser. He then loaded it with two cartridges, and pointed at a white post in the distance which was used as a target. He invited the stranger to have a go.

Macarthur fired one shot at the target and then turned the gun on Dónal Dunne and shot him through the side of the head at point-blank range. The young man died instantly.

# 10

# NO ORDINARY BOYHOOD

"I carried on in the tradition that I had been brought up in,
that is that children are seen and not heard." Irene Macarthur

In older schools in Ireland, you sometimes find rows of black
and white photographs of sports teams from the distant past
on corridor walls.

The Christian Brothers school in Trim, County Meath, is a
good example. Among the framed photographs is one that
shows an under-14 team from the parish of Summerhill that
took part in a GAA football 'street league' organised by the
school in 1959.

The photograph was taken over six decades ago. All of
those boys in the picture would be in their late 70s now. Some
have passed away.

The boys are lined up in two rows: the front row kneeling;
the back row standing with their arms folded. Most of the boys

have the sleeves of their jerseys neatly rolled up in readiness for the game they are about to play. Virtually all have broad smiles creased across their faces.

There is an innocence around it. These are uncomplicated country boys living uncomplicated country lives: teeming with vitality and joy and anticipation.

Except for one small detail.

On the far left of the photograph, we see a boy standing clearly apart from, and some paces behind, the rest of his team-mates.

He is a handsome boy with hair that is bristle-thick. He is conspicuously wearing a jacket over his football jersey. He is staring right at the camera. He is not smiling like the rest. His expression and posture are ambivalent.

Is he a part of the team? Or is he apart from it?

It almost looks like this boy has deliberately distanced himself from the rest of the group as if he does not belong; as if he is, in some way, an outsider.

The caption at the bottom of the picture identifies him.

"M. Macarthur."


Stories abound surrounding the childhood of Malcolm Macarthur. They differ in detail but follow similar themes. He was a lonely child, ignored by his parents, largely brought up by the family's housekeeper. He was a pawn in his parents' volatile relationship. His mother was cold and absent. His father was stern, fiery and controlling. He was a painfully shy boy who was tongue-tied in the company of other children. Whatever the precise truth of Macarthur's early life, his was no ordinary boyhood.

Malcolm Daniel Edward Macarthur was born on 17 April, 1946, in a nursing home in Hatch Street in Dublin, the first and only child of Irene and Daniel Macarthur. Even among the wealthy land-owning County Meath set, the family were outliers, being both Catholic and, even second generation in, still 'blow-ins'. His father Daniel was the son of Daniel Sr and Mary, who had arrived in Ireland from Scotland in 1906. Even though Daniel Jr had been born in Meath, the neighbours still regarded him and the family as Scottish. Indeed, Daniel's own wife Irene – who hailed from County Meath – described the family she married into as "wild highlanders".

Although the Macarthurs didn't tend to socialise with the poorer Catholic families of the area, neither were they fully embraced by the Church of Ireland landowners. They were neither one thing nor another.

Daniel Sr was 36 years old in 1906 when he set out with his wife, Mary, 30, from their home in the lowlands of Scotland for Ireland, a country with which they had no connection. The move is said to have been suggested by a missionary priest from County Meath, to free the family from the religious discrimination that they, as Catholics, were experiencing in the predominantly Protestant region of Scotland where they lived.

The same year, Daniel Sr bought Breemount House – described as a "gentleman's residence" – at public auction. The large Georgian farmhouse in Stokestown, Laracor, County Meath, came with 362 acres of prime land. Laracor was a parish best known for its association with author Jonathan Swift, who was Church of Ireland rector there between 1700 and 1745.

The farm was about two miles outside Trim on the road that led to the village of Summerhill. It spanned across one of the few hills in the plains of County Meath, Bray Hill.

The house, a handsome mansion, dating from the early 19th century, was approached by a pretty avenue lined by beech trees. There were three reception rooms, a study, six bedrooms, servants' quarters, and a kitchen and pantries.

The byre was substantial for the time: big enough to accommodate 100 cattle for feeding during the winter. There was a walled garden extending to two acres, with a large glasshouse, which provided fresh produce for the house; and stables where as many as 30 horses could be kept.

At the time of their move to Ireland, Malcolm Macarthur's grandparents had three young children, two girls and a boy. By the time of the 1911 census, two further boys had been born, completing the family.

The census returns showed the family was of substantial means and employed a governess, domestic servants, coachmen, and farm labourers.

The family was welcomed by other land-owning families in the area and they were quickly absorbed into the social set, which revolved mainly around horses and hunting. However, the fact they were Scottish and Catholic did set them apart from the local Protestant landed gentry.

All the children went to private schools abroad, the boys to Fort Augustus, an austere Benedictine boarding school in the Scottish Highlands.

Daniel Sr never lost his Scottish accent. He was a small man who was very religious and said to be odd in his ways. He had run a successful tea and wine importing business in Glasgow along with his mother, Mary, and continued to travel to and from Scotland for many years. There was a curious family story behind it. When he was a young child in 1872, his own father, John, went on a trip to buy wine in Bordeaux and never returned. It was never established if he died or set up a new life. Mary, who had been a weaver, built up the business to become one of Glasgow's largest tea and wine merchants.

A local story went that one of the many rooms in Breemount House was kept locked because it was haunted, but that old Daniel had inadvertently let the ghost out soon after arriving in Ireland. "They had to get a Redemptorist to exorcise the place after that. The penance for Dan was to attend Mass and evening devotions every day for the rest of his life," a farmer from the locality told the *Meath Chronicle* many years later.

Whatever the reason, Daniel Sr was a daily communicant. He cycled every day to Mass in Dangan church, a little over two miles away. While there were no designated seats in the chapel, the Macarthur family always occupied the same pew, and all would dress impeccably for Sunday Mass.

The older Macarthur retained his fervent religiosity until he died in 1946 at the age of 75. Indeed, he died on his way to devotions, after crashing his bicycle on a dark, damp evening as he descended Bray Hill on his way to the local church.

His widow, Mary, was also very religious. She was from the town of Lanark outside Glasgow. Her father, Thomas Bowie, had converted to Catholicism in the 1830s after coming under the influence of leading Catholic convert John Henry Newman at Oxford University. He had married late in life and Mary was his only child. His occupation was a particularly

Scottish one: he was a "portioner" – a person who owned a portion of an estate of land, sometimes going back centuries, with options to increase their share over succeeding generations. Bowie, Malcom Macarthur's Scottish maternal great-grandfather, lived off the proceeds of a large estate, dying a wealthy man in the early years of the 20th century. He left a substantial sum to his daughter Mary, Macarthur's grandmother.

However, by 1946, 40 years after moving from Scotland to Ireland, there were signs that Mary's inheritance from her father's fortune was diminishing. When her husband, Daniel Macarthur Snr, died from his bike crash in 1946, Mary had to sell off almost 200 acres of Breemount to pay death duties.

Mary and Daniel Macarthur Snr's youngest child, Daniel Jnr – Malcolm's father – took over the running of the farm in 1946 after his father died. Born in 1910, Daniel would farm Breemount until his death in 1971. His four older siblings would all emigrate as adults to Britain and the USA.

By the time of his father's death, Daniel had married Irene Murray and they were expecting their first child. Irene was over a decade younger than her husband. Like him, she came from a well-to-do family of 'Castle Catholics', the Murrays of Tanderagee, who lived on an estate near the village of Rathmolyon in the south of County Meath. They were one of the largest landowners in the county, with 900 acres between Longwood and Ballivor, and more land in County Westmeath. Almost unheard of for a Catholic family, they could trace their fortune back to the 17th century, when they originally settled in County Armagh (hence the Tanderagee label).

Irene's grandfather, Thomas Murray, was a leading member

of the Irish Parliamentary Party (IPP) in County Meath. In 1895 he proposed John Howard Parnell, elder brother of Charles Stewart Parnell, as the IPP candidate for South Meath in the Westminster parliamentary elections, an election that John Howard Parnell won.

After Thomas Murray died, his son Edward (Irene's father) took over the estate. The family's wealth was enormous compared to their neighbours, but there were headwinds in store. While Catholic families like the Murrays supported Irish independence, this did not insulate them from the sharp end of the political direction of the new state. During the 1930s, the Land Commission began breaking up the large estates in County Meath and distributing the land to tenants, smallholders and landless families from the west of Ireland. The Tanderagee estate was broken up, with the Murray family losing much of its land. (The Macarthur family also lost some of its land on foot of a Land Commission ruling.)

These changes signalled the beginning of what would be a terminal decline in the wealth and sway of estate-owning families in Ireland. But for the two daughters of Edward and his wife, Anne Monica – known to everybody as Queenie – life in the 1920s and '30s remained idyllic. Irene and her younger sister, Sheila, had a governess, and both went to a convent finishing school in County Wexford. The girls were passionate about horse-riding and hunting and it occupied most of their spare time.

Irene was vivacious and extroverted, and socialised at local hunt balls. She became engaged to a local landowner, but they split up. Soon after, she met Daniel Macarthur through their shared social circle, and they married in 1943. Locally, some thought she had married Daniel 'on the rebound'. Her new husband was known for his stern temperament. As time would tell, theirs was not to be a match made in heaven.

Tragedy befell the Murray family a year after Irene and Daniel Macarthur married when, in 1944, Irene's only sibling, Sheila, died after a hunting accident. She was in her early 20s. She had fallen from her horse while jumping a ditch. She seemed to have recovered despite some of her ribs bruising, but unbeknownst to anyone, she had perforated her appendix in the fall. This led to sepsis, which killed her some days later.

Sheila and Irene had been very close and Irene was bereft at her sister's death, although her upbringing – with its stiff-upper-lip mentality – did not lend itself to overt displays of emotion. In an interview many years later, she sadly reflected that Sheila's death had left her with no close family.

When Malcolm was born in 1946, it is said that his father was very attentive to his young son, until around the time he entered education at the age of eight. For her part, Irene did not have a strong maternal instinct and had a distant relationship with the boy. She spoke of this in a remarkably candid interview with broadcaster David Hanly in early 1983.

"I never was a very great person with children. I carried on in the tradition that I had been brought up in, that is that children are seen and not heard. And therefore I saw him every day, and I went out to do my gardening and my horses and whatever else was on, and this girl came in and taught him."

Malcolm was a painfully shy boy, who spent a lot of time

in the company of the housekeeper, Mary Kate McCann, a widow who sometimes took the child to her home, a short distance from Breemount, at night.

"At first you could not get a word out of him," a former Breemount farmhand told the *Meath Chronicle* in 1983. "He would not speak and if you addressed him he would run and hide his head behind his hands. The poor little lad was scared stiff of everyone. Eventually he came out of his shell and began playing with youngsters. He was even then a quiet lad but you knew he was very, very bright."

His mother, Irene, concurred. "As a child, I think he was probably very shy. And I think when he grew up, he was very shy. And being an only child, of course he didn't have other children to play with. But to be fair to him, he has always said in recent years that his childhood was very happy."

The evidence, however, suggests a more complex picture than this. From the outset, his parents' marriage was strained. While Irene was outgoing and involved in many activities, Daniel was a stern and forbidding man, who had a reputation for being a skinflint as he became older. He was tall and imposing, and always dressed smartly. On Irene's part, there were rumours of rows and long absences from the home, and also of affairs.

That increasing dissonance in the Macarthur marriage – and the rumours – were referred to by the late Homan Potterton, former director of the Irish National Gallery, in his memoir, *Rathcormick*. He grew up in County Meath and recalled meeting Malcolm Macarthur as a child.

"My father acted as a sort of land-agent for many people . . . One of his clients – who like many others became a friend of my father – lived outside Trim on a farm of several hundred acres with an attractive Georgian farmhouse called Breemount.

"This was Daniel Macarthur, a gentleman. On some occasions in the school holidays, my father would take my brother Alan and me with him as he visited clients and we would wait in the car, or get up to some mischief, while Father discussed business.

"At Breemount, it was different. There was a small boy of our own age there with whom we could play about the farmyard. He was called Malcolm and was an only child: he was also a lonely one. His parents' marriage was not a happy one – in fact it was a disaster – and his mother, Irene, was rarely at Breemount. Malcolm was very much neglected."

One anecdote recounts Malcolm leaving Breemount for school while his parents were having a huge row. As he walked down the curved driveway, his mother's car sped past him as she stormed off. Moments later his father's car did the same. Neither had bothered to stop for their son, who was left to walk the half mile to the bus stop for school by himself.

"The poor lad had a dreadful childhood," says the farmhand, "never knowing whether his own wanted him or not. His parents would pass him on the road in hail, rain or snow without ever giving him a lift."

Irene spent a lot of time, while in Breemount, with her horses or in the garden. Malcolm never acquired the same passion for either. Perhaps that lack of interest stemmed from a serious incident that happened when he was four years of age, when one of his mother's mares kicked him in the head, leaving a scar that was still noticeable in adulthood.

"I thought he was a goner," recalled the farmhand, "but he came through it alright, poor Malcolm."

He did learn to ride and to jump, but unlike his mother, who rode out regularly with the Meath Hunt and the Trim Harriers, he never had any interest in hunting. He was more interested in fishing on local rivers or along the banks of the River Boyne four miles away. As a child, he and his father would travel by car through the villages of Meath and Westmeath until they arrived at Dysart, a tiny village on the far side of Mullingar. They would take a boat out on Lough Ennell and fish for trout and perch. While he was the only child in Breemount, in many ways he was a regular boy who liked climbing trees, playing with marbles, and flying kites.

There was a billiards room in the house, although the baize on the table had become somewhat faded and worn by the time Malcolm was a child. In the grounds there were two tennis courts, and a field that was used for cricket.

Daniel Macarthur loved cricket and organised what was called 'country house cricket' games against teams from the other big houses scattered throughout Leinster. They were irregular occurrences during the summer and farm workers or neighbours were hauled in to make up the numbers. Breemount played against teams from Dunsany Castle, Mount Juliet and, indeed, from Shelton Abbey – where Macarthur would later end up in prison, after the ancestral seat of the earls of Wicklow was sold to the Irish state and re-opened as a penitentiary.

One of those interviewed many years later in the *Meath Chronicle* described Daniel Macarthur as an unlucky farmer and businessman. There was a rich lime deposit on part of his land and he leased it out to a quarry company, which was eventually taken over by Roadstone. Despite the substantial income he made from it, he still struggled to make ends meet. "Nothing ever seemed to go right for him," said the farmhand.

While Daniel was contrary and difficult, he was also found to be principled and honest by those who dealt with him. A person who knew him very well said he did not tolerate people cutting corners or using underhand methods.

Until he was almost eight, Malcolm received a private education, with a governess coming to Breemount each day. This may now seem anachronistic but was par for the course as far as his parents were concerned. Both had been privately educated at home as young children and had been sent away to boarding school from around the age of eight.

Malcolm was primed to attend the salubrious Gilling Castle in Yorkshire at around this age. It was the preparatory school of the highly exclusive Catholic boarding school Ampleforth College, also in Yorkshire. Daniel's sister lived in the county and had recommended both schools as suitable for Malcolm. The problem was the fees. The farm at Breemount was not going well and the Macarthurs were feeling the pinch. Irene later said that the price of cattle had fallen dramatically at the time, leaving the family short of funds.

Irene still wanted Malcolm to go to Yorkshire but ultimately Daniel decided otherwise. Plans for a private education were put aside, and instead Malcolm was sent to primary school in Trim, progressing onto St Michael's secondary school, run by the Christian Brothers.

It was a big wrench for the young boy. His few friends until then came from big houses. Now he was mixing with a totally different social class. By the time he started secondary school, though, he had blended in somewhat.

"You could not say he was a loner, he was just an ordinary fellow," said a schoolmate of his who gave his first name, Jim. "He had a very ordinary Meath accent, nothing beyond the ordinary local rural accent. It was not an educated accent. There was a bit of sport in him too. He could joke. Lads used to have the craic with him. And they started playing tricks on him and he played tricks back and he was absolutely no different than anyone else. He didn't like doing sports. But that was nothing, there was nothing wrong with that. He was a very intelligent fellow."

One of those who went to school with him told the *Meath Chronicle* in 1983 that Macarthur had not intended to return to school after his Intermediate examination despite getting good results. He understood Malcolm had made arrangements to keep accounts for a farm. However, the school principal intervened and convinced him to come back, saying that leaving school at 15 would be a waste of his talents. According to Jim, however, this was not so – Malcolm had always intended to go to university while attending St Michael's.

At home, life was becoming more difficult. As Malcolm grew older, relations with his father came under increasing strain. At this stage, his parents' marriage was disintegrating, and his mother had sought an annulment. It involved Malcolm taking sides in the ongoing war between his parents. Now a teenager, and showing signs of rebellion, he and Daniel – whose default mood in the face of Breemount's dwindling fortunes was stern or angry – began to clash. Where once there had been over 20 staff at Breemount, the complement had been reduced to a housekeeper and a cook.

The tensions culminated in a violent encounter between father and son in the farmyard in 1962, when Malcolm was 16. There was no food in the house and Daniel announced they would not have Sunday lunch. It escalated into a full-blown row resulting in a physical fight between the pair, during which Daniel bit Malcolm's hand between the thumb and forefinger, leaving a gash that required five stitches.

Malcolm was put out of the house and stayed with housekeeper Mary Kate McCann in her cottage. He would not return to live in Breemount on a full-time basis for over five years. At this stage, his parents had split up and Irene was now living about half a mile away in an apartment in another grand house, Freffans, which belonged to a friend of hers, Norman Potterton.

Later reflecting on her stormy marriage, Irene said, "Malcolm saw violence at an early age. And who's to know what will happen against that."

Escape from Breemount presented itself the following year, in 1963. Malcolm's uncle, Jack Macarthur, was a lawyer who had emigrated to California in the 1930s. He offered to take Malcolm over to the US where he would try to gain him a place in the prestigious Stanford University. Malcolm achieved good results in the Leaving Certificate and travelled to California at the end of that summer to live with his uncle there.

At 17, though, he was too young for Stanford and his application was turned down on the grounds of age. He then attended a pre-university school called Diablo Valley University for a year before again applying for Stanford, but he failed to win a place. Instead, he went to Oregon State University for two years and studied economics. He liked university life but complained to his mother in a letter that Oregon was cold and wet, with more miserable weather than Ireland. There was also the problem that Oregon was not Stanford, not Harvard and not Princeton. At this stage, for him at least, prestige and social advancement mattered.

For the final two years of his college education, Malcolm transferred to a constituent college of the University of California, Davis, a sleepy college town of about 15,000 people. Unlike just about everywhere else in the US, the town had a reputation for being bike-friendly from the 1960s onwards. Most of its students were studying agricultural science but there was a small liberal arts faculty, which allowed Macarthur to complete his economics degree.

By this stage, the flower power movement had overtaken Northern California, but the young Macarthur eschewed it, cultivating a dress style that set him distinctly apart: that of a foppish young toff, wearing tweeds and corduroy jackets, as well as cravats. His view of hippies was that they were escapist. He saw himself as a humanist, a rationalist and a realist – a rather posh one. Any residual trace of the broad vowels of the Meath accent had been ironed out. His mother remarked years later to broadcaster David Hanly that it was in the US that Malcolm's accent became an ascendancy one.

Macarthur graduated in 1967. He had no intention of hanging around in the US and taking a risk of being put on the draft for a possible call-up to the Vietnam war. He was now 21 and much changed from when he had left Ireland behind four years ago. The small-town country boy now cut the shape of an aristocratic figure.

He returned to Ireland to live with his father at Breemount in 1967. That autumn, he commuted in and out of Dublin on a motorbike each day, telling his parents that he had enrolled in a postgraduate course in Trinity College Dublin (TCD).

This was not the whole truth. He had registered as a temporary student on a short-term course, which gave him access to the library. There he spent long hours studying what was of interest to him, namely mathematics and quantum physics, without any intention of taking any course. Later, he would acquire a library pass for Cambridge University and do the same thing, pursuing his own academic interests without ever enrolling. He frequently mentioned both TCD and Cambridge when talking about himself. It was part of a by-now identifiable trait of his that was reflected in his dress, his accent, and his disposition – a need to project an air of grandeur. All who knew him assumed – right off the bat – that he had post-graduate degrees from some of the most prestigious institutions in the world.

Malcolm and his father had a relationship that varied between passive and quarrelsome. Initially, after his four years abroad, they got on well, but soon enough the old habits re-emerged and they began rowing frequently. Daniel believed in the value of work and wanted Malcolm to take a job in the office of the lime quarry situated on the land. Malcolm refused. He wanted to continue his studies. He relied on his parents for money and that led to more rows. It came to a head right at the end of 1970, when the pair parted ways again.

Irene recalled: "His father put him out again on New

76

Year's Eve in 1970. I had a flat in the wing of Freffans. And he stayed there for about eight months."

Unexpectedly, Daniel, who suffered from heart disease, became very ill in August 1971 and was admitted to a nursing home in Dublin where he stayed for two months. Malcolm returned to Breemount and lived there alone. In October, Daniel had recovered sufficiently to return to Breemount. However, he took ill again soon after returning home and died three days later. He was only 61 years old.

Malcolm took over the running of the farm for a year or so before it was put on the market as part of the settlement of his father's will. When probate was completed two years later, Malcom Macarthur found himself to be a wealthy young man. His proceeds from two-thirds of the estate amounted to between £70,000 and £100,000 – the equivalent of €1.25 million to €1.75 million in today's terms.

The sale marked a severing of the Macarthur family's connection to Breemount going back almost seven decades. Irene remembered clearly that moment when Malcolm learned of his inheritance. They were both standing in the kitchen of their soon-to-be-sold home with their cook. "He turned round to the cook at Breemount and said, 'I'm going to leave my mark on Western Europe.'"

# 11

## OUTSIDE THE RULES
## OF THE GAME

"The first impression this man gives is that he is an 'oddball' of some type. He gives the impression that he is cultured and educated." Garda Síochána internal bulletin

On Sunday, 25 July 1982, as the blast of a shotgun echoed on the empty stretch of bog near Edenderry, Dónal Dunne fell motionless on the ground, instantly dead. There was no traffic to be seen on the nearby Edenderry to Rathangan road that crossed the vast brown expanse. Nothing moved save the occasional jet drawing a line of white across the blue sky.

The killer dragged his victim's body into an area with longer grass and tried to cover it with dried branches lying on the bog. It was a cursory effort.

He then grabbed the gun and ran back to Dunne's silver Ford Escort. He placed the gun in the well between the car's front seats and drove across the track until he reached the

78

metalled road. Instead of going back through Edenderry, he drove south to Rathangan, across the border in County Kildare. He then drove back to Dublin via Prosperous and Maynooth. When he reached Chapelizod on the outskirts of Dublin, he took a southern route into the city, which took him to the Grand Canal.

At Chapelizod, unknown to Macarthur, a car slipped in behind him and began following him as he drove through Drimnagh and Crumlin, before crossing the canal at Portobello Bridge near Rathmines. He drove into the city centre via Camden Street, still unaware that he was being followed. When he reached Dame Street, he turned left and parked the car on a side street, in the shadow of the Central Bank building.

The car that had been following him stopped there too. It was a group that were travelling from Offaly to Dublin for the Leinster hurling final against Kilkenny. Not sure of the way, they had spotted the Offaly registration of the Ford Escort and concluded it was travelling to Croke Park. But the man who emerged did not look the hurling type, with his tweed jacket and aristocratic bearing.

They watched him walk down Fownes Street towards the Liffey quays carrying his blue hold-all bag, before they reversed the car and navigated their own way to Jones' Road and the hurling final.

Malcolm Macarthur ambled a while at the quays on that sunny afternoon before taking a number 8 bus back to Dún Laoghaire. From a public phone box near his lodgings on George's Street, he called Brenda Little. He told her he was in

Ostend in Belgium sorting out finances. He assured her he would return to the Canary Islands within a week once he was back in funds.

That evening, on the Offaly bog where Macarthur had discarded Dónal Dunne's body earlier in the day, a seven-year-old boy out picnicking with his family followed a trail of blood to a place of undergrowth on the bog. He was shocked to discover a half-hidden body lying there.

The following day, as members of the garda murder squad arrived in Edenderry to begin investigating the murder of Dónal Dunne, the young nurse Bridie Gargan finally succumbed to her injuries, four days after being brutally attacked. Both victims were around the same age. Both were single. Both had been cut down in broad daylight. And both killings were equally mysterious.

Back in Dublin, the investigation into the death of Bridie Gargan was progressing. Detectives began following new leads. Two gardaí went to speak to Bridie Gargan's family and learn more about her private life, her circle of friends, especially male acquaintances.

Detectives contacted wholesalers to find out what hardware shops sold that particular lump hammer and shovel. The hammer was an unusual brand, made in China and with the figure '1,000' embossed on the metal. Lenehans, the hardware shop on Capel Street, was one of the few outlets which stocked it, but none of its staff could remember selling it.

At this point, no physical description had been issued to the public. But crime correspondents were unofficially getting information from their contacts within the ranks and a picture of the events was beginning to emerge. Among them was Peter

Murtagh, security correspondent of *The Irish Times*. Murtagh was 29 at the time, young to be a correspondent, but with a growing reputation for thoroughness. He reported that the suspect was seen on the South Circular Road between 5.30 and 6pm on the day the nurse was attacked.

"He was running towards the city centre and carrying a blue hold-all bag," he wrote. "Eyewitnesses have told the gardaí that he looked dishevelled and was out of breath. When the man was seen in the park, he is thought to have been wearing a dark pullover. However, on the South Circular Road he may have been wearing just a white shirt. Gardaí believe there may have been blood spots on the shirt and detectives say there were two marks on his back, possibly blood."

Not all the information was reliable. The suspect had, in fact, been wearing a light-coloured pullover.

This and other media coverage triggered a flood of calls and contacts from the public. By Monday morning, several officers were sifting through a growing pile of witness statements and reports for useful information. Despite extensive canvassing among local residents and workers, nobody until then had come forward to say they had seen him leave the South Circular Road area, or who had spotted him elsewhere.

If there was no shortage of leads in the early stages of the investigation, there was a dearth of good ones. Every day scores of people rang the helpline to suggest sightings of the suspect, or to finger-point a local eccentric or oddball who seemed to fit the loose description. None could be discounted. For the investigation team, every small detail was a lead and all the leads had to be followed. With each, detectives embarked on a path through a maze that they sensed would, more likely than not, lead to a dead end.

Then came a lead that landed. When flicking through the telephone call log, Tony Hickey came across a record that piqued his interest. On the previous night, a Sunday, a woman contacted gardaí to say she had encountered a man the previous Thursday, who matched the description of the suspect.

On foot of the call, Hickey and a colleague, Joe Shelley, visited Odyssey Travel on the South Circular Road, situated close to the large Player Wills tobacco factory. There they met the woman who had phoned in, Rita Brennan. She told them of the strange encounter she had with a breathless jogger. She had thought nothing of it until she saw a news report on RTÉ about the attack on Bridie Gargan on Sunday night. Her information came to the investigation a little late. Nonetheless, it was striking.

Brennan's account enabled investigators to stitch together the attacker's escape route. Like the gardener, Paddy Byrne, who'd witnessed Macarthur's attack on Bridie in the Phoenix Park, Rita Brennan of Odyssey Travel was also able to give a good description that fitted with the consistent picture emerging.

Guards flooded the buses on all the out-of-town routes that passed the travel agency to see what they could uncover.

For a small and tranquil town like Edenderry, news of Dónal Dunne's murder hit like a thunderbolt. "Of course, it was a massive shock," said retired local journalist Henry Bauress.

"The Dunne family were very well known and respected in

the area and Dónal Dunne was only 27 at the time his life was taken."

Dónal Dunne was single, full of vitality and action. His life revolved around farming and outdoor pursuits. He fished in all the local rivers and lakes and was passionate about shooting, which he took very seriously: he was a leading member of the local clay pigeon club and went out at least once a week to the shooting range on the Rathangan Road. He also kept gun dogs and regularly went game shooting, roaming happily through the boglands of Offaly in search of pheasant.

Bauress shook his head at the thought of the seven-year-old boy finding the body. "Everything about that day was awful, it was a black day," he said.

The Dunnes were a large and close family and were deeply distraught at the loss of Dónal. As they waited for his body to return from the pathology lab so they could prepare for his funeral, Dónal's brother Christy told investigating gardaí what the family knew: that a man had rung up responding to Dónal's advert for the shotgun in the *Evening Press*, and that Dónal had travelled from the farm into Edenderry to meet with him around noon.

By this stage, scores of gardaí had arrived in the town, including trainees from Templemore Garda College in County Tipperary. At the shooting range on the Rathangan Road, the gardaí panned out across the bog and combed the peat looking for any additional clues. In the town, detectives interviewed hundreds of people.

Unlike the Dublin attack, the investigation made very quick headway in establishing the movements of the killer. Within a day of the shooting, numerous witnesses had come forward to describe an unusual visitor who arrived in Edenderry on Saturday evening and hung around the Harbour area of the town. He was spotted in a shop on Sunday morning, and then reading a paper and drinking milk on a bench at the Harbour. Several people who were coming out of Sunday Mass in the town centre told gardaí they saw a thin, stooped figure leaning over the passenger side of Dónal Dunne's silver car.

Henry Bauress lived in the Harbour area but was in Dublin that weekend. As soon as he heard of the murder he returned and began talking to locals.

"Most of the descriptions of Malcolm Macarthur at the time indicated he stood out from the crowd," he said. "It was his clothing, or, if anybody had spoken to him, it was his accent. It helped people to maybe put two and two together."

The reports coming back to Kevin Street Garda Station in Dublin of the dress, demeanour and accent of the stranger immediately aroused suspicions that the same man was responsible for both the Dunne and Gargan murders. But for now, gardaí treated them as separate cases.

"People from the murder squad were also in Edenderry investigating the case," said Tony Hickey. "Notes were swapped and it began to seem on the face of it that the same man may well be the common denominator. But again, despite inquiries that were carried out, there was no obvious connection between Bridie Gargan and Dónal Dunne, except that both were from farming families."

In Edenderry, a scenes of crime unit searched the dustbins in the area where the stranger had been seen and retrieved the copy of *The Sunday Press* and the discarded milk carton. From those they were able to lift fingerprints.

Thanks to the multiple sightings and encounters of the suspect in Edenderry, the gardaí were able to issue a detailed description of the killer in the internal confidential bulletin, or *fógra tóra*, which was sent to all garda stations.

It read:

DESCRIPTION: 30 to 35 years. 5ft 8ins to 5ft 9ins, medium to light build. Dark hair, neatly groomed but appears bushy or long at the back.
Clean shaven though may now have a light growth of beard.
May wear dark horn-rimmed square type glasses. N.B. He has a habit of wearing the glasses on the tip of his nose and looking out over them.
His hands and finger nails are well kept – they would give the impression that he is a professional type person.
Speaks with what is described as a soft cultured educated accent. The accent has been described as upper-class Dublin to English. It is possible that the accent is English.
The man's complexion has been described as sallow to pale and sickly looking.
The man has a peculiar gait. He walks with a slight slouch with his head held forward. He gives the impression that he is walking against the wind. He has the habit of walking with his left hand in his pocket.

DRESS: Normally wears some type of head dress. N.B. usually a peaked cap which he wears towards the front of his head with the peak down over his eyes. Dark coloured brownish/green tweed jacket. The jacket may give the impression that it is a poor fit i.e short in the sleeves.
Dark coloured open neck shirt.
Dark pants.
Black leather laced boots, nicely polished.

May be in possession of a dark coloured mackintosh coat, which he may wear, or carry over his arm.

PECULIARITIES:
Normally carries a bag, which has been variously described as –
Black polythene refuse sack.
Blue hold all.
White plastic shopping bag.
The man has a habit of carrying some type of implement wrapped in brown paper or black plastic.
He appears to have a craze for the sport of clay pigeon shooting.
He likes water i.e. rivers, canals and boats.
Usually travels on foot or on bus.

GENERAL:
The first impression this man gives is that he is an 'oddball' of some type.
However, when he speaks he gives the impression that he is cultured and educated.

He is quiet and will not speak unless spoken to. He has been described as the 'French Artist Type', a Geologist and an Engineer.

The Commissioner directs that enquiries be made at the following premises in a determined effort to locate the man.

Hotels, Lodging Houses and Licensed Premises.

Shops and Cafes (urban and rural).

Firearms Dealers.

Mental Institutions, Homes, Rehabilitation Units, Drug Units, Hostels etc.

Hospitals.

Clay pigeon shoots (both official and flapper meetings). It is possible that this man may turn up at a clay pigeon shoot. With this in mind, particulars of all clay pigeon shoots in each Division should be obtained.

The bulletin was uncannily accurate in its description of the mystery killer, down to his studied manner, the air of a cultured and educated person, his habit of not speaking until spoken to and the "oddball" gait, including his habit of stuffing one hand into his jacket pocket. But the investigation would remain completely in the dark as to the strange man's whereabouts for some time yet. Indeed, it was over a week later, on the morning of Monday, 2 August, when the next significant development came.

A detective in the incident room in Kevin Street Garda Station got a call from the fingerprint section of the garda technical bureau. It had examined the fingerprints lifted from the milk carton and the Sunday newspaper in Edenderry. The process had taken some days, but the bureau concluded that the Edenderry fingerprints matched with those left on the polythene bag that was used to wrap the shovel abandoned in the Phoenix Park.

It was a major breakthrough. The murders of Bridie Gargan and Dónal Dunne had been conclusively linked. The same man was responsible for both homicides. But the investigation was no closer to finding out who, or where, he was.

# 12

# A GARGANTUAN SEARCH

"We realised very quickly that it was another wild goose chase." Detective Tony Hickey, murder squad

The man leading the murder investigation, John Courtney, was a figure not to be taken for granted by those who worked under him.

One detective, Brian Sherry, said, "He was a tough man to work with. You didn't bullshit Courtney. You daren't bring in a statement that was only half done, or where you had failed to ask all the relevant questions.

"If you prepared a statement you made sure you asked everything. You drained the witness of every scrap of information they had in their head, you bore into them to try to get it.

"Courtney would be there at the table at six o'clock in the morning reading the statements. And if your statement was not up to scratch, when the conference started he would tear ribbons off you. He would roar at you: 'Why did you not ask that man this question? Get back out there. Get back out there and go back to the man and ask him that question.'"

Courtney had a controversial career – not least because it was alleged he used 'heavy gang' tactics years earlier to coerce confessions out of suspects. But no one would deny he was dogged, obsessively thorough in his work. He was phlegmatic and curt in manner and expected all who worked with him to put in the long hours that he did.

"I didn't tolerate slackers or hangers-on," he wrote in his autobiography, *It Was Murder*. "Many could not stick the pace and disappeared off the investigation team altogether. I was very happy to get rid of them. Officers who made excuses of going on holidays, or whatever, were dropped. I wanted total commitment."

By that he meant that while a murder case was ongoing, there was no such thing as a weekend, or knocking off a little early on a weekday, or avoiding early mornings.

"From eight o'clock in the morning until 10 or 12 o'clock at night, you were just focused on the jobs you had to do," said John O'Mahony, the young detective involved in his first murder investigation.

And so it was for the team of detectives on the hunt for Ireland's possible serial killer at large. Edenderry had provided an eye-witness-rich environment for statements. When news of the Dunne murder broke, many people came forward with descriptions that gardaí were able to assemble into a very precise description of the killer who loped around the town and around the Harbour between Saturday and

Sunday. The forensic evidence that had arrived over a week after his death only confirmed what gardaí knew: both murders were connected.

It would take a further four days before the gardaí would publicly make the connection between the two killings. On 6 August 1982, DSI John Courtney would tell *The Irish Times*: "The description of the culprits tally. And in both cases, the murderer used his victim's car to get away from the scene. We don't overlook those sorts of facts when we are investigating murders."

However, despite the detailed profile of the killer, the tried and tested methods of the garda murder squad, under the control of Courtney, were failing to turn up anything of use. The suspect did not fit the profile of any known criminal or paramilitary. They could establish no connection between him and his victims, nor any connection between him and his victims' work, their acquaintances, or their localities. Nor could they establish any link between the two young victims.

Despite the Hansel and Gretel trail left when fleeing after the first attack on 22 July, it took gardaí many days, and hundreds of interviews, to establish that Macarthur had taken the 19 bus to Finglas on Dublin's northside. The search wasn't helped by the fact that nobody from the Fingal House pub came forward with information. This, despite a strange man with a bloody shirt appearing in the pub on the evening Bridie Gargan was attacked, a man who then went into the toilet and spent fifteen minutes hacking off his beard with dry razor blades.

In the early days of the week following the Gargan attack,

a large team of detectives were scouring the northside of the city, calling door-to-door and distributing flyers. They were under the command of Detective Superintendent Hubert Reynolds, another murder squad veteran, who was also leading the related Dónal Dunne investigation in Edenderry. The theory that the suspect might be hiding on the northside of the city was buttressed by members of the gun clubs in Balheary and Ashbourne, who came forward to describe a strange, bearded man with bottle-thick glasses who hung around while their shoots were in progress.

The piecing together of the suspect's movements was laborious and frustratingly slow. It was only when gardaí called into the Fingal House pub as part of their routine inquiries in the first days of August that they learned of the bearded man with the bloody shirt who arrived into the pub on the Thursday evening of 22 July. And it was 3 August, 12 days after the attack on Bridie Gargan, when they finally tracked down the taxi driver who had taken the suspect from the pub.

Unlike the Dublin murder, the trail that ran from the murder scene in Offaly was pieced together quickly. Within days of Dónal Dunne's murder, the Offaly hurling supporters who had inadvertently followed the stolen Ford Escort into Dublin came forward. The men were able to describe where the car had been parked and gave a good description of the man they saw getting out of it. Gardaí arrived in Fownes Street to begin a detailed examination of the abandoned car.

Beyond this point, however, the trail ran cold. The savage killer with the posh accent and distinct mannerisms had seemingly evaporated into that summer's haze. There was a growing sense of urgency.

DSI Courtney reflected this concern when he appeared on television and radio later that week, pleading with the public not to shelter the murderer, hinting that he could kill again.

The Gargan and Dunne murders were not the only active cases, however. Although they came at a time when murder was a rare occurrence in Ireland – the official garda report for 1981 noted a total of 24 murders in the Republic for the whole of that year – the summer of 1982 produced an unusually high cluster. In a remarkable run of events, over the course of the two days from 22 July to 24 July 1982, four people had been fatally attacked: Bridie Gargan, Dónal Dunne, Robert Belton and Patricia Furlong. It meant the resources of the murder squad were spread across four separate events and left things stretched to breaking point.

"Four killings in two days, the violence was quite shocking," recalled journalist Peter Murtagh. "My memory is that there was – hysteria is the wrong word – extreme anxiety amongst the public and extreme anxiety amongst the gardaí, naturally enough, who are charged with ensuring public safety and solving crimes. Suddenly, they had four murders on their plate in a matter of a couple of days."

Robert Belton was shot by an IRA gang during an armed raid of the north Dublin post office where he was postmaster. Patricia Furlong was a 21-year-old woman who attended a music festival in the Dublin mountains on the night of Friday, 23 July – the day after Bridie Gargan had been attacked and left for dead. The following morning, a farmer discovered

Patricia's body in a field a few hundred metres away. She was partially naked and her blouse had been used as a ligature to strangle her.

Very briefly, gardaí considered the possibility that there might be a link between her murder and that of Bridie Gargan, given how proximate the attacks had been to each other. But within hours this was ruled out. The motive for the Furlong killing was sexual violence, the method very different, and the killer was, in all likelihood, known to the victim. Whoever the Furlong killer was, gardaí quickly formed a view it was not the same person who had killed Bridie Gargan.

An incident room was set up in Stepaside Garda Station on Dublin's southside for the Furlong murder. People willing to give statements queued outside the station for hours. By the time the investigation came to an end, over 1,350 statements had been gathered from people who attended the festival alone, all of which had to be checked and cross-checked.

An English DJ, Vincent Connell, who attended the festival, was one of those interviewed by gardaí. He subsequently emigrated to South Africa but was arrested almost eight years later, in 1990, and charged with Patricia Furlong's murder. He was subsequently convicted but was released four years later on appeal. His appeal was grounded on a claim that the guards had deprived him of sleep and had subjected him to verbal and physical abuse. Key witness evidence that put Patricia Furlong in the company of other men, including a distinctive-looking young man, much later that night (long after it was agreed Connell had gone home), had never been put to the jury.

*

Once the link between the Gargan and Dunne cases was established, garda operations scaled up greatly. There were teams of detectives working in north Dublin, in Edenderry, and around Dublin city centre.

DSI John Courtney's tried and trusted method was to carpet-bomb everybody in the locality of a crime with questionnaires. As with the Patricia Furlong case, a huge volume of statements on both the Gargan and Dunne cases was taken. There were also many tip-offs from the public identifying possible sightings of the strange suspect.

Inevitably, some of those leads led on to false trails. The very first assignment the young detectives John O'Mahony and Frank Hand received when they joined the team was to check out psychiatric hospitals in Dublin. The savagery of the attack on Bridie Gargan had raised the possibility of a criminally insane killer on the loose.

O'Mahony thought they had struck gold when a psychiatrist in St Patrick's Hospital told them that a man who had been admitted on the day of the attack fitted the attacker's description. The man could not be interviewed as he was under sedation in a secure unit. A few hours later he was ruled out. He had been nowhere near the Phoenix Park on the day in question.

Brian Sherry was an experienced detective with the Central Detective Unit (CDU), which tracked major criminals and armed robberies. His partner in the CDU was another experienced investigator, Kevin Tunney. Both were seconded to the murder inquiry.

Long retired, Sherry now lives in a neat suburban home in north Dublin not too far from the site of the Fingal House pub, which is now a Tesco Express. "Kevin and myself were plods in this investigation," he told me. "It sounds terrible. But that's what we were. We were investigators. We made inquiries, we interviewed people and took statements from them, all that sort of stuff, and brought it back to the incident room in Kevin Street."

A member of the public contacted Kevin Street to identify a potential suspect. Sherry visited the person identified in his flat in Rathmines. The first thing he noticed was that the man came from money. The second thing he noticed was the pungent – and unmistakable – smell of hash.

He was dressed in a bohemian manner, and wore a hat not dissimilar to the tweed fisherman's hat the attacker had worn. The man quickly made a full confession and seemed to know a lot of details around the murder. But something seemed off to Sherry, even as he brought him back to the station for questioning.

"I went to John Courtney and told him this guy had made a full confession. 'Look,' I said, 'I went into the flat and there was the distinct smell of cannabis. I think he's a bit affected. I don't think this guy is the real McCoy.'"

Courtney went downstairs and chatted with the self-confessed "murderer". The conversation did not last long. He came back up within minutes, told Sherry his instincts were right, and ordered the man to be "returned to sender" as quickly as possible.

John O'Mahony had his own share of wild goose chases that summer. It was the driest July since records began in 1837, and he knew all about it. He was working purgatorial hours in purgatorial heat.

He, along with the more experienced Tony Hickey and Kevin Tunney, spent the guts of the last week of July travelling around the south-east of the country trying to check out a suspect. Gardaí had received an anonymous call that a man who travelled the country was a good fit for the suspect for the two murders.

When they caught up with the man, they discovered he was a bible salesman, a flim-flam man who scammed and tricked his way through the countryside, high-tailing it without paying from guesthouses and removing the number plates from his car before robbing petrol from garages as he journeyed around.

O'Mahony recalled that this man had been identified by a member of the public as a suspect and his appearance and mannerisms were not unlike the mystery killer's.

"He proved extremely difficult to rule out," said O'Mahony. "We had everything ruled out except the critical two or three hours on that Thursday afternoon."

Eventually he told them that he was selling bibles house-to-house off the main road between Arklow in County Wicklow and Gorey in County Wexford, and the detectives' painstaking follow-up revealed it to be so.

Out on the road, as they were from dawn to dusk, the detectives were not contactable. It would be a decade yet before mobile phones became common. "Nobody could contact you. When you were in Gorey you were gone."

The elimination work was slow, painstaking and mundane. As July drifted into August, they seemed no closer to finding the killer, despite the mountain of information that had come into the incident room at Kevin Street. The murder squad was coming under increasing pressure – from the upper echelons of the force, from politicians, and from a wary public – to find the possible serial killer.

"The suspect we were seeking wasn't your ordinary criminal," said Sherry. "Your ordinary criminal is street savvy and he is crime savvy." Sherry said there was none of the hallmarks of the experienced criminal in either of the crimes, describing how detectives were confused about the motives behind the killings, with no rational explanations suggesting themselves at that moment. "We didn't know who he was at the time," he said. "We didn't know at that stage if this was a chance intervention in life between two people that just happened."

Tragically, that is exactly what it was. For that reason, the killer remained elusive, unknown, just beyond reach. For now.

# 13

## A DOUBLE-KILLER PREPARES HIS NEXT STRIKE

"I brought the gun with me to my digs at Mrs Hughes' house.
A couple of days after that I cut about 12 inches off the
barrels of this gun." Malcolm Macarthur

Macarthur had lain low for several days after the Dunne
killing, emerging from his Dún Laoghaire guesthouse only to
buy newspapers and food. At some stage he went to the local
hardware store, Murdochs, and bought a hacksaw. He used it
to shorten the length of the barrel of the Miroku shotgun by
12 inches. That task took him most of a day. All the while he
was listening closely to news bulletins on the radio to find out
details of the garda investigations into his attacks.

By midweek, his confidence grew that gardaí were not
closing in on him. His caution about venturing out too soon
was offset by the knowledge that time was running out.
After all, he had told Brenda Little he would return to Tenerife

the following weekend. It seems clear that at this time he recognised his grand plan to rob a bank was beyond his capabilities. Yet, he was desperate to get his hands on money fast and so needed to find an easy mark. Having acquired his shotgun, he prepared for his next strike.

On the Wednesday evening of 28 July, he travelled from Dún Laoghaire to Dublin city centre and his old stomping ground of Fitzwilliam Square. An acquaintance lived there, an elderly man whom Macarthur knew to be wealthy.

When the man opened the door, he was surprised to see Malcolm Macarthur standing there. The pair had not met for several years. Macarthur said that he had been passing and had decided to call in on a whim. The man invited him in.

Macarthur was wearing brown vinyl gloves that he did not take off when he entered. When the man pointed to them, Macarthur explained he needed to wear them because he was suffering from a skin condition.

He led Macarthur into the sitting room and the pair sat down. Macarthur placed the blue hold-all bag he was carrying on the floor beside him. Inside was the loaded Miroku over-and-under shotgun with a sawn-off barrel and ten cartridges.

They had a polite, tentative conversation. Macarthur told the man he had been living in Tenerife for some time but had come back to Ireland to sort out financial affairs. Within minutes, however, the doorbell rang again. The man's son and daughter-in-law arrived. They were coming for dinner and the owner invited Macarthur to stay too, which he accepted.

If Macarthur was displeased when the couple arrived, he didn't let it show. On the contrary, he quickly settled into dinner party mode as the conversation took off on a wide range of topics. He spoke at some length and with great authority about the importance of preserving the Georgian character of the square, showing off his knowledge of the architecture and history of the fine houses which surrounded them, with their colourful doors and elaborate fanlights.

It made for a pleasant evening. When he removed his gloves in the heat of the night, it wasn't lost on his hosts that the skin on his hands appeared to be unblemished.

The family bid farewell to Macarthur at 1.30am, blissfully unaware of what a lucky escape they'd had. The unassuming intervention by the son and daughter-in-law was likely a lifesaving one, averting the old man from being held at gunpoint and robbed.

Six days on from the murder of Bridie Gargan, three days on from that of Dónal Dunne, the killer vanished into the night, acutely aware of how badly he was failing in his attempts to restore the fortune he once had but frittered away.

# 14

## THE MAN WHO
## WOULD BE KING

"You've got to throw your ambition far enough ahead if you want to succeed." Charles J Haughey

August could not have come a moment too soon for Charles J Haughey. His long-awaited holiday on his private island of Inishvickillane was within his sights. The first six months of his second term as taoiseach had turned out to be a white-knuckle ride. Every Monday of every week since February the odds were stacked against his fragile government surviving until the following weekend. But, somehow, it had survived. Haughey's unshakeable belief that he had been born to lead had served him once more.

Charles J Haughey's ability to succeed was apparent from his early days. The headline of an *Irish Press* report from 17 August 1938 read, "First of 500". Underneath was a photograph of a boy one month shy of his 13th birthday, his features striking: a wide forehead, Grecian nose, and hooded eyes with a steady, all-knowing gaze. The short report read:

> Twelve and a half years old, Cathal Haughey of Belton Park, Dublin, won first place among 500 entrants in this year's Dublin Corporation Scholarships to secondary schools.

The young boy was destined for greatness. He would win scholarship after scholarship, excel on the sports field, and show a natural leadership instinct, matched by ambition and confidence, that were obvious to anyone who met him.

"You have to remember the Roman centurion," Haughey once observed. "He would throw the standard into the ranks of the enemy and dare his troops to follow. You've got to throw your ambition far enough ahead if you want to succeed."

Haughey's ascent was not a smooth one. But the perilous and lengthy route he chose finally brought him to the summit in December 1979, when he was elected leader of Fianna Fáil and taoiseach of the country.

In his early 20s, Cathal was dropped in favour of the more worldly Charles J. Gary Murphy has observed in his eponymous biography, *Haughey*, that the two names provided a neat shorthand for the dichotomy that characterised the man: Cathal, the smart, able and visionary public figure; Charles J, the vain, greedy and corrupt politician.

Haughey had risen through the political ranks, becoming a minister in the 1960s. At the same time, he amassed a huge fortune in mysterious circumstances. He owned Abbeville, a grand Georgian mansion on an enormous tree-lined estate in

Kinsealy, just seven miles north of Dublin city centre. He was living "high on the hog", as the journalist Peter Murtagh put it, enjoying a lifestyle that was far beyond the reach of an Irish politician at the time.

Those who knew Haughey say he was obsessed with distancing himself from the penury he experienced as a child. That desire for trappings and financial security was a huge motivating factor in his life.

Haughey's father, Johnny, was an Old IRA and War of Independence hero who contracted multiple sclerosis at a young age and was effectively invalided. His wife, Sarah, was a determined and hard-working woman who kept a tight leash on her seven children as they grew up, ensuring each won scholarships. Charles was the second eldest, considered the brightest and the most precocious.

Emily O'Reilly, a political journalist at the time Haughey was taoiseach, has no doubt that escaping from poverty was a huge motivating factor in his life, and why the wealth he accumulated as an adult was so important to him.

"I remember talking to a friend of Charlie's, who said when he was a young man he remembered going into the kitchen and the father was in a wheelchair, a particular chair from which he rarely moved.

"He remembered that the carpet was worn, it was worn from just that chair. It's an image that resonated with me. [The friend] said that Haughey had a fear of poverty and he certainly got over his fear, because he became instantly, and quite miraculously, very rich."

Haughey was an exceptional student. He was awarded a first-class honours degree in commerce and qualified as a barrister the following year. He started seeing Maureen Lemass – daughter of a founding father of the state and future taoiseach, Sean Lemass – while they were students in University College Dublin. The pair married in 1951. He was elected to the Dáil later that decade.

Running in parallel with his public life was his relentless pursuit of riches. Through his accountancy practice, Haughey struck up a friendship with the developer Matt Gallagher of the Gallagher Group. He bought a period house, and lands, in Raheny off Gallagher which was later rezoned, and Haughey made a killing on it when selling it back to Gallagher. It was a murky deal, and was the first known instance of Haughey accepting the patronage of wealthy business people. The politician had effectively been bankrolled by one of Ireland's most powerful property developers. The profits allowed him to buy Abbeville, an impressive ivy-clad mansion with 300 acres of prime land in Kinsealy, designed by the celebrated 18th-century architect James Gandon.

With the acquisition of Abbeville, the northside boy from Donnycarney had arrived. The lavish spending did not stop there. He bought a stud farm, rode to hounds with the Fingal Harriers, drove expensive cars, wore bespoke suits and shirts tailored in Paris, and ate at Dublin's finest restaurants like the Mirabeau and Le Coq Hardi. Despite being married with young children, he also had a reputation as a Lothario and began an affair with socialite and columnist Terry Keane in 1972 that lasted for almost three decades.

Later Haughey would acquire an impressive yacht, travel by helicopter, and buy his own island, Inishvickillane, off the coast of Kerry. The satirical magazine *The Phoenix* referred to him as 'Squire Haughey'.

Haughey left the handling of his finances to an accountant named Des Traynor, who had done his articles with the Haughey Boland firm in the late 1950s. A chain-smoking, behind-the-scenes type of presence, Traynor was as tough as nails when negotiating. Utterly devoted to his old accountancy firm boss, he effectively became Haughey's bagman, negotiating ever-bigger loans with banks, and cajoling more businessmen to contribute to the Haughey fund. All the while Haughey's spending became more lavish and his debts accumulated. Traynor and Haughey brazened it out, calculating, correctly, that nobody would have the courage to call them out on it.

TK Whitaker, the most accomplished civil servant who ever served the Irish state, could not but notice the change from Cathal to Charles J.

"There was a spectacular change psychologically from the young man who grew up in ordinary surroundings, probably liked a packet of Woodbines and a pint, to an ascendancy figure who liked horses and champagne and so on. There is a big psychological question there as to how that transition occurred."

The trappings with which Haughey now surrounded himself – the lifestyle he adopted, his taste for the better things in life – were exemplified in his Abbeville mansion, which was on a par with Breemount where the Macarthurs had prospered, until they didn't. But while Haughey had risen from poverty to seemingly great wealth, by the late 1960s the Macarthurs' pendulum had swung the other way.

At the time Haughey moved into Abbeville in 1969, he was minister for finance. He was seen as favourite to succeed Jack Lynch as Fianna Fáil party leader. It seemed he was on the cusp of achieving his lifetime ambition.

However, by April 1970, the high-flying finance minister found himself trapped in a political bunker, from which there was no escape. When communal violence flared up in the North of Ireland in 1969, the Irish government approved a sum of £100,000 for the relief of besieged nationalist communities in the six counties. Haughey was a key member of the committee that controlled the funds.

A secret consignment of arms was due to arrive into Dublin Airport from Vienna. Garda special branch became aware of it and put a "ring of steel" around the airport. The weapons never arrived despite a phone call by Haughey to have the consignment pass unhindered through customs. The arms were allegedly part of a batch funded by that same special committee – of which Haughey was an influential member – whose job was to control the funds designated for the relief of nationalist communities. Under pressure from the opposition, Taoiseach Jack Lynch immediately sacked Haughey from his position as minister for finance.

The secret plot to import arms created an enormous scandal that cleaved cabinet unity and sharply divided opinion. Haughey denied he was involved in the plot.

Nevertheless, he was arrested and tried in the Circuit Court in October 1970 on a charge of illegally importing arms into the state. His defence was that he did not know the shipments were arms. The case was convoluted and revolved around who knew what. The jury sided with Haughey, acquitting him on all counts.

The Arms Crisis was to prove a grievous wound for Fianna Fáil that suppurated for many years afterwards. Enmities were created that lasted for the whole of political lifetimes, with the party divided into Haughey and Lynch factions.

Politically, Haughey was at a dead end. His ministerial career was over and his ambitions had been set at naught. He remained within Fianna Fáil but he was now on the back benches, defenestrated by the taoiseach, ostracised by his former cabinet colleagues.

It was the equivalent of a once-famous actor doing pantomime at the end of a pier. Haughey had little choice but to play a long game, an unglamorous comeback, most of which would be played facing into the wind.

Over the next seven years until 1977, Haughey visited almost every branch, or *cumann*, of Fianna Fáil throughout the country. There were hundreds of them. Fianna Fáil was the largest political organisation in Ireland, with over 20,000 members. It had a presence in almost every hamlet and crossroads in the state. That masochistic exercise of midweek and weekend trips to distant parish halls – arriving back to Dublin in the dead of night – became known as the "rubber chicken circuit". It was a reference to the bill of fare invariably offered when they stopped for dinner at country hotels and pubs.

Haughey was cultivating faithful followers within the grassroots. But for those who were at the upper echelons of the party, there was a mutual distrust that would never fade.

As far as his finances were concerned, Haughey was also facing mountainous obstacles. Out of office, with neither power to wield nor influence to offer, he could no longer fund his extravagant lifestyle. His debts began to mount. The solution he came up with for his money problems was simple, brazen and effective.

On a morning in June 1973, Charles J Haughey walked into a branch of Allied Irish Banks (AIB) on Dame Street in Dublin. While no longer a minister, he remained an instantly recognisable figure and his presence still caused a frisson in the building.

He was there to open an account. Gerry Scanlan, later a chief executive of the bank, described a customer like Haughey as a KBI, shorthand for 'key business influencer'.

The bank made one fatal flaw with its prestigious new KBI. It gave him a chequebook. Within weeks Charles Haughey was spending heavily on it and ordering replacements. To its cost, the bank belatedly realised the kind of KBI he was. The only business he had a key influence on was AIB, and not in a good way.

Haughey's spending was prodigious. Within a year, his debts to AIB had surpassed six figures. He had also massively overdrawn his accounts with other banks.

At the time he bought his island of Inishvickillane for £25,000 he owed £600,000 to the bank.

The flagrant spending continued. By 1976, AIB decided it would adopt a hard-line approach to Haughey. JJ Denvir was the eastern area general manager and a buttoned-up kind of guy. At a meeting in October that year, Denvir demanded that Haughey return his chequebook.

What happened then was so surprising that even the dry minutes of an internal bank memo capture the drama and shock. The then 51-year-old Haughey turned on the officials with a tirade of abuse.

As Denvir noted: "Mr Haughey became quite vicious. He said he would not give up his chequebooks as he had to live and we were dealing with an adult and no banker would talk to him in this manner. He further stated if any drastic action were taken by the bank he could be a 'very troublesome adversary'."

The bank retreated and continued to issue him with chequebooks.

The forbearance of AIB, along with a number of other banks, allowed Haughey to keep a Daimler and a Mercedes, wear bespoke suits and Charvet shirts from Paris that each cost the equivalent of a month's average industrial wage, and dine regularly with his mistress, social diarist Terry Keane, in the exclusive Le Coq Hardi restaurant. His favourite dessert was, apparently, Gateau Diane. He was also known to spend lavishly on the restaurant's notoriously expensive wine list. A friend once saw him spend £500 on a bottle of 1967 Château d'Yquem when dining with a group of guests.

Meanwhile, given his popularity with the party's foot soldiers around the country and his growing influence, Lynch had no choice but to bring Haughey back to the front bench in 1975 when the party was in opposition.

Lynch won a landslide general election for Fianna Fáil in 1977 with a manifesto promising tax cuts and increased spending. The one silver lining for Haughey was that most of the new intake were "his people". Within a year, however, the economy was in decline and the fortunes of Lynch's government also plummeted.

Haughey was appointed minister for health. He looked for the kind of "wow" policies that had got him noticed in other portfolios earlier in his career, such as free travel for pensioners. He increased spending significantly and got approval for two major hospitals in Dublin, Beaumont (in his own constituency) and Tallaght, plus county hospitals everywhere. He also committed publicly to give up smoking, to lead by example, as it were. It was a stunt but it worked with the public – Haughey's popularity was at an all-time high.

He and his supporters were biding their time to make a move. The tipping point came in late 1979 when Fianna Fáil lost two by-elections for seats the party had held in Lynch's stronghold of County Cork.

Frank Dunlop, then government press secretary, was with Lynch on an official visit to Washington when news of the by-election losses came through. Recalling Lynch's reaction, Dunlop said he "was absolutely flabbergasted and shocked. Physically he showed it in his features."

When the official visit moved on to Boston, Lynch called Dunlop aside one evening when he was at a loose end. "We had a long chat. Jack was very fond of a glass of Paddy. And I think he had one or two glasses of Paddy. And he said, 'Look, I want to tell you something. I'm going to resign.'"

The taoiseach was as good as his word and stepped down by the end of the year, paving the way for Charlie Haughey's comeback after a decade in exile. George Colley, who was in the same class as Haughey in O'Connell's School, was his rival in the leadership election. Both politicians were not on good terms and Colley was the preferred candidate of the Lynch camp. In a sense, all those rubber chicken dinners came home to roost for Haughey. While Colley was backed by the vast majority of ministers, Haughey had cultivated the grass roots and was revered by the ordinary members. Most of the new intake of TDs were also his "people". After a bitter leadership battle, Haughey won the backing of 44 of the party's TDs to Colley's 38. At the age of 54, he became taoiseach, and leader of the country.

In public, he had triumphed. In private, his finances were out of control. Haughey's debts to AIB totalled £1 million at that stage.

As 1979 turned to 1980 and a new decade, it was evident that the country's economic prospects were bleak. All the indicators were pointing to a stark reality – after three years of spendthrift giveaways, Ireland was facing a bitter recession.

Soon after becoming government leader, Haughey made a famous live TV address to the nation, in which he spelled out the grim realities the government was now facing. "As a community, we are living way beyond our means," he said.

The irony of that was not lost on many people when, years later, the secrets of Haughey's finances and lifestyle were revealed.

Haughey came into government in mid-term and the adulation given to him by the party's grass roots was not shared elsewhere. He had many enemies outside his party, but also enemies within. His leading internal critic in Fianna Fáil, George Colley, in a cutting put-down of Haughey, referred to "low standards in high places".

It went beyond a lack of trust, and beyond the Arms Crisis

schism. For some, Haughey was a flawed politician with questionable motives. As journalist Olivia O'Leary has observed, "What always strikes me about Haughey was this guy was so bright, he would have become leader of his party, and he would have become taoiseach without ever having to take shortcuts.

"Deep down, he didn't believe in himself. And that's why he took shortcuts. And the other reason he took shortcuts was he had become used to a lifestyle that involved a private island, racehorses, helicopters, whatever. In order to maintain that lifestyle, he needed to be in power . . .

"There was a sort of a Faustian pact there, that if he hadn't had the rich lifestyle, he could have just gone steadily and straight to the top. But because he had become wedded to that, because he was indebted, because he needed that sort of money, he needed to be in power by hook or by crook and was probably ready to use whatever methods were needed."

The Troubles seeped into the politics of the South in 1981. Across the border, a hundred miles to the north, ten republican prisoners, all in their 20s, died that year after going on hunger strike in the H-Blocks.

Haughey could have waited until 1982 to call an election but was determined to go early. He enjoyed a big majority in the Dáil but that had been won by Jack Lynch when he was leader. He was determined to get validation and secure a majority of his own.

On 21 May 1981, Haughey called a general election for 11 June. That allowed for a tight three-week campaign. Minister for Agriculture Ray MacSharry, one of the few who was not afraid to confront Haughey, implored him not to run. "We are up to our eyes in Provos and hunger strikes. Why would we want to run now?" he challenged him.

In the election, Fianna Fáil's vote fell by 5 per cent. Two H-Block candidates were elected, winning seats that would have, in the normal course of events, gone to Fianna Fáil.

To his surprise and consternation, Haughey found himself back in opposition, with his great rival, Garret FitzGerald of Fine Gael, becoming taoiseach. It was a blow to his confidence and gave succour to his own internal enemies.

The June 1981 election marked the beginning of a volatile and shambolic 18 months in Irish politics. FitzGerald's government's majority was as fragile as gossamer wings, relying on the support of two independents. The government lasted a mere seven months, falling over a controversial budget proposal that would have imposed new taxes on children's shoes.

In the subsequent election in February 1982, Haughey's advisers prevailed on him to take a more sober, less flamboyant, approach to the campaign. It was another close-run thing. Haughey increased his party's vote share and secured 81 seats, but was still three seats shy of a majority. He and FitzGerald each began to barter with the few independents in the Dáil as well as the three TDs elected from the left-wing Workers' Party.

As both vied to form a government, all eyes turned to a newly elected teacher from one of Dublin's poorest areas, the north inner city. Tony Gregory was a left-wing republican independent, then aged 35. He was intense in nature and slightly humourless in personality but had a self-assuredness and purpose that belied his novice status. On his first day in Leinster House, he caused consternation among officials by flouting the rule that required TDs to wear a tie while in the Dáil chamber.

He was courted by both Haughey and FitzGerald. Despite his wealthy lifestyle, Haughey had not departed from his working-class north Dublin roots and had no trouble travelling to Gregory's base in Seán McDermott Street for the crucial negotiations. FitzGerald, a product of Dublin's affluent southern suburbs, lacked that common touch. Gregory found little about the Fine Gael leader that was relatable to him or his life.

The encounter between Haughey and the new TD was to go down in history. Famously, Haughey's opening gambit to Gregory was, 'Well, you know what I want, so what do you want?'

The new TD wanted a lot and got most of it. It included at least £100 million in support to the north inner city. Despite the eye-watering sums involved, Haughey readily signed what became known as the Gregory Deal. He delivered a parting shot to the young TD as he left the final meeting: "As Al Capone said, I like doing business with you."

With Gregory onside, Haughey had the support he needed to form a government. He got on with the job of appointing ministers. His choice of attorney general was particularly interesting as it harked right back to the Arms Trial, and a member of his legal team at that time. He chose his old friend, a low-profile, old-fashioned senior counsel named Paddy Connolly. As August 1982 veered into sight, Connolly had been in the role of attorney general for six months, negotiating the tough transition from the Law Library into the cut and thrust of the highest legal office in the land. As with Haughey, what lay just ahead for Paddy Connolly would place any recent challenges in the ha'penny place.

# 15

## SILENT WITNESS

"When I told her that I thought I knew the murderer she just laughed." John Monks, news vendor

It was the red racing bicycle that first caught John Monks' eye on that sun-splattered day in early August 1982. It seemed at odds with the well-dressed man who brought it to a halt at the kerb near the newsstand that Monks operated.

Monks recognised the man immediately even though it had been a fortnight since he had last seen him, and even though he was now markedly different in appearance. Back in July, the man had been wearing a beard; now he was clean-shaven. His clothes were different too. Gone were the military jumper, bottle-lens glasses and fisherman's hat. He was now wearing a beige jacket, white shirt and sunglasses.

The man stood for a long time, his hands in his pockets, looking at the news vendor. "At first I thought he was about to buy a paper as usual, but then I realised he seemed to be checking to see if I recognised him," Monks said.

Monks felt "creeped out" by the experience. It struck him that he was being subjected to some kind of identity parade.

The following day, Wednesday, 4 August, Monks spotted the man again, this time at lunchtime, outside the local Allied Irish Banks branch in Dún Laoghaire. He was curious to see what he was up to and discreetly followed him into the bank.

The man was wearing a corduroy jacket, grey trousers and a yellow silk cravat. He went up to the counter and seemed to withdraw money. Monks hung back and watched him from the shadows.

"I made sure he didn't see me. He was carrying a weekend case with some design on it – the sort of weekend case you often see girls carrying. And he had a blue rain Macintosh which covered something underneath it.

"I was very suspicious of that rain Macintosh. If you have ever seen anyone carrying a shotgun, it looked exactly like that."

It was on that day, 13 days after the attack on Bridie Gargan, that Monks first asked himself whether this man could be the murderer the whole country was talking about. It was only a hunch. Back at his flat that evening, he had a conversation with his girlfriend about it.

"When I told her that I thought I knew the murderer, she just laughed," he said. "I suppose anybody would have. That's another reason why I wasn't too keen to go to the police. I thought they would think I was spinning a yarn."

Despite the extraordinary detail about Macarthur's appearance and mannerisms in the *Fógra Tóra* internal bulletin, for reasons unknown, the gardaí had given only a generic description of the killer to the public, noting the wavy black hair, thin frame and posh accent. "One man's description was that he looked like a white-collar worker," DSI John Courtney had told *The Irish Times* in late July. That kind of information was not particularly helpful, as it described a significant portion of the adult population.

Monks' hunch might never have gone any further than his own private suspicions, were it not for a suggestion from a garda involved in the team that would change the course of the investigation. He had seen crime-scene re-enactments on BBC TV, and suggested a similar exercise be broadcast on RTÉ. The Garda Síochána and the Department of Justice were conservative bodies and their approach to communications had changed little since the foundation of the state. Surprisingly, it was agreed.

"There was a detective called Steven Sheehan who had a beard," recalled Detective John O'Mahony, "and he looked something like the suspect. They got him to dress up and wear the fisherman hat. He walked along the joggers' path in the Phoenix Park."

The re-enactment was broadcast on Thursday, 5 August on an RTÉ programme called *Garda Patrol*. For the first time, the public got a real sense of the killer's appearance and manner. There was a huge public response.

John Monks was in his flat that night with his girlfriend and saw the programme. "Something clicked when I watched it. They had a man dressed up in the sort of crazy gear that this guy used to wear and it was probably that what got through to me."

He now felt sure that this man was the murderer. On Friday morning, August 6, John Monks went to his boss George Davis, himself only in his twenties at the time, with his bombshell news and asked for his advice on what he should do.

"He said he was spooked and told me there was something funny about this guy who bought papers off him," Davis recalled to me. "I thought it was strange because the guards were up in the northside of the city using helicopters and all. I told John to contact the guards immediately."

Monks was reluctant to go to the gardaí. He was also a committed republican, which made for an uneasy relationship with the apparatus of the state. Davis persuaded him to go, however. He went down to the local station in Dún Laoghaire and told the desk sergeant what he knew. The information was passed onto the 'book man' in the incident room in Kevin Street Garda Station, who assigned two detectives to take a statement from this new witness.

"Later that day, these two rookies came out to talk to John," said George Davis.

The rookies in question were detectives John O'Mahony and Frank Hand. They met Monks and took down a full statement from him.

Recalls O'Mahony, "I dropped the statement back into Dún Laoghaire on Friday evening. And that was my job done. I went home and got a phone call around 10 o'clock that night with instructions that I was to go to Kilmainham Garda Station because the superintendent wanted to see me."

O'Mahony had seen DSI John Courtney administer a few tongue-lashings over the previous few weeks, and as he set out for the station that night, he thought that he had left out some question when taking the statement, that he was about to be the latest to feel a lick of Courtney's verbal whip. "I was a young detective on my first case, and I kept on thinking, what did I do wrong? If the super wants to see you, you are in real trouble."

However, it turned out the conversation was all about the details of the statement. Monks was an unusually good witness and had provided detailed observations.

What had piqued Courtney's interest, however, were other salient details.

"Monks had described a jumper," said O'Mahony. "It was an unusual jumper, a military-style jumper with patches on the sleeve and shoulder. He said it was a fawn colour which was unusual enough because the common colour for that style of jumper was green or navy. I think I had the navy one myself, with the patches on the shoulder and elbow.

"He also said he had seen the man with a beard and then seen the man without a beard."

Senior murder squad detectives had picked up on these specifics, as the official description had purposefully withheld the information about the military jumper. Courtney was interested to find out whether O'Mahony had been let in on this detail himself.

"The one question he asked is did I know anything about this jumper? I didn't. It transpired afterwards, for me anyway, that it was the jumper which was found in the laneway near where Bridie Gargan's killer had abandoned the car, with bloodstains on it. Some of the key detectives knew about it, but I didn't."

O'Mahony was told to leave and went back to routine inquiries and thought no more of it.

Monks was to be the missing piece in a jigsaw that was finally coming into formation. In the previous days, as the RTÉ re-enactment was prepared for broadcast on 5 August, the murder hunt had already taken a decisive sweep to the southern coastal suburbs around Dún Laoghaire, after gardaí finally tracked down the taxi driver who had taken the killer from the Fingal House pub on Thursday, 22 July. He had told them that he had left his passenger near the dock for the mail boat in Dún Laoghaire.

Then on Wednesday, 4 August, the day before the RTÉ broadcast that led Monks to report what he knew to gardaí, another astonishing incident was reported. It occurred in the nearby suburb of Killiney, and it would bring the beleaguered investigation one step closer to the killer who had been at large for almost a fortnight.

# 16

## RETURN TO CAMELOT

"I hope you have a sense of humour." Malcolm Macarthur

Killiney Hill was shrouded in fog on the evening of Wednesday, 4 August, as the man with the blue hold-all made his way along the suburb's salubrious Vico Road. It was a week on from a foiled attempt to rob his old acquaintance in Fitzwilliam Square, and his money difficulties were no closer to being resolved. He trudged up the steep ascent – passing Killiney Beach and the Victorian mansions built into the hill, with their commanding views of Dublin Bay – until he finally reached an unmissable landmark close to the apex, an ornate castellated arch that extended across the road. It was attached to a round tower and turret, all with decorative battlements. The 1853 granite building, once the gate lodge of Victoria Castle (located further down the hill), was now a private home: Camelot.

At about 5.45pm, the owner, Harry Bieling, answered the door. There stood the slim man with curly dark hair wearing a crumpled jacket, a white shirt and a grey silk cravat. In his hand was a blue hold-all bag.

"Hello," he said. "Do you remember me? I was at a party here about seven years ago. I particularly remembered the panoramic view from the sitting room. Would it be okay if I took some shots?"

The view indeed was a commanding one, taking in the coastline as far as Bray Head, with the Sugarloaf mountain in the distance.

Bieling discerned an ascendancy accent, and the thought struck him that he really ought to know this man who seemed a stranger to him. But seven years ago was a while back, and although he looked vaguely familiar, he could not recall the man.

If Bieling had company, he could come back another time, he offered. No, no, said Bieling, I am alone. And thus Harry Bieling invited Malcolm Macarthur into his house.

Harry Bieling was a 48-year old American, from Stewart Manor, just outside New York City. Born in 1934 to a prosperous family, Bieling had studied at the prestigious Ivy League college, Dartmouth College, in Hanover, New Hampshire, graduating in 1956.

The pen picture of him in the Dartmouth yearbook shows a slim young man with thick fair hair brushed back, a bony nose and slightly jutting ears.

After studying politics and history at Dartmouth, Bieling did a postgraduate degree in politics at the University of Michigan.

Soon after, in 1958, he joined the US Foreign Service. The following year, having taken intensive German lessons, he was posted to Hamburg in West Germany as a diplomat. It was plumb in the middle of the Cold War era and it is likely that Bieling's role would have involved a degree of espionage and intelligence-gathering. He did military training during that time.

In 1964, Bieling was transferred from Hamburg to London where he served as vice consul, or second secretary. The following year, in 1965, he was appointed to a similar role as vice consul to Glasgow, which seemed – at best – a sideways step.

He never had another posting. Within a few years he had left the diplomatic service. Part of the reason behind this may have been that Bieling harboured a secret. He was gay. The US federal government prohibited gay people from joining the civil service until 1975. Its code required its employees to be of 'good moral character'. That excluded people who were known to be homosexuals. The paranoia about gays and lesbians undermining national security and public morality was particularly evident during the Cold War. A diplomat who was gay needed to live a double life if they had any hope of continuing their career. Was Bieling compromised or outed as a gay man? Or did he tire of living a double life?

In the late 1960s, Bieling visited friends in Dublin for a short stay of a few days. He was so taken with the city that he decided to put down roots there. He bought Camelot. By the 1970s he had retired from the foreign service. He did some work: he later set up as a bespoke agent for higher-end travel and – maintaining his interest in politics – also volunteered as an election monitor, in countries where nascent democracies were taking hold.

Bieling quickly immersed himself into the Dublin scene. He was a tall man with fair hair and a natural charm. He became friendly with a group of Trinity students and postgraduates and they met regularly in city-centre bars such as Bartley Dunne's. Bieling hosted many parties in Camelot. They tended to be classy affairs, with caterers, canapés and wine.

It was one such party in 1974 that drew Malcolm Macarthur to Bieling's Camelot for the first time, along with others from the bohemian set who socialised in Bartley Dunne's and The Bailey. He went back several times that year and the following year. Given Macarthur's laconic nature and lack of sociability, it was not surprising that Bieling had difficulty recalling him.

Macarthur entered the house and Bieling led him to the sitting room, which had a large window overlooking Killiney Bay. The American noted that it was very misty: "You're not going to get a good photograph today," he said.

"Well, this is exactly as I remember it," replied Macarthur.

The pair moved from room to room, taking in the view, and then returned to the sitting-room window where they stood for a while. Macarthur chatted about some of the people who attended the party that night in 1974. In fact, he told Bieling, he had attended several parties at his house [in '74 and '75]. He told Bieling how, at one party, he was chased by "some slut from Ballymun". He mentioned some other names in a staccato fashion. Some chap from the North, Macarthur said. Mr So-and-So. A woman friend of his, who attended all the parties.

Bieling had no recollection of most of the people Macarthur mentioned. But there had always been gate-crashers at his famed Camelot parties, soirées he'd long since stopped hosting. He recognised a few names, but he had not met those people in years. At this stage there was a pause in the conversation as both men continued to look out the window. Bieling glanced at the blue hold-all bag and reminded his visitor about the photographs he wished to take.

Macarthur began rummaging in the bag and said to Bieling, "I hope you have a sense of humour." He produced a sawn-off shotgun which he pointed at Bieling, then gestured for him to sit down.

"What kind of nonsense is this?" a shocked Bieling blurted out.

Macarthur was calm. He settled himself in the armchair opposite Bieling and told him he expected to rob a great deal of money from him.

Bieling had some military experience from his time in the US foreign service and he managed to collect himself. He asked Macarthur's permission to pour himself a drink to steady his nerves. Macarthur agreed but accompanied him to the drinks cabinet to ensure there was no funny business. Bieling poured himself a large vodka. He offered a drink to Macarthur but he declined.

Bieling knew he needed to keep his assailant talking and he found that Macarthur was quite happy to respond to his questions. The first was almost naive but Macarthur took the bait. Bieling asked him how long he had been carrying out robberies.

"A little over a year," Macarthur said. Before adding the truthful rider, "Ever since my patrimony has run out."

He confided that he disliked the idea of working. Another silence ensued. Bieling then asked about the dangerous nature of the life of crime to which he had committed himself. Macarthur replied that it was easier than one would think, as long as you were able to disguise yourself and change identity.

"How are you going to get away with it?" Bieling asked.

He reminded the intruder that no crime had yet been committed and if he were to go, he would not mention it to anybody, and nothing more would be said about it.

What the former diplomat did not know was how desperate Macarthur regarded his situation at that moment. Even the modest luxury of the Dún Laoghaire guesthouse was no longer affordable.

Macarthur responded by saying he expected at least £1,000 in cash from Bieling. He boasted he himself used to spend that much a week or a fortnight in Dublin when he was in funds. Surprised by the demand, Bieling said he did not have that kind of money in his house, telling Macarthur he had only £23 or so in cash lying around.

Macarthur said he was surprised by this admission. Bieling replied he had money in the bank, but it would be no good to his would-be robber as he would have to withdraw it in person. Macarthur suggested Bieling could write him a cheque for €1,000 which he could then cash in a bank. The conversation went back and forth in this way for a while.

Casting his eyes around the sitting room, Macarthur

spotted the telephone. He said he needed to phone his accomplice and tell him to come the following morning to guard Bieling while Macarthur went to the bank. He intended to spend the night in Camelot.

He informed Bieling that his current accomplice was his second one, that he had a young guy the previous year who was not up to the job.

"It's very hard to get reliable people these days," he said.

By now it was close to 7pm. Macarthur seemed content to sit languidly in an armchair, with his gun across his lap, reminiscing about mutual acquaintances that Bieling could not remember. The American was now on his second vodka, trying to remain calm.

He decided that it was time to force the issue. He told Macarthur that his housekeeper, Bridget, would be there shortly as she had to cook dinner. Macarthur told him to get the cheque book and gesticulated with his gun.

Bieling said he kept it upstairs in his bedroom. The room was situated at the top of the round tower, reached by a spiral staircase. The American climbed the stairway first with Macarthur immediately behind, pointing the shotgun at his back. When they reached the bedroom, Bieling went over to a chest of drawers and began rummaging. He stood up and said he could not find the cheque book.

Macarthur reacted angrily and shouted at Bieling that he was trying to make a fool out of him. Bieling said he must have made a mistake, that the chequebook was downstairs and he would easily retrieve it.

They made for the staircase, Bieling going down first, Macarthur following behind with the gun.

Halfway down the spiral, just as it turned towards the front door of the house, Bieling grabbed his opportunity. He bolted down the last steps and sprinted towards the front door, Macarthur in hot pursuit. By the time Macarthur got to the bottom of the stairs, Bieling was already out on the street, running for his life. He ducked into a garden and dived into a rhododendron bush, trying to control his panicked breathing.

Macarthur ran out onto the street, the shotgun in his hand, looking up and down the hill to see if he could spot the fleeing American. He quickly realised he was beat.

# 17

# THE QUIET MAN

"It is a daunting task." Diary entry of newly appointed
attorney general, Paddy Connolly

In mid-July 1982, Paddy Connolly received a phone call one
evening at his home in Pilot View, Dalkey. When he answered
he immediately recognised the cultured accent and
characteristic sombre tone. It was Malcolm Macarthur.

Macarthur told him he was in Liège in Belgium sorting out
some financial business, while Brenda and Colin remained in
Tenerife. "I shall be visiting Dublin later this month,"
Macarthur told him, "and may call by." Connolly replied he
would be welcome but said it would have to be before 14
August when he left for his holidays.

Macarthur, or course, was not in Liège. He had called
Connolly from a public phone box in Dún Laoghaire, less
than two miles away.

Connolly was at that time coming to the end of a frantic first six months in his new position as attorney general, having moved there from the rarefied atmosphere of the Law Library. Politics was a tough profession at the best of times, but in 1982 it was visceral. His first half-year in the job had been spent in the deep end.

Connolly had known Charles Haughey since the 1950s. Though two years younger than the taoiseach, and behind him in UCD, they were both in the King's Inns Law School in Dublin city at the same time, after Haughey decided to qualify as a barrister on completing his accountancy exams. The pair strengthened their personal friendship when Connolly, then 43, was appointed to Haughey's legal team twelve years previously for the 1970 Arms Trial.

That bond would develop during the 1970s. Connolly became a frequent visitor to Haughey's home and corresponded with him regularly. They shared a passion for fine food, wine, the arts, and theatre.

Connolly's nephew and godson, Stephen Connolly, said that Paddy often stayed overnight on his regular visits to Haughey's estate, Abbeville. "Paddy often told a story of one occasion when Haughey offered his guests a choice of wine, one of which was a rare and expensive bottle. Paddy knew his wines really well," said Stephen.

As soon as he showed both bottles of wine, Haughey realised the expensive wine would be uncorked. "I knew I was making a mistake by offering you that choice," he told Connolly.

Stephen spoke at length to his uncle about his friendship with Haughey. "I suppose they had an intellectual connection,"

Stephen said. "They both were followers of and interested in the arts, opera music, that type of thing. At the same time, Haughey was a very different person because he had that political side to him, whereas my uncle Paddy was a very reserved person. He was a background person."

Their upbringings were quite similar. Like Haughey, Connolly was born in modest enough circumstances in north Dublin and had been a scholarship boy at school and at university. The son of a County Galway schoolteacher, he grew up in Oldtown in north County Dublin. He and his brother Tony – Stephen's father – were very close throughout their lives, both attending Garbally College in Ballinasloe, Galway, and then UCD.

In their youth the two brothers had been accomplished Gaelic football players and regularly attended GAA games together in adulthood.

"They used to attend Croke Park on a religious basis," recalled Stephen. "They would cycle from Oldtown during the Second World War to Swords and then take the bus from there into town. For them, GAA was an absolute religion."

Tony was to become a senior manager with the Irish Sugar Company. Paddy studied law in UCD. He excelled academically and was also a champion debater. He was elected auditor of the Law Society in 1948 and called to the Bar in 1949, at the age of 22 (in the same class as Haughey).

He forged a successful career as a barrister, mainly working in commercial law and personal injuries. While he was a friend of Haughey's, he did not expect Haughey to turn to him to become his attorney general.

"I remember talking to Paddy about it at the time," said

Stephen. "It must have been a huge transition for him to move from dealing with personal injury cases in the rarefied atmosphere of the Law Library to this."

Connolly kept a diary all his life. In his entry for the day he was offered the position in February 1982 he wrote: "It is a daunting task."

And so it would be. But there was a strong tradition in the Law Library that if offered the position of attorney general, it was to be accepted. Connolly was close to Haughey, enjoyed his company and his intellect, and admired his skills as a politician greatly. It was a great honour to be asked, but there was no escaping how daunting the task was that lay ahead.

Before his appointment, before even the deal with Tony Gregory was agreed, there were controversies and crises surrounding Haughey that suggested a volatile period ahead. Haughey's close friend and solicitor Pat O'Connor was arrested on polling day, accused of voting twice. He was later acquitted but acquired the unfortunate nickname "Pat O'Connor Pat O'Connor".

Haughey's failure to get a majority then prompted a heave against him, spearheaded by Des O'Malley, a 43-year old solicitor from Limerick, who had been close to Haughey's predecessor, Jack Lynch.

The media immediately installed O'Malley as odds-on favourite, with the *Irish Independent* naming 46 TDs who would support him. O'Malley's challenge fizzled out: Haughey enjoyed a rare moment of schadenfreude towards the political correspondents, whom he detested.

It turned out to be one of the rockiest and most turbulent periods in Irish political history, with the government operating on the basis that, at any moment, its existence could be sundered. In some ways, Haughey contributed to the mayhem.

In March 1982, after just six weeks in power, he tried to pull an old-fashioned stroke to create an extra Dáil seat. He offered Richard Burke the lucrative post of Ireland's commissioner to the European Economic Community. It was unheard of for a taoiseach to offer this highly sought-after position to a politician from a rival party. But Burke was a sitting Fine Gael TD in the Fianna Fáil stronghold of Dublin West. Taking up the commissioner post would mean he would vacate his seat, and a by-election would ensue. This, Haughey predicted, would be won by Fianna Fáil, leaving it only one seat short of a majority. However, the plan backfired when Fine Gael wheeled the scrum and won the by-election.

Haughey's government also incurred the wrath of British prime minister Margaret Thatcher after it withdrew its support for EEC sanctions against Argentina for its invasion of the Falkland Islands. The move came after the sinking of the cruiser *Belgrano*. While the withdrawal played well with the party's more republican base, Haughey's relationship with Thatcher was already poor and this further poisoned the well.

Reflecting on this period, Paddy's nephew Stephen Connolly says, "That cabinet, as you know, was fraught with difficulty. There was internal fighting. There was the constant leaking of information into the press, which was happening at an extraordinary rate.

"It was something that Haughey was extremely conscious of. I remember Patrick saying two things about the cabinet. He said he had never seen somebody so in command of his brief like Haughey was. He knew every ounce of detail that was on every other minister's brief. And he would go through them if they didn't know what he knew."

The other thing Patrick Connolly found extraordinary, recalled Stephen, was the respect that existed between Haughey and Des O'Malley, despite the fact that there was such political enmity between them. "Paddy said that with the exception of Haughey, O'Malley was streets ahead of the rest of those who sat around the cabinet table."

Fianna Fáil TD Bertie Ahern, himself no slouch when it came to realpolitik, was chief whip at the time, the youngest person sitting around that table. He recalled the political era as like watching a car veering out of control in slow motion.

"It was an extraordinary year because it was just one crisis after another. And it looked as if there would be an election any day. We had a tough Finance Bill which Ray MacSharry brought through somehow.

"I was the chief whip. So every vote, you were never sure whether you were going to win or not. It depended on who turned up and who'd support it. Then we won the by-election in Galway West. That gave me a bit of hope going forward. But that summer it was all about hanging on to see if we could get back after the break and how long would we be able to stay on."

If Ahern was wishing the government could survive long enough to return in September, Connolly, for his part, was hanging on to the prospect of his holiday in mid-August like a lifebuoy. He had booked the trip soon after becoming attorney general. His itinerary would take him to London for one night, then by Concorde to New York. He planned to travel on from there to New Orleans, Phoenix, Salt Lake City and Washington DC before returning to London by Concorde again. At the time, flying by Concorde was extremely expensive – the equivalent of six months of an office worker's salary.

Away from his work life, Connolly had another life, and another set of friends, very different to those in the Law Library and in politics. Those two parallel worlds, at such a remove from one another, would collide spectacularly that summer. Unbeknownst to Paddy Connolly, within weeks he would have the mischance of being the bridge that spanned those two very contrasting worlds.

# 18

# GUEST OF THE NATION

"A silly joke gone sour." Malcolm Macarthur

On the evening of Wednesday, 4 August 1982, Paddy Connolly answered his intercom. "Hello, Paddy," said the unmistakeable voice of his friend, Malcolm Macarthur.

Connolly was pleased to hear Macarthur's voice, having been concerned in the previous days as to his friend's whereabouts. Brenda Little had called him from Tenerife the previous Saturday, expressing worry that she had not heard from Malcolm for some days. She was anxious. He had been due to return to the Canary Islands that weekend.

Despite being very busy in work in the period running up to the summer recess, Connolly took time to ring Little on three consecutive days leading up to Tuesday, 3 August, to see if there was any news. Despite reassuring Little that things would be fine, privately he too was worried. But now here was Malcolm, turning up right at his door. He felt palpable relief as he greeted him. He told him Brenda had been worried sick about his whereabouts, not having heard from him for a week.

Macarthur told Connolly he had travelled to Ireland from Belgium and had been staying with friends for the past few days. "She must have misunderstood when I called her from Ostend," he lied.

Connolly managed to contact Brenda in her apartment building in Tenerife and relayed the news that Malcolm was with him. She sounded relieved and asked to speak to him. They chatted for several minutes before Malcolm handed the receiver back to Connolly, saying Brenda wanted to speak to him again.

Brenda, who was always direct in style, asked Connolly if he would put Malcolm up for a few days. She said Malcolm was too shy to ask.

Once the call ended, Connolly extended the invite. Initially, Macarthur demurred but Connolly insisted. They went back and forth like this for a while until Macarthur finally agreed. And so Malcolm Macarthur became the house-guest of the Irish attorney general, on the understanding, as Connolly later said, that "he was going to be around for a few days dealing with financial affairs.

"I told him that he would be perfectly welcome to stay with me while he was so doing," said Connolly, who could never excise courtroom-speak from his daily conversations.

"In the beginning," said Connolly, "Malcolm said he did not want to intrude upon my privacy, and he also told me that he had been staying for a couple of days already with some friends from Trinity. I indicated to him that I would not regard his stay as intruding on my privacy."

Connolly accepted his visitor's account of his recent movements at face value, having no reason not to. He had known him for eight years, and recognised him as a shy man who was always courteous and had "impeccable manners".

He added that his guest was never one to volunteer information, even when asked. "Malcolm Macarthur was not the kind of person of whom you would ask what he had been up to."

What he had been up to included an aborted armed robbery only half an hour beforehand, which might have ended up as his third homicide, had his would-be-victim, Harry Bieling, not had the survival instincts to pick his moment and run for his life, leaving his assailant defeated.

The following morning, Connolly's state car, with its garda driver, arrived to take him to work shortly after 8am. Macarthur lolled around the apartment after breakfast, listening to music on the stereo system.

At about 9am, he looked up the telephone directory for a name and, on finding it, rang the number.

The previous evening, after coming out from his hiding place of bushes in a house on a neighbouring street, Harry Bieling immediately reported what had happened to Dalkey Garda Station. He explained how the man who had held him at gunpoint had not given his name and although he said he knew Bieling of old, Bieling had no memory of him. However, he was able to give a detailed description of his would-be attacker, including the slim build, wavy dark hair, cravat and cultured accent.

The American, who lived alone, was naturally nervous about returning to his home by himself that night and invited a friend over. As the aftershock of his close shave began to sink in, both drank heavily, draining a bottle of whiskey between them. It was after 5am when Bieling finally fell asleep.

He awoke to the sound of the phone ringing at 9am. On answering, he immediately recognised the voice and accent. "Hello, this is your friend from yesterday. Why did you run?"

Bieling was dumbstruck. In the background, he could hear the strains of Beethoven's Seventh Symphony playing loudly.

"Oh, you must have been scared," said the man whose name Bieling could not recall. "A silly joke gone sour."

Now – despite having had only four hours' sleep and the beginnings of a hangover kicking in – Bieling was fully alert.

Macarthur did all the talking. He asked had Bieling contacted the gardaí. Bieling did not reply. After a long pause, Macarthur said it might be a good idea to contact the gardaí to let them know it was just a joke.

"Should you call them or should I?" Macarthur asked.

"You do it," Bieling replied.

His next question astonished Bieling further. "Can I call over to your house next week?" he asked.

"Yes, but telephone first," he replied, before putting down the receiver.

Shortly after calling Bieling, Macarthur wrapped his gun in a plastic bin bag and ordered a taxi into Merrion Square in

Dublin's city centre. There, in the park, he crawled into thick bushes, where he hid the gun. He then hailed a taxi back to Dalkey.

At around midday, a call came in to Dalkey Garda Station. The caller, who identified himself as a freelance journalist, told the guard he was the man who had called to Bieling's house the previous evening. He explained that his threat to rob Bieling had been "a joke gone wrong".

"It was a practical joke and no harm was intended," he added. He also said he had phoned Bieling earlier that day and explained everything.

Sergeant Pat Fitzgerald, who had answered the call, was incredulous.

"What's your name?" he asked.

"Malcolm Macarthur," the caller replied.

"And what's your address?"

He replied he was born in Gardiner Street before hastily ending the call.

# 19

## A WITNESS DISAPPEARS

"I am followed by two goons who look like the mafia." John
Monks, news vendor

Back in Dún Laoghaire, Detective John O'Mahony did not
expect to see John Monks again after taking a statement from
him on Friday, 6 August. But within 24 hours, on the evening
of Saturday, 7 August, O'Mahony was called back in, this
time to track down John Monks, who had gone missing
earlier that day.

This had happened on the back of a surveillance plan
senior detectives in the murder squad had put in place,
dispatching two young guards to shadow Monks as he went
about his business on Saturday, in case he came into contact
with the suspect. The plan had one flaw – they failed to tell
John Monks that he was under surveillance.

From early that day, Monks worked the newsstand, as

usual. The pattern was to close the stand in the mid-afternoon, then take the evening papers down to the thronged seafront in a satchel and sell them along the promenade.

The two plain-clothes policemen were dispatched. Both were wearing suits. They followed Monks at what they thought was a discreet distance but lost sight of him in the crowds. In fact, Monks had cottoned on that he was being followed and, feeling nervous, had scarpered. Now not only had a killer apparently vanished into thin air, but so too had one of the key witnesses in the investigation.

DSI John Courtney hit the roof when he learned that Monks was missing. He gave the two unfortunate plain-clothes gardaí who had lost the witness in the crowds a tongue-lashing. Courtney then called in the young detectives, O'Mahony and Hand. Monks had spoken to them the previous day. On that basis, Monks might be more inclined to trust the two younger men, if they found him.

First, they had to track down Monks. The pair spent the next 12 hours looking for him. They spoke to his girlfriend, who said he had just taken off on Saturday afternoon without saying a word. They called around to the Marine Hotel in Dún Laoghaire where he worked at night but he had not showed up there either. They trawled the local pubs and walked the length of the seafront looking for him, to no avail.

Monks' girlfriend lived in a house that was set out in flats. One of the other flats happened to be let out to Detective O'Mahony's sister, a student. O'Mahony and Hand camped themselves in her flat on Saturday evening and remained there overnight. Every time they heard a sound, they peeped out the door to check who it was. The ploy came good on Sunday morning. Hearing the front door open, they looked out to see Monks ambling up the stairs.

The news vendor told the detectives he had panicked the previous day when he noticed two burly men in suits and ties were following him. When he got a chance he had bolted. He told O'Mahony and Hand: "I made a statement to you on Friday and the following day I am followed by two goons who look like the mafia."

The two detectives cooled Monks down and then spoke to their superiors back at the incident room. A plan was devised, this time with the newspaper seller in on it, where a team of plain-clothes detectives, dressed casually, would accompany Monks around Dún Laoghaire but hang back a little.

An unmarked Renault van was parked continually near his newsstand pitch within easy sight of him. There was a pre-arranged signal. If he spotted the suspect, he was to raise his left arm and wave a rolled newspaper as if he was greeting somebody.

The four detectives who were assigned to him were O'Mahony and Hand, along with Brian Sherry and Kevin Tunney. They followed him throughout the day and the night. They also got him to walk through just about every bar in Dún Laoghaire to see if he could spot the suspect.

Monks was an understandably reticent collaborator. When he was asked by the detectives to walk through the tightly packed crowds at the beaches near Sandycove, to see if he could spot the man, he was less than enthusiastic.

This was partly grounded on fears for his own safety and that of his girlfriend. If the man was the killer, he had seen Monks and likely knew Monks was aware he had changed his appearance. Given the callous nature of the two killings, Monks told gardaí, he was nervous that he would end up being shot.

"The guards stayed behind me all the time but not so close that they could have stopped him if he wanted to snuff me," he said.

Detective Brian Sherry, who drove the surveillance van all over the coastal town that week, sensed they were getting close to their quarry despite the lack of sightings. By this stage, many of the senior detectives on the case, including Inspector Noel Conroy and Det Sergeant Tony Hickey, had decamped to Dún Laoghaire.

"I knew in my gut this guy was out here. We all said to each other, we know he's out here," said Sherry. "Tony Hickey, Noel Conroy and another case detective Denis Donegan were picking up other things. It was all pointing to here."

Yet despite days and nights of trawling the seafront, Monks would never see the strange man on the red racing bicycle again. The reason was, he was no longer in Dún Laoghaire. The man with the blue hold-all bag had found a more agreeable pied-à-terre.

# 20

# A SUSPECT IN PLAIN SIGHT

"He was wearing a white shirt and it was dirty and it also had grass stains on it. I thought that was odd." Stephen Connolly, nephew of Paddy Connolly

As the days passed, Malcolm Macarthur made himself at home in Connolly's plush penthouse. After arriving on the evening of 4 August, he almost immediately began ordering deliveries by taxis, under Connolly's account, of bottles of Perrier water, copies of *The Irish Times*, and the English satirical magazine *Private Eye*.

Just after 8am each morning, Connolly's state car arrived, driven by an armed garda driver. On at least two occasions during the following week, Macarthur accepted a lift into the city centre.

Before departing on his US holidays, the attorney general was looking forward to attending a big GAA game. He and his brother Tony were lifelong GAA supporters and went to all the major matches. Sunday, 8 August was a big occasion in the sporting calendar. Galway were playing against Kilkenny in the All-Ireland hurling semi-final.

That morning, Tony Connolly drove down from Carlow with his 18-year old son Stephen, who had just completed his Leaving Certificate exams. They all gathered in the attorney general's apartment in Pilot View in Dalkey, before departing for Croke Park.

Paddy, because of his status as a member of cabinet, had two tickets for the *Ard Chomhairle* section of the Hogan Stand, effectively a VIP ticket. Stephen was going to buy a ticket to watch the game from the lower stands. Connolly also invited Macarthur to attend. A little to his surprise, he accepted. In the eight years they had known each other, Macarthur had shown no interest in sport.

Paddy, Tony and Stephen were driven to Croke Park in a state car, along with Macarthur.

In the years that followed, a myth was propagated that Macarthur sat alongside Paddy Connolly in the *Ard Chomhairle* section of the Hogan Stand. Embellishments include that he stood in close proximity while Connolly and the garda commissioner had a conversation about the dreadful recent murders of the nurse and the farmer and the hunt for the mystery killer.

The truth, however, was more mundane. Stephen and Malcolm bought their own tickets at the stadium. They filed in through the turnstiles with thousands of other hurling fans and took their seats in another section of the Hogan Stand.

Stephen had met Macarthur several times before but on

this day, he noticed something that was not right. "I remember turning around to my father afterwards and saying, 'Did you notice something strange about Malcolm?'

"My father said, 'No,' and then asked, 'In what way?'

"I said, there were two things. We were sitting in the Hogan Stand watching a hurling match. So the sun is pointing towards the Cusack Stand [on the opposite side of the ground], whatever sun there was that day. It was hard enough to follow the flight of the sliotar [where he was in the shade]. But when you're wearing sunglasses, in the Hogan Stand, it's impossible.

"Malcolm was looking around the whole time. When I'm looking at a match, I want to see everything that's happening on the pitch. [Macarthur] just looked uncomfortable, on edge."

The second thing that Connolly noticed was Macarthur's clothes.

"He was wearing a white shirt and it was dirty and it also had grass stains on it. How would you get grass stains on your shirt? I thought that was odd."

Stephen was a young man, half Macarthur's age. On the previous occasions he had met Macarthur, he had found conversations with him hard work.

"He was very aloof and very withdrawn. He's not someone that you go and have a friendly chat with," said Stephen.

"It was like fly fishing. You would throw something out in the hope of getting a bite. More often than not you would get nothing.

"Sometimes with those types of people, they don't pay huge amounts of attention to what they wear and whether their shoes are scuffed. But with the benefit of hindsight, clearly money was an issue because it was running out."

Stephen's uncle Paddy was less observant: "Perhaps I should have noticed," he later reflected. "If I had really looked, I would have noticed, for example, that his shoes were very run down."

The morning after the match, Monday, 9 August, Macarthur got a message to his mother asking her to meet him the following day in the Greville Arms Hotel in Mullingar, near to her new home in County Westmeath.

It was the first Irene Macarthur knew her son was back in Ireland. From Irene's point of view, it was a social visit. Later events would cast this in an altogether darker light.

On Tuesday, Macarthur accepted a lift alongside Connolly in his state car to Merrion Square, and then walked to Busáras bus station about a mile away. He bought a ticket for the next bus to Mullingar.

He arrived early and traipsed around the town for a while, looking in shop windows. Just before noon, he went to the Greville Arms Hotel and ordered water.

When Irene arrived at the appointed time, she noticed that her son seemed ill at ease. Without preliminaries, he asked if she was having any problems with her income tax. She said she was not. He then asked if he could use her address as his forwarding address. He did not tell her why, but she readily agreed.

At this point, Malcolm began talking in a somewhat sinister fashion.

"He told me there had been some skulduggery going on and I was not to be surprised or worried if I was interrogated by the Italian police," she later said.

She was taken aback by this but could make little meaning of it. She did not question her son about it but took it to be some reference to a six-month period that Malcolm and Brenda had spent in Milan and Florence in 1976 or 1977.

"I did not understand what he was talking about," she said.

Even though it had been the first time they had met in nine months, within half an hour the conversation had ended and Malcolm had departed. Despite being on his uppers, he had not requested any money from her, as he so often had in the past. It was not clear as to the purpose of the meeting. It didn't appear to have been social given how truncated it was. Later events would bring it into sharper focus.

Macarthur returned to Killiney to spend his seventh night as a guest of the nation in the apartment of the attorney general. Connolly had told him he was departing on his holidays the following Saturday; Macarthur told him that he would have concluded his financial dealings by then and would return to Brenda Little and their son in Tenerife on the same day.

It was 10 August. That evening, Macarthur pored over *The Irish Times* to see if there was news relating to his activities. There were no reports of the Harry Bieling incident and he assumed the gardaí had not pursued the matter.

The naivety of the assumption reflected how detached his thinking was from reality. The gardaí were all over the Harry Bieling incident and actively pursuing all leads, knowing that they were closing in on the killer. The local area was swarming with detectives carrying out enquiries practically under the killer's nose. The simple reason they did not publicise the

Bieling incident is they did not want to alert their quarry just in case he would bolt.

Three days later, on the morning of Friday, 13 August, Macarthur again cadged a lift from the attorney general as far as government buildings. He entered nearby Merrion Square and recovered the shotgun from where he had hidden it in the bushes just over a week before, on the day after his aborted robbery of Harry Bieling. Then he returned to Pilot View and considered the gun. He had already sawn off 12 inches from the barrels but decided he needed to shorten them more.

He rang the taxi company in Dún Laoghaire with which Connolly had an account and asked for the driver to pick up hacksaw blades in Murdochs Hardware, as well as a bottle of Perrier water.

Despite two failed attempts at armed robbery, Macarthur was hatching a plan for a third attempt, unaware that his time as a house-guest in Pilot View was fast coming to a dramatic end.

# 21

# THE MANHUNT CLOSES IN

"I think we have your man out here." Superintendent Mick
Sullivan, Dún Laoghaire Garda Station

Bridie Gargan was left for dead on Thursday, 22 July, and
succumbed to her injuries four days later. Dónal Dunne was
shot dead at point-blank range the day before Bridie died. The
scale of the garda investigation to find the perpetrator was
unprecedented: a fifty-strong team was working on it round
the clock. Yet it would be a full two weeks into the investigation
before the moment arrived that pivoted it in the sure direction
of its quarry.

Detectives were already on the right track. In recent days,
on the back of the taxi driver testimony that located the killer
in Dún Laoghaire, DSI John Courtney had moved his most
senior people to begin inquiries in the area. They included Det

Sgt Tony Hickey, Det Sgt Denis Donegan, and Det Inspector Noel Conroy.

Tony Hickey happened to be in the incident room in Kevin Street Garda Station when a call came in from Dún Laoghaire on August 5.

The caller was Superintendent Mick Sullivan and he asked to be put through to John Courtney, who was leading the investigation. The team gathered around Courtney and listened in.

"Mick Sullivan described an incident which we weren't aware of at that stage, an aggravated burglary attempt in Killiney," said Hickey.

Sullivan described how a man with dark wavy hair, wearing a cravat, with an upper-crust accent, had shown up at the house of a retired American diplomat, Harry Bieling, and produced a gun, demanding money from the home-owner.

"I think we have your man out here," Sullivan told Courtney. On the back of that call, Courtney ordered Noel Conroy to mobilise his team and canvass every home within a mile of Camelot. Conroy's team soon rooted out new information about the suspect. In door-to-door inquiries at the crest of the hill, only 50 metres above Bieling's house, a woman told them about a "dodgy man" in an agitated state who had called to her door claiming there had been an accident and he needed her car to bring his brother to hospital. She said she had slammed the door in his face once she saw a rifle butt peeking out from under his jacket. Her description tallied with the Bieling intruder.

The decisive link was not offered from a witness, nor did it land off the back of astute work. Instead, as we've seen, it was handed up on a plate by the perpetrator himself, when he called Dalkey Garda Station on Thursday, 5 August, the day after his doomed heist in the home of Harry Bieling.

"What's your name?" Sergeant Pat Fitzgerald had asked the caller.

"Malcolm Macarthur," the caller replied.

And there it was, at last. After two weeks of grasping at every possible lead, pursuing too many wild goose chases to count, finally something tangible had landed. Now the task in hand turned to finding out who this person was, whether he matched up to the killer, and, most importantly, where he was hiding out.

When no record of a Malcolm Macarthur could be found in their files, detectives set out that afternoon for Gardiner Street, where he'd told the guard at Dalkey he was born, to see if the man's name meant anything to any of the hundreds of people who lived in the flats and tenements of the north inner city. Nothing came of the exercise, however.

But the trail to his whereabouts was revealing itself all the same. Two days after the attempted robbery at Camelot, a man made contact with gardaí. He and two friends had been driving a van down Killiney Hill on their way to do a spot of fishing. He said that just before 7pm the previous Wednesday, a man flagged him down. He sensed the man had been trying to get away from something.

He described the man's unusual clothing and the tale the man had spun about a friend taking ill. The occupants of the car dropped him off at the requested destination of Pilot View in Dalkey. Struck by his oddness, they lingered a little to watch him. They noticed that instead of going to Pilot View, the man turned on his heels and headed in the direction of Harbour Crescent.

Detective Hickey picked up one salient detail, and that was that the suspect mentioned an injured or sick brother to two different people – the woman whose house he'd tried to enter, and the van driver – as he tried to make his escape from Bieling's home. There was a pattern emerging and for the following week, DSI Courtney's team wore out shoe leather by day, and burned the midnight oil by night, following the leads provided by Harry Bieling and the witnesses who told police about Macarthur's movements after the attempted armed robbery.

Public interest in the case had escalated even further after the TV re-enactment that had been broadcast on RTÉ on Thursday, 5 August. However, the garda team which had been regularly briefing the media in the first fortnight of the investigation had now gone silent. When reporters like Peter Murtagh rang they were given the standard line that investigations were ongoing. The impression being given was that the investigation had stalled. In reality, the team was beginning to close in on its quarry but did not want to do anything that would make him flee.

As the days wore on, a game of sliding doors was playing out, each party unaware of how close they were to the other. Hickey and Tunney spent their evenings knocking on doors along Harbour Road, to see if anybody had a sighting of the suspect. It was early the following week, around the time Malcolm Macarthur was setting out for a meeting with his mother in Westmeath, when detectives first gained access to the gated community of Pilot View.

Alan Solomons was chairman of the residents' association

there. He told gardaí that it was unlikely they would find a killer among the wealthy and mostly retired residents. Gardaí learned from Solomons that the attorney general, Paddy Connolly, lived in Pilot View, when Solomons told Detective Hickey of a "particularly rude" man currently staying with Connolly, who he took to be his nephew.

Meanwhile, on the weekend just passed, as Macarthur had set out for Croke Park courtesy of the attorney general's state driver, senior members of the investigating team, including Courtney, had reviewed Harry Bieling's statement in light of the new name being suggested and had set up another interview with him. Detective Hickey recalls that interview, as gardaí pressed him for the name of his would-be attacker who claimed to have attended parties at his house less than a decade before. "He said he had held lots of parties, and there were many people there and he didn't know or could not recall everybody." They pressed him further, asking about the people the intruder had mentioned during their strange conversation. Finally, a name sprang to mind.

"Betty B," he said.

Betty Braughan was an old friend of Brenda Little's – the two had hung out together back in the Bartley Dunne days. Bieling had only ever known her as Betty B, but she had been a regular at his house parties in the mid-70s.

Bieling found an old number for her, which led the guards first to Terenure. Betty had long departed the social scene and also the southern suburbs. It took gardaí a few days to track her down, to a northside local authority housing estate, Marigold Court in Darndale, Dublin 17.

A pleasant woman with neat blonde hair and an open disposition, Betty willingly agreed to be interviewed in Dún Laoghaire Garda Station, where she travelled with detectives on Wednesday, 11 August. There, she was filled in by Detective Hickey on what happened at Bieling's house. He described the man with his wavy dark hair, his lord-of-the-manor accent and the silk cravat who had produced a shotgun and demanded £1,000 off Bieling.

The hairs stood on the back of Hickey's neck with her unhesitating response. "That can be only one person," she said. "Malcolm Macarthur."

Betty described a wealthy, eccentric man from County Meath, with a distant personality, whom she knew from the Dublin pub scene. He had started a relationship with her friend, Brenda Little, and although she knew the couple had a young son, she could not tell Hickey or Donegan where they now lived as she had not been in touch with them for several years.

Betty Braughan mentioned another person who might know of Macarthur's whereabouts. It was Victor Melia, the elderly mathematician who used to frequent Bartley Dunne's. He was the only customer to whom the otherwise unapproachable Macarthur was willing to converse with at length on his pub visits.

By Thursday, 12 August, gardaí had managed to track Melia down to his home in Trees Road in the southside suburb of Mount Merrion. Hickey and Donegan called out to him and within minutes realised they had struck gold: Melia, now in his 70s, had a black book of contacts for Dublin's bohemian and alternative set.

"He kept track of people, he was a collator for a certain group," said Hickey. "If somebody went abroad for a few years and came back, and they wanted to find Tom, Dick, or Harry, he'd be likely to have an idea of where they had been most recently, and would have their phone number and address."

Melia had kept in touch with Macarthur, with whom he shared an interest in astronomy. The man they were searching for, he told Hickey and Donegan, was very wealthy, spent a lot of time abroad, lectured occasionally and wrote academic articles. He used to meet Macarthur regularly in Bartley Dunne's, he said, adding the proviso, to buck the gay association with the pub, that he did not believe he was homosexual. Melia told the detectives that after Macarthur had a child, they would occasionally meet in the Shelbourne Hotel for drinks. He also mentioned, in passing, that Macarthur and Little were friends of the attorney general, Patrick Connolly.

# 22

# 'WHATEVER IT IS, YOU'RE ON YOUR OWN'

"He could see us. He knew we were on to him." Detective Brian Sherry

Events in the search for the killer were finally beginning to gather pace. The person who had been for so long almost spectral had in fact laid down what looked like a very obvious trail.

This latest information on Macarthur, from Victor Melia, was that he, Brenda Little, and their son Colin had left Ireland a few months beforehand and were now living in Tenerife. Prior to that, they had been living in a flat in Donnybrook. Melia did not have an exact address but did have a telephone number.

The gardaí now knew who they were looking for, and that the man had some connection with the attorney general, Paddy Connolly. They knew that Connolly lived at Pilot View.

The man described by Pilot View residents' association chair Alan Solomons as likely to have been Connolly's nephew fit Macarthur's description. It was still a theory, and during his career, Hickey had seen enough theories blown embarrassingly apart to jump too soon to any massive conclusions. "You'd be reluctant even in the incident room to say what you were thinking, or what you had discovered," says Hickey.

But it clearly warranted further investigation, and before making a move, gardaí needed to be sure.

On Wednesday, 11 August, Courtney ordered for Harry Bieling to be interviewed for a third time, on this occasion in Dún Laoghaire Garda Station. He instructed his officers to go through everything in minute detail. The murder squad detectives questioned him for five hours that day.

They repeatedly asked about Malcolm Macarthur, Pilot View and Patrick Connolly. He insisted he knew nothing about any of them and could not recall having met Macarthur before the night he arrived to rob him with the possible intention of killing him.

Pursuing a possible line of enquiry that the suspect might be a homosexual serial killer, detectives brought up the case of Charles Self, a gay man who was brutally murdered the previous January in nearby Monkstown. The killer had not yet been found. Bieling insisted he did not know Self and could not recall ever meeting him. *The Boss* by Joe Joyce and Peter Murtagh gives a detailed account of this interview and Bieling's impression that detectives thought "they were onto a series of murders involving the gay community".

Bieling, who was himself gay, was nonplussed by the questioning. He repeatedly said he knew nothing that could add or subtract from the theory of homosexual murders that was being canvassed.

Already traumatised – and now fully realising how close his own brush with death had been – Bieling was exhausted by the time the long session came to an end.

Early on the morning of Friday, 13 August – the same morning Malcolm Macarthur cadged a lift from the attorney general as far as government buildings and recovered the shotgun he had hidden in nearby Merrion Square – Detective Denis Donegan checked out a telephone number that Victor Melia had passed on to the gardaí. He traced it to a flat called Sleepy Hollow at 4 Seaview Terrace in Donnybrook. As he arrived, he met the young Malaysian doctor who lived there as she was departing for work at St Vincent's Hospital. She recalled that the previous tenants were a young couple, with a small boy, who were now living in the Canary Islands.

Donegan asked her for the name and number of her landlord. When he contacted this man, he was not very receptive but when pressed, he revealed that the couple and their child were not the tenants but were guests of the person who held the lease. And the name of the actual tenant? Patrick Connolly SC.

Once Connolly's identity was established, it was quickly conveyed to the incident room and on to Dún Laoghaire that this was the same Patrick Connolly who was the attorney general in Charles Haughey's Fianna Fáil government. The investigation had now narrowed down to a single location: Connolly's home in Pilot View. While detectives were closing in on their prey, they were now also embroiled in a high-wire act which carried, should anything go wrong, enormous political ramifications.

Detective Superintendent Courtney was not a politician, however. He was a policeman, and his one and only consideration at that moment was tracking down Malcolm Macarthur.

Which was how, just after noon that day, the first of the team drove up discreetly to Pilot View. Tony Hickey and Denis Donegan made their arrival in an unmarked Renault 4 van. As they approached the gates, they spied a grey Mini Minor parked a little askew from the kerb. They were taken aback by what greeted them when they looked through the window. Inside was a black pistol sitting in full view on the passenger seat. Alarm bells began to ring. The suspect in the Phoenix Park murder had brandished a black pistol when the gardener, Paddy Byrne, had confronted him. Could this be it?

The door of the car was unlocked and after closer inspection, they saw that despite how real it looked, it was only an air pistol.

"It was another red herring," said Hickey. "A few local lads who were in college had done some summer work abroad and bought an air pistol on their way back to Ireland."

The two detectives drove on through the gates and parked at the side. The council was doing some work on the roads and footpaths inside Pilot View and had erected a small hut there. Posing as council workmen, the pair wore donkey jackets and stood around the hut. To allay suspicion, they occasionally came out to sweep some stones from the footpath.

Other detectives were in position at the front and back of

the apartment. Brian Sherry and Frank Hand were deployed on the lawn. They were told to pass themselves off as residents and just to sit and watch. Another experienced murder squad detective, Joe Shelly, was stationed at the front of the block, where John Courtney and Noel Conroy were.

Connolly's penthouse took up the upper two storeys of the Carnsore block in Pilot View. The upper level opened out to a generous balcony. Hickey and Donegan had a good view of the sitting room where the curtains were drawn back. They spotted a man moving around the room and occasionally coming out on the balcony. Hickey could see he had "wavy hair, a nice tan and was well-dressed". Their prime suspect was in situ.

Very soon, the man was at the window again, but now looking directly at the undercover detectives in the hut, and the two "residents" sitting at the edge of the lawn.

"He could see us. He knew we were on to him," Sherry said.

It was after 5pm when a taxi arrived outside the block. The young driver was astonished when his car was surrounded by armed gardaí. When they asked him what he was doing he said he was making a delivery to number 6. The items included a bottle of Perrier water and two hacksaw blades.

The gardaí knew immediately why the blades had been purchased and, by implication, that the man in the apartment was likely armed. Some of the detectives were armed: Sherry was carrying a revolver in a holster inside his jacket.

By this stage, John Courtney and Noel Conroy had entered the foyer after being let in by another resident. They were joined there by Hickey. They rang the intercom bell for number 6 and Courtney identified himself as a garda to the man who answered. "I made repeated pleas for the man to open the door," he said. "My pleas were ignored."

The three held a quick confab and decided not to make any move until the attorney general came home. A resident who was passing told the guards it was possible for somebody to escape from the roof. Frank Hand was sent around the back and told to watch the upper floors.

Patrick Connolly was greatly relieved to finish up work at 6pm that Friday, 13 August and head for home. It was the start of summer recess and his long-awaited holiday.

"He had a spring in his step," said Hickey, recalling his entrance into the lobby at around 6.40 pm. It didn't last long.

When asked by Courtney if there was a man staying with him in the flat, Connolly responded, yes, his friend, Malcolm Macarthur. When Courtney told him that the same Malcolm Macarthur was wanted for armed robbery, Connolly was stunned. "Poor Paddy, God love him," recalls Detective Brian Sherry. "I had never seen a man so shocked. He could not believe it.

"He said, 'This is crazy, Malcolm is a lovely guy. It is crazy. There is no way he could have done this.'"

Despite his disbelief and his protests, Connolly was immediately cooperative, according to Hickey. "He said, 'What can I do?' And he went and he tried the intercom but there was no response. We went to one of the apartments downstairs and he rang the phone number. There was no answer."

It was decided that they would approach the flat and try to talk to Macarthur directly. The gardaí warned Connolly that he might be armed, but Connolly said he did not believe Macarthur was capable of harming anybody. Nonetheless, he was cautious. There was a turn just before the last flight of stairs to the door of number 6. Connolly stopped there and would go no further. He shouted up towards his door: "Malcolm, there are some gentlemen here to see you. They are gardaí and they want to talk to you."

Connolly then handed his keys to Tony Hickey. Hickey quietly and carefully climbed the remaining stairs to the door. Alongside him were Noel Conroy and Brian Sherry, both of them with their guns poised. Courtney followed the three detectives up to the door of number 6.

Detective Sherry recalls his instruction from Detective Courtney: "If he comes out with a gun, shoot him."

"I said to myself, 'Fuck, this is mad stuff.' I had a standard 38 revolver, a Smith and Wesson. It had a four-inch barrel though, it was a cannon."

Hickey tried the lock but Macarthur had turned the deadbolt inside. The guards demanded he open the door. Eventually they heard his voice. He wanted to speak to Connolly. The attorney general came up a few steps and pleaded with Macarthur to open the door. He replied that he would.

The moment he opened the door the three detectives rushed in.

"We ran and pushed back the door and he went flying over a couch that was directly behind the door. Hickey was on top of him immediately. I had also dived on top of him," recalls Sherry.

Just after 7pm on Friday, 13 August, the biggest manhunt

for a killer in the history of the state had come to a successful conclusion. The man wanted for the murders of Bridie Gargan and Dónal Dunne put up no resistance as gardaí handcuffed him.

Connolly arrived into the apartment and looked at Macarthur. "I don't know what this is about, Malcolm," he told him. "Whatever it is, you are on your own."

Hickey asked Macarthur if he had a gun and he replied that he had. He showed them where he had hidden it in an attic space upstairs, under the eaves of the roof. Hickey crawled in and retrieved the gun, which was wrapped in a plastic bag. He used a tissue to handle it. Courtney was not too worried about niceties, Sherry recalled, and told Hickey "Fuck the fingerprints, open the bag."

When Hickey examined the gun it was unmistakably a Miroku with its elegant design. The serial number confirmed it was that of Dónal Dunne.

Macarthur had been closely monitoring newspapers and TV news on his own case since the Bieling incident and had taken the lack of coverage as a positive sign that gardaí were not closing in on him. He mentioned to Hickey later that evening that if he had known, he would have been long gone.

Sherry later recalled the sense of anti-climax when the killer was revealed. The man who had held Ireland in the grip of fear for over three weeks cut a pathetic figure standing before them now, a deflated-looking fool lacking guile or self-awareness. It was hard to equate this person with the cold brutality he had displayed.

"What had just happened was a combination of huge pressure on us to get a result, the off-chance we had got it wrong, and then a really tense stand-off at Pilot View. Yet this fellow, when we caught him, he was a nobody.

"He was a guy who had inherited money years before when his father had died and had spent it. He was highly educated and gave the impression he was an academic.

"But he had never worked. He had no skill set like everybody else who had to learn how to go out in the world and make a few bob and do whatever they had to do.

"It was incredible. This is the only way you could describe him, as a nobody."

For the gardaí involved, it was the culmination of three weeks of relentless toil and effort during one of the hottest summers on record. Mixed with relief, though, was a clear contempt for Macarthur, a man whose misdeeds had caused terror and devastation.

"I remember Courtney saying, 'Get that fucker out of here. Get that fucker out of here,'" Sherry recalled. "And he was dragged out and brought to the car."

# 23

# THE MEDIA DESCENDS

"Holy cow, what is going on here?" Peter Murtagh, journalist

August is known among newspaper people as "silly season", because all the institutions of the state are shut down, the country is in holiday mode, and there is little real news around. August of 1982 was an exception, though. The slew of four murders in late July kept the newsprint flowing. There was an air of heightened tension among the public, too. As of mid-August, none of the killings had been solved. Not that of postmaster Robert Belton, nor of Patricia Furlong, the young woman strangled at a music festival in the Dublin mountains. Nor, of course, those of Bridie Gargan and Dónal Dunne. The fact that the latter two had died at the hands of the same killer meant they imbued more fear among the public than the others.

By the second weekend of August, however, news coverage

of the manhunt had quietened. *The Irish Times* had not covered it for six days, since Saturday, 7 August. Then, it reported that the investigation for the double murderer was being conducted on the northside of the city. That was around the time Detective Courtney had secretly shifted the investigation's focus to Dún Laoghaire, after the evidence there had emerged.

On Friday night of 13 August, the front of *The Irish Times* had been 'put to bed' in the D'Olier Street newsroom. Most of those finishing their work walked the ten paces from the back door of the offices to Bowe's pub, directly across the narrow street.

"It was the end of the week, things are winding down a bit," says Peter Murtagh. As he and other journalists sipped pints and balls of malt in Bowe's, a skeleton staff remained in D'Olier Street to add any breaking stories to later editions that came off the printing press, which was clattering away in the bowels of the building.

Sometime around 10pm, that all changed. "News came through that something was going down in Dalkey, that there was a big garda operation," recalled Murtagh. "We made an assumption it must be related to all of these murders, that maybe they had a breakthrough."

The reporters and editors in the pub were immediately mustered. Others were called in from their homes into the office or sent out to the southern suburbs.

As security correspondent, Murtagh was one of a team dispatched out to the Dún Laoghaire area. "I would have been tasked to find out whatever I could about what had happened. Pretty soon I became aware that it was around this flat complex over Bulloch Harbour. I don't think we knew it was called Pilot View at that stage, but I certainly was aware of it because it was quite a prominent landmark: it was fairly new, was quite big and was, obviously, quite upmarket."

Reporters congregated near Dún Laoghaire Garda Station, which had closed its doors to the public – in itself a sign. The journalists took up vigil, and a stream of the force's senior investigating officers arrived at the station.

Murtagh shuttled between the garda station and Pilot View, where reporters congregated outside the gates. They settled in for a long wait, trying to pick up snippets of information from garda contacts and any residents who had wandered out that night to see what was going on.

"By that stage, word had come through that Pilot View is where the attorney general lived. And I thought, Holy cow, what is going on here?" said Murtagh.

"That was Friday night and into the early hours and Saturday morning. I was running around trying to put the pieces together. Was all of this connected to one of the murders that the guards were doing their damnedest to try and make progress on? Was it anything to do with the attorney general?"

A resident in the Pilot View complex came out and told reporters he had been informed by a detective that a man had been arrested. The man may have been armed, he added, but was detained without a struggle. The reporters could see a lot of garda activity in one of the apartment blocks, Carnsore. The resident told them Connolly's penthouse was in that block, but the journalists couldn't determine for sure that the suspect was arrested in the attorney general's home.

Work on the last, or city, edition of all the papers had continued into the early hours of Saturday morning, extending its latest deadline by several hours. "Charges Expected Today over Killing of Nurse, Farmer," read the headline in *The Irish Times*.

"Big Break in Murder Hunt," read the more declamatory headline in *The Irish Press*, with a subhead: "Man Held for Double Killing". In all likelihood, the media had Malcolm Macarthur's name at this stage but did not use it.

The official garda spokesman, Supt Noel Anderson, told media that the suspect had been arrested under Section 30 of the Offences Against the State Act. Anderson would not confirm it, but it was taken that the man arrested had a firearm in his possession – one of the grounds for arresting a suspect under the emergency powers of the act.

Some details about the detained man, not all of it accurate, were trickling into the reportage. "There was a suggestion the man was titled," reported *The Irish Times*.

"Reporters in all the newspapers were running around like headless chickens for a day or two, trying to put the pieces together to find out what was going on," said Murtagh.

Long after other residents of Pilot View had retired for the night, the reporters remained huddled outside its gates, in view of the still-blazing lights of the penthouse at number 6. Although the connection between the arrested man and Connolly had not been confirmed, every journalist there fully knew its import, if true.

The watershed moment came from the charge sheet the following morning, Saturday, 14 August: that the man wanted for two brutal murders was named Malcolm Macarthur and he had given his address as 6 Carnsore, Pilot View, the same address as that of the state's top law officer, Paddy Connolly.

Even now, so long afterwards, Murtagh finds it hard to convey the enormity of that bombshell. "It was one of the most sensational stories that I can think of in my career and, indeed, at any stage over the last 50 years. It was absolutely extraordinary.

"The questions came at 100 miles an hour. How did this happen? What was the relationship between these two people? The urgency surrounding those questions was frantic. If you think of something like this happening in the age of social media, Twitter would implode, Facebook would melt down. It was that sort of situation. And of course, the terrible thing was that people started making connections and assumptions and allegations, most of which – as they frequently are – would be wrong."

# 24

# A DIFFICULT CALL

"It is very difficult to exaggerate exactly how dumbfounded I was." Paddy Connolly

Ireland's attorney general was in a state of shock. He had come home from work to pack for his holiday, only to learn that his houseguest and good friend was being sought for armed robbery and, to boot, had hidden a shotgun in the eaves of his home.

Connolly watched in dismay as gardaí led Malcolm Macarthur away just after 7pm. Then more detectives arrived to conduct a detailed search and to sift for evidence. He led them into the guest bedroom where Macarthur had been staying, and also showed them items which he had stored for Brenda Little and Macarthur when they left for Tenerife.

The scene inside the penthouse was chaotic, with gardaí conducting searches and collecting evidence, and emotions running high. Aghast and drawn, Paddy Connolly was pouring himself the first of several stiff drinks he would have that night. Two of the detectives, Brian Sherry and Frank Hand, stayed in the apartment and spoke to him at length. Connolly could not believe that Macarthur was wanted for any crime. At that stage, nobody, least of all the attorney general himself, had any awareness whatsoever of the scale of the pending eruption.

"He was very upset," said Sherry. "He kept on saying, 'Malcolm is a decent fellow. He is living with Brenda Little and they have a child. He is a decent man.'

"Paddy himself was a gentleman. I was trying to calm him down. He told me he was going on holiday the next day. I told him, 'If I were you, I would not go, it would be a mistake to go now. You can always go later.' He kept on saying he had planned it for months."

Connolly's brother, Tony, was in Carlow, unaware of what had happened. He knew Paddy was due to go on holiday the next day and called the brother whom he fondly nicknamed 'Lord Dalkey' to wish him well.

Tony's son Stephen recalls his father's return from that call. "He sat down and said to me, 'Something very strange is happening.'"

Tony told his son that Paddy's apartment was full of gardaí and they had arrested Malcolm Macarthur for burglary. He'd asked his brother if he wanted him to travel up from Carlow, but Paddy declined, saying he was okay.

Soon after speaking to Tony, however, Paddy was to receive news that deeply shocked him. The head of the serious crime squad, Supt Pat Doocey, arrived at the apartment. He took

Connolly aside and informed him that Macarthur faced two further serious charges, the murders of Bridie Gargan and Dónal Dunne.

In Carlow, meanwhile, Stephen Connolly told his father that it all sounded odd, and that he should call his brother back to make sure he was alright, which Tony did. "[My father] came back in after the [second] call and he sat down," says Stephen. "He was absolutely white. He told me that it was a lot more serious, that Macarthur had been arrested for murder."

Within minutes, Tony Connolly was sitting in his car setting off on the hour-and-a-half journey to Dublin. Stephen said he knew that Paddy would find it difficult to handle the situation.

"My father was the common-sense person. He was a practical person. Paddy, in terms of stuff like that, could be naive."

As he waited for his brother, a dumbfounded Paddy Connolly had another drink to try and pull himself together and to brace himself for several very difficult phone calls he would have to make.

He did some cursory and half-hearted packing for his trip. Going into his bedroom, he made an entry into his personal diary. What he wrote was laconic but there was no doubting the sense of utter devastation.

When I came home this evening ready to pack for holidays, I found that there were detectives waiting to arrest Malcolm Macarthur. I was absolutely stunned. The most shattering day of my life. He is wanted for two murders of a violent nature. Unbelievable news.

When Tony Connolly arrived from Carlow, there was a ferocious argument between him and the senior gardaí in the apartment. Tony was incensed at the guards, assuming that Macarthur had been allowed to remain in situ in Paddy's flat for a number of days without Paddy having been informed.

It was explained to him that it was not as clear-cut as that, that the circumstances had all come together very quickly. It was only in the last 24 hours before they moved in on the apartment that they were certain that Macarthur was their prime suspect for the murders.

Nevertheless, this led to tensions between the gardaí and the Connollys. When investigation lead John Courtney arrived back at the flat later that night, Tony Connolly confronted him. Courtney said Tony Connolly subjected him to a barrage of criticism for not tipping off his brother earlier. It led to a prolonged rut between both men, with some choice language used. For his part, Courtney stood his ground and gave as good as he got. He said he was doing his job, and told Tony, "I am not in the business of cosying up to anyone, however elevated their position."

What galled the Connollys was that the gardaí knew for some time a suspected double killer was staying with the attorney general and nobody had given any consideration to the risk that might have been posed to his wellbeing.

Stephen Connolly said that in the years that followed, he had asked his father, Tony, and uncle, Paddy, the same questions: what would have happened if Paddy had found the gun in the apartment? Would Macarthur have used it? Both

Connolly brothers had said they did not think so. Stephen had his doubts.

"They knew only a part of Macarthur. Did they know the part of Macarthur that went off and did the actions that he did?"

As throngs of photographers and reporters continued to gather outside the apartment building, Paddy Connolly felt as isolated and helpless as a submarine commander cut off from his fleet. He was reeling from the shock of his good friend having been arrested for two murders. He rationalised that while it was an incredible coincidence, he himself was a wholly innocent party who had no inkling that anything was amiss until armed gardaí greeted him at his own doorstep. He continued to prepare for his holidays the following day.

"It is very difficult to exaggerate exactly how dumbfounded I was," he said in the aftermath. "When I was later informed that he was wanted for murder, I was even more astounded. Even though I rather pooh-poohed it at the time, I was actually in a state of shock for the next few days, with the sense of all this being unreal."

But that night, as scenes-of-crime gardaí methodically combed every inch of his flat, there were nettles to be grasped for Connolly. He made the dreaded phone call to Brenda Little in Tenerife. The apartments in the Torres del Sol complex in Los Cristianos did not have individual phones. He left a message for Little at reception, asking for her to return his call urgently. She telephoned him shortly afterwards.

He informed her that Macarthur had been arrested on suspicion of committing two murders. Initially, she did not believe him, but as the reality sank in she became very distressed and sobbed uncontrollably. Paddy struggled to keep back his own tears.

After the call to Little, it took Connolly some time to compose himself. He knew, however, there was one other important phone call he needed to make.

He braced himself and called Taoiseach Charles Haughey, who had arrived on his remote holiday island of Inishvickillane the previous day.

# 25

# INISHVICKILLANE

"Bon voyage." Taoiseach Charles J Haughey to Attorney
General Paddy Connolly

The telephone system in west Kerry relied on a manual
exchange in the village of Ballyferriter. Each call had to be
routed through a telephonist and finding one on duty late on
a Friday evening could be tricky. After several unsuccessful
attempts, Connolly eventually managed to make contact with
the taoiseach at 10pm. When he did so the line was very bad.
He explained what had happened as best he could.

Haughey did not fully catch the gist of what his attorney
general was telling him. He asked if he, Haughey, knew this
Malcolm Macarthur fellow, and had they ever met? Connolly
replied no. Haughey seemed reassured by that. It is not exactly
known what was imparted or understood during that fateful
conversation, given the quality of the line, but it is clear that

Haughey's attorney general did not inform him of one important piece of information within his possession: that gardaí had recovered a shotgun from the apartment.

Towards the end of the short call, the attorney general told the taoiseach that he was departing on his holidays to the United States the following morning. Haughey raised no objections to Connolly's travel plans.

"Bon voyage," Haughey rasped, before hanging up. For now, he was under the impression that Connolly had rung to inform him about the arrest out of courtesy. He thought no more of it.

In his Dalkey apartment, Paddy Connolly was sure Haughey had given him clearance to proceed with his holiday plans. As Stephen recalled, both men may have been at cross-purposes in that conversation. "Our understanding was that he talked to [Haughey] on Friday night. It was the end of the week, people were relaxing. So we don't know how clear the message was that was relayed, or how clear was the message being received."

Paddy Connolly spent the rest of the night packing and talking to his brother. It was early in the morning by the time both went to bed.

The attorney general did not get much sleep that night. Just before 8am on Saturday morning, 14 August, John Courtney and Noel Conroy arrived at Pilot View. They informed Connolly he was obliged to make a statement and should not depart on his holiday. He was in no mood to capitulate. He refused point-blank and it prompted an expletive-laden exchange between himself and Courtney. The latter insisted the attorney general needed to be questioned as to why a man wanted for two murders was found in his flat. He told Connolly in unvarnished terms that he would not be treated differently than any other citizen.

Connolly stood his ground and forcibly reminded Courtney he was attorney general. His only involvement was allowing a friend to stay in his flat. He was wholly innocent of any wrongdoing. The two gardaí eventually backed down and did not try to impede Connolly's departure.

At 9am, Connolly left the apartment to take an Aer Lingus flight to London, to begin the first leg of his holiday. He may have thought he was escaping the nightmarish trauma of the previous night. Nothing could be further from the truth. His decision to proceed despite the protests of the gardaí was to prove a lapse of judgement of gargantuan proportions. For Ireland's US-bound attorney general, his troubles were only beginning.

# 26

# THE INTERROGATION

"Desperate situations require desperate remedies." Malcolm
Macarthur

After his arrest at Pilot View, Malcolm Macarthur was
bundled into an unmarked blue Talbot Solara for the short
journey to Dún Laoghaire Garda Station. Two detectives
squeezed in beside him on the back seat. DSI John Courtney
sat in the front passenger seat. Little was said as they drove
along the coast, save for the occasional pointed barb from
Courtney, who did not disguise his contempt for the arrested
man.

As the four senior detectives marched through the station
doors with Macarthur in custody, every garda in the station
knew they were witnessing a fateful moment. They arrived
downstairs and clamoured for a look at the notorious killer
with the aristocratic airs and raffish cravat.

News spread quickly, by mouth or car radio. Within minutes, other detectives began arriving at the station, including some senior officers such as Det Supt Hubert Reynolds and Det Inspector Colm Browne. Reynolds, a native of Leitrim, was a murder squad veteran, having been there since 1969. He had been in charge of the massive investigation around north Dublin after Macarthur had been spotted at the clay shooting grounds and later at the Fingal House pub. That part of the operation had involved the gathering of many hundreds of statements across a swathe of Finglas, Glasnevin and Ballymun.

Detective Browne was another experienced investigator who had been in charge of the inquiry into Dónal Dunne's murder in Edenderry.

The evidence against Macarthur was compelling. There was a clear set of fingerprints left on the polythene bag that concealed the shovel he'd abandoned in the Phoenix Park. He had also left fingerprints on a milk carton he bought in Edenderry on the morning he murdered Dunne. There were important eyewitnesses – the retired US diplomat Harry Bieling; the gardener Paddy Byrne who saw him attack Bridie Gargan; the travel agent Rita Brennan on the South Circular Road; the news vendor John Monks; people who spotted him shaving off his beard in the Fingal House pub; those who saw him at clay pigeon shoots, or in the town of Edenderry. He had been caught in possession of Dónal Dunne's rare Miroku shotgun. The blood-stained military-style pullover he'd worn in the Gargan attack had been recovered, as had his tweed fisherman's hat, and the lump hammer he'd used.

The gardaí could still have successfully prosecuted without

a statement from Macarthur, but Courtney favoured a belts and braces approach and wanted Macarthur to admit he had committed both murders.

Until the Criminal Justice Act was enacted in 1984, gardaí had no general powers to question suspects who were suspected of serious crimes, including murder. There were exceptions, but they related to emergency legislation designed to combat terrorism and subversion, namely the Offences Against the State Act. Section 30 of that act allowed a person to be detained, and questioned, if they were suspected of a schedule of offences, including firearm offences. Macarthur had been in possession of a shotgun during his unsuccessful armed robbery of Harry Bieling and so – by dint of that technicality – he was arrested under a law whose original intention was to tackle organisations like the IRA. That power gave investigating gardaí 24 hours – and a further 24 hours if necessary – to question the suspect.

After being processed, and having his fingerprints taken, Macarthur was brought to an inspector's office for questioning.

There was an established protocol for interrogations. Pairs of detectives would question the suspects in relay during the interrogation period. The guards who arrested Macarthur knew relatively little about him, other than his name and some scant details about his background. Tony Hickey and Noel Conroy were the first to interview him.

"He was quite condescending," Hickey recalled. "It was kind of, how dare you ask me questions like that. So we carried on a certain conversation about his background and his family and all that type of thing, which is routine. You try and build up a rapport with somebody."

Macarthur spoke for some time about his family and upbringing, giving the two detectives a lengthy treatise on his atheism and why he opposed the institution of marriage. He had sufficient means not to work, he told detectives, and it allowed him to spend his time studying – he mentioned his fictional Cambridge degree – writing, travelling and reflecting.

The dissolute life he described was at a distant remove from the detectives who had been slogging 16 hours a day for the previous three weeks. After an hour or so, Hickey and Conroy began to steer the interrogation to the crimes themselves. They took Macarthur back to 22 July and described in detail his movements on the day.

John Courtney was keeping a watching brief on the interviews as they progressed. He noticed how preternaturally calm the suspect was. He later said of this first encounter: "Some killers are just thugs, pure and simple. Macarthur was different. He was very well spoken, obviously well educated – you could imagine meeting him in a social situation and having a normal conversation with him."

When questioned on the crimes, Macarthur initially used a combination of denial and bluster. He claimed he found the shotgun under a bush on Killiney Hill and repeated his line that what had happened in Harry Bieling's house was a prank gone wrong, that they knew each other, and that he'd attended eight or nine parties at Camelot back in 1974 and they were friends.

When Macarthur finished speaking, gardaí conveyed the

picture of events as they knew it. This short, sharp reality check was to quickly burst any bubble Macarthur had managed to keep inside up to this point. Hickey and Conroy now started a hard press. They said they knew everything he had done. They knew it was he who had crawled through long grass in the Phoenix Park towards a woman in the hope of stealing a car, only to be warned off by her husband. They could place him some minutes later at the roundabout near the US ambassador's residence, drinking water underneath the statue depicting a phoenix. The gardener Paddy Byrne had given a detailed description of the man who bludgeoned the nurse with a lump hammer and who had pointed a pistol at him. It matched his description. There was a shovel left behind wrapped in polythene which gave a fine set of prints, which were sure to match the fingerprints that had been taken off him in the station earlier. They also told him that they had recovered the blood-stained pullover and the fisherman's hat he had abandoned near the South Circular Road.

The ambulance crew who had unwittingly escorted Macarthur from the Phoenix Park could pick him out in an identity parade. So could Rita Brennan, the woman in the travel agency, who gave him three glasses of water. Gardaí knew what bus he had taken, that he alighted in Finglas, that he had bought razor blades and shaved in the toilet of the Fingal House, before taking a taxi to Dún Laoghaire. Customers in the pub had seen him there, had seen him shave, had seen the blood flecks on his white shirt.

Eventually, Hickey said, Macarthur's guard began to crumble. He spoke of his financial woes. "I did not invest my money wisely," Macarthur told them. He then admitted that all the money he had inherited had been spent or lost and he had found himself in debt with no way of paying it back. It was clearly dawning on Malcolm Macarthur that there was no talking his way out of this; he was well and truly trapped.

"He stopped talking and he got very pale," said Hickey. "His eyes kind of focused and then lost their focus. He asked for a glass of water, which he got."

Another team of two took over and began asking direct questions about his motivation, why he needed a gun and a car. He said that with no job and with mounting debts, committing a robbery was the only solution he could think of to overcome his financial difficulties.

"Desperate situations require desperate remedies," he told detectives.

It was well after midnight when Macarthur requested to talk to Detectives Hickey and Conroy again. "When we went into the room," said Hickey, "he said, 'I want to get my thoughts in categorical order. I will tell you everything that has happened in the morning.'"

# 27

# A MURDERER CONFESSES

"I affirm that I am responsible for the deaths of nurse Bridie Gargan and farmer Dónal Dunne." Malcolm Macarthur

The suspect was allowed to rest on a mattress in the room until seven o'clock the following morning. The first detectives in to question him that Saturday were Det Sgt Joe Shelley and Det Sgt Denis Donegan. At around 8.45am, Macarthur began his statement. It took over four hours to dictate and ran to 21 hand-written pages and some 4,000 words.

What was striking to the gardaí about the statement was how matter-of-fact it was. Macarthur described his actions as if he were an observer to them. It was a full admission of his misdeeds but without any of the upswell of emotion or release of tension that gardaí were used to seeing in those moments.

Courtney later observed, "He did not show any kind of emotion at all. He appeared totally calm about everything."

Despite all the exposition to follow, the very first line was the clincher. "I affirm that I am responsible for the deaths of nurse Bridie Gargan and farmer Dónal Dunne."

The motive was clear: his obsessive need for money. So was the *mens rea*, or criminal intent: he said he was quite prepared to kill anybody who got in the way of his enterprise.

Everything else afterwards was detail, and there was a lot of it.

It was a textbook example of an inculpatory admission. Macarthur began by describing what he called the "Miss Gargan incident" in the Phoenix Park and how he had acquired the hammer, shovel, and the pistol crossbow. He stated:

> The reason why I bought this all goes back to money. For the past two years my finances have been diminishing. This was something I could not cope with because during the years 1974 to 1976 I inherited the sum of roughly £70,000, part of the proceeds of the sale of my father's estate at Breemount, Trim, Co Meath. All this I spent because of mismanagement and unwise use. I now realise that I should have invested this money in a profitable manner.
>
> I wanted this hammer to injure somebody [in order] to get a car, to travel down the country to get a gun, because I had no transport. In turn I had planned ahead to stick somebody up and the object was to get money. I had read

in the newspapers about all the [IRA] robberies, and this seemed a way out of my obsessive financial situation.

Part of that plan also involved a shovel, because my attitude was that I wanted this venture to succeed, and if by chance I did kill anybody in this venture, I would use the shovel to dispose of the body.

My finances were bad. I left my wife [sic.] enough to help her for about two months. I told her I would return to her in between two weeks and three weeks with some money, but my wife Brenda did not know where this money was going to come from or any of my plans.

Macarthur recounted in detail how he created his imitation pistol, and his appearance as he walked through Phoenix Park on the exceptionally hot afternoon of 22 July 1982:

I was wearing the fisherman's hat, beard, a fawn coloured crew-necked jumper, army type, with patches on the elbows and shoulder. I wore a white shirt, a grey pants and orange shoes.

I walked between two straight lines of trees. Before I got to the American Ambassador's residence I looked at a few cars but they did not seem easy prey and I walked on. As I walked along the row of trees I saw somebody lying in the long grass to the left of these trees. I saw a car parked beside this person and I think the driver's door was open. The car, which was silver in colour, was facing out towards the main road.

I walked past the car and I decided to make an approach. I did not know at this stage whether it was a man or a woman who was lying beside this car. I then put my shovel, which was wrapped in black plastic, on the ground beside a tree, and I approached this vehicle. As I walked towards the car I had this imitation gun in my right hand and the holdall bag in my left. When I came within a few feet I saw that it was a lady who was sunbathing topless. I pointed the gun at her and told her to get into the car.

She was very calm and she said: "Is this for real?" and I said: "Yes, it is."

She then calmly said: "May I put back on my clothes?" and I said: "Yes."

She put on a blousy top and she did not appear to have any bra on. She then got into the back seat of the car. I assured her that I wanted her car. I told her to lie on the back seat and that I would tie her up.

She then began to panic, and I panicked because she would not lie on the seat. I was afraid that she was going to draw attention to us, so I took out the hammer from the bag and I hit her a couple of times, because the first blow did not do what I expected it to do. There was blood all over her, and some on the window and more on the seats. I used a newspaper to wipe some of the blood off the left side window. When I was cleaning this window, I saw a gentleman walking towards the car.

He walked around the front of the car and he said: "Is this serious?" or something like that. I got out of the car and produced the pistol. I pointed the weapon at him. He stood there for a while and then he ran at me and grabbed the gun. We wrestled for about ten seconds and this man, who was bigger and stronger than me, eventually let me go. If it had been a real gun, and he had made a more successful attempt to block my escape, I may have shot him. I then jumped into this Renault 5 car and drove off along the dirt track. As I did so, I saw this man out on the main road trying to hail down a car.

As Macarthur drove the car away at high speed in a low gear across the dirt track, he said he could see the girl moving in the back seat. He described how, by chance, an ambulance driver gestured to follow him when he got stuck in traffic at an exit gate from the Phoenix Park, and how he followed the ambulance, with its blue lights flashing, to the entrance of St James's Hospital.

> During the time while I was following the ambulance I was less desperate, but when I turned into the hospital I felt that my need to escape reasserted itself and I wheeled around the driveway and back out the same way. I think I turned to my left after going out that gate and drove in towards town. I then got the feeling that I should leave the car and run away. I took a left turn into a narrow laneway and I abandoned the car there.

Macarthur expressed no misgivings about leaving Bridie Gargan bleeding in the back of the car. He went on to describe arranging to meet Dónal Dunne in Edenderry two days later, on Saturday, 24 July.

> [Dunne] told me that he had the gun with him in the boot. He passed a remark like, "We won't look at it here in the middle of the street", so he drove some distance outside town, at the edge of a bog, in a flattish area. He told me that this was their gun club grounds.
>
> We got out of the car and Mr Dunne took the gun from the boot. It was in a case. He told me that he did not really have to sell it but

that if he got what he paid for it, he would sell it. He told me that it cost him £1,100 but that he would not sell it at a loss. I wanted a gun badly but I did not want to buy it or I could not buy it.

Mr Dunne put two cartridges in the gun and I shot at a target which was a white post. I don't know if I hit it or not. I was trying to think of a way of getting this gun without paying for it and I was playing for time. Mr Dunne then got a bit angry and reached out and put his hand on some part of the gun to take it.

I pulled back and pulled the trigger and I shot him in the head. He fell down. I ran towards Mr Dunne's silver car and I left the gun beside it. I then went back to Mr Dunne and I saw that his head was in a mess. I pulled his body into some bushes and I broke some branches to cover him up. I then went back to his car and I put the gun inside lying between the two front seats. I drove off in this car towards Dublin.

In the same unemotional way, Macarthur went on to describe how he went back to his digs, bought a hacksaw, shortened the barrels of the gun and planned to carry out robberies. He neglected to mention his first foray, to the elderly man's home on Fitzwilliam Square, as the gardaí were not aware of it at the time. He then began recounting the Harry Bieling incident.

# Harry McGee

On Wednesday 4th of July I left my digs at approximately 4pm and I got a bus to Killiney. I walked to a house called Camelot on top of Killiney Hill. This house is like a small castle and is owned by Mr Harry Bieling. I thought that he would have money. I was in his house eight or nine times in all, around 1975, and we were friends then.

I pretended that I wanted to take some photographs from his window but instead produced the gun that came from Edenderry and I pointed it at him and I demanded £1,000. He told me that he did not have that kind of money. I then suggested to him that he could give me a cheque for £1,000 and that a fictitious accomplice, who I said was working with me, could go to the bank and cash this cheque.

I had earlier opened an account in the Allied Irish Bank opposite the shopping centre in Dun Laoghaire village for the amount of £10. I opened this account in the name of John Eustace, using a false address at Oak Road, Dun Laoghaire. I later withdrew £7 from this account to give the bank staff the impression that the account was being used.

Harry Bieling made good his escape by running out the front door. I don't know whether I would have shot him or not. After Harry

196

Bieling had run away from his house, I ran over Killiney Hill. After that I called to another house on the same road and a lady answered the door. I had the gun with me and I wanted her to ring a taxi for me. She told me that her phone was out of order and she did not open the door for me.

I then left and a car came along with some people in it who were going fishing. They gave me a lift to Dalkey. I think the man who was driving this car was American but he said that he lived in Killiney. I then went to a friend of mine in Pilot View and I have been living there ever since.

The next morning I brought the gun away and left it under a bush in Merrion Square. I only brought the gun to this address again on Friday 13th of August. That is the same gun that I handed over to gardaí yesterday.

This statement has been read over to me and it is correct.

Signed: Malcolm Edward Daniel Macarthur.

In the minutes after Macarthur signed the statement, the atmosphere inside the station became calm. There was no triumphalism or joy, just business and procedure. The Director of Public Prosecutions' office needed to be contacted. Macarthur needed to be charged. A district justice needed to be contacted to hold a special sitting as soon as possible. The charge sheet had to be filled out in precise detail. Arrangements had to be put in place to bring the prisoner to the nearby courthouse.

It was now late afternoon on Saturday. The detectives involved in the capture and interrogation were exhausted, but adrenaline would carry them through the final acts of that day's drama.

At 4.25pm Det Insp Noel Conroy formally charged Macarthur with the murders of Bridie Gargan and Dónal Dunne. When he was asked for his response, Macarthur replied: "I wish to withhold comment for the time being."

Macarthur's statement contained at least 40 different admissions of culpability, prime of which were two outright admissions of homicide. For the investigation team, no stone would be unturned in corroborating his testimony, to ensure the killer's swift passage to a long prison sentence at the earliest possible time. By Saturday evening, the garda sub aqua unit were already at Bulloch Harbour searching for the refashioned crossbow Macarthur had thrown into the sea on the night of Bridie Gargan's murder.

We can only guess at the shock of guesthouse owner Alice Hughes, who opened her door to two plain-clothes gardaí the same night, to learn that the quiet and polite lodger who had checked out the previous week was suspected of committing the two murders that had absorbed the public throughout the recent weeks of summer.

# 28

## BEST DRESSED IN COURT

"Malcolm Macarthur wore a white shirt with a red spotted bow tie, a fawn cord jacket, grey trousers and laced brown shoes." Report in *The Sunday Press*, 15 August 1982

Malcolm Macarthur's arrest for the double murder was already shaping up to be the biggest story of the year. The public were aware that the suspect was some kind of aristocrat. Even before the place of arrest was officially confirmed, the rumour mill was at full tilt, with rampant speculation around Macarthur's relationship with the attorney general.

Dozens of reporters had been camped outside Dún Laoghaire Garda Station since early morning on Saturday, 14 August. Word soon filtered out that Macarthur had been charged and would be brought before a special sitting of the District Court in Dún Laoghaire. Courtroom officials arrived to open the small Victorian-era courthouse just around the corner from the station, which was normally closed at weekends.

Soon a large crowd was gathered outside the courthouse, there to catch a glimpse of this exotic killer arriving before the judge. By afternoon the place was thronged. A line of teenagers sat on a high ivy-clad wall overlooking the lane, letting out occasional shouts at people down below.

Shortly after 4.30pm, Malcolm Macarthur emerged from the doorway of the garda station at the other end of the laneway, flanked by officers. He was handcuffed and a blanket had been thrown over his head. The crowd began jostling and hurling abuse at him. Macarthur was shunted along the laneway that led to the courthouse. Even though he could not see where he was going, he cleaved to his affectation of stuffing his hands into the pockets of his jacket.

Tony Hickey held on to his elbow to steer him in the right direction. A dozen gardaí formed a protective doughnut from the baying crowd, with people screaming "murderer, murderer". Macarthur was brought into the courthouse, which was packed with gardaí, reporters and some members of the public.

Blanket removed, Macarthur made an Agatha Christie drawing room entrance, walking slowly across the courtroom, his hands still in his jacket pockets. It made for an impressive sight. He had somehow managed to put a bow tie in his pocket at the time of his arrest. He now wore it in court. His big shock of wavy hair had been combed back. *The Sunday Press* reported that Malcolm Macarthur wore a "white shirt with a red spotted bow tie, a fawn cord jacket, grey trousers and laced brown shoes". *The Irish Times* described the colour of the bow tie as claret with white spots. It also noted his wavy dark hair. Those two particular features of Macarthur's would forever burnish his image in the public mind.

He sat in his designated seat flanked by two detectives. As they waited for District Justice Mary Kotsonouris to arrive, Macarthur studied the courtroom, looking at the ceiling, its large shutter windows and, finally, scanning the packed public and media benches with a look of disdain. This might have been unconscious on his part, but the sense of hauteur it gave was picked up by reporters.

Despite his apparent indifference to the grave charges he faced, Macarthur showed small signs of tension and nervousness. He was pale and dishevelled and seemed distracted. Reporters noticed barely discernible tremors in his hands and his shoulders, as if he were struggling to maintain control.

Outside in the laneway, the crowd of onlookers had swelled to several hundred. Their muffled shouts and taunts could be heard clearly inside the room.

The hearing lasted all of 11 minutes. Det Insp Conroy described the arrest of Macarthur at 6 Carnsore, Pilot View, and told the court that Macarthur had been charged that afternoon with the murders of Bridie Gargan and Dónal Dunne, as well as the aggravated burglary and possession of a firearm at Harry Bieling's house in Killiney.

Asked by Judge Kotsonouris if he could afford a solicitor, Macarthur said he was not working. He was then granted legal aid. He told the judge he did not have a particular solicitor in mind as he did not know any.

Once the hearing was over, Macarthur continued sitting with the detectives for several minutes as the court was cleared. Reporters could overhear the conversation between the three. It was banal. He described in detail his interest in astronomy. Both listened attentively and politely, feigning interest. All newspapers reported the myth the following day that Macarthur had a major degree in astrophysics from Cambridge University.

The blanket was again placed over Macarthur's head and he was rushed out to the laneway, where two unmarked Talbot Solara cars were parked. As he emerged onto the street, crowds surged forward. The youths sitting on the wall ripped clumps of ivy off it and hurled them at the cars. Macarthur was spat at, thumped with fists and people shouted abuse through the windows as the two cars slowly made their exit from the laneway, before speeding away towards Mountjoy Prison.

Macarthur continued to talk incessantly to the detectives for the duration of the journey. He asked about the remand process and the court hearing and how long it would take. He may have been uncharacteristically talkative, but he was characteristically detached, as if experiencing some interior version of events entirely at odds with the shattering reality unfolding around him.

# 29

## AN UNLIKELY FUGITIVE

"Irish Biggie Flees Here After Slay Scandal" *New York Post* headline, 16 August 1982

People would long remember where they were the moment they heard news of the shocking location of Malcolm Macarthur's arrest, which hit the evening newspapers on Saturday, 14 August, the same day as Macarthur's hearing at Dún Laoghaire courthouse. Emily O'Reilly, who was then an intern journalist, recalled it: "I remember being at the 15B bus stop in D'Olier Street on my way home and getting a copy of the *Evening Herald*. It was just starkly there – Malcolm Macarthur found in the A-G's flat.

"It is hard at this remove to convey just what a departure, what an astonishing turn of events it was. The attorney general was the state officer who would be prosecuting Macarthur. And Macarthur had turned up in his lovely, beautiful apartment in the most sought-after address, possibly, in the country. It's hard to even think of something currently that would generate as much surprise as that did at the time, because that was a very different world."

But if newsrooms were nimble in terms of reacting to quick-moving events, the apparatus of government was a different affair. Charles Haughey had been informed by Paddy Connolly the previous evening that Macarthur had been arrested at his flat. But as of the following morning, nobody else in Government Buildings in Merrion Street knew an iota about the dramatic events unfolding.

Frank Dunlop was the government press secretary at the time. He was a 35-year-old political appointee who had risen through the ranks of Fianna Fáil at a precociously young age, becoming its head of communications at only 27. He had been government spokesman since 1977, first under Jack Lynch, and since late 1979, with Haughey. Curly-haired and bespectacled, Dunlop was self-confident, smooth and loquacious, and was seen – in terms of the Fianna Fáil internal power struggle – as very much in the Haughey camp.

Dunlop was at home in County Meath that weekend. From very early on Saturday morning his colleague on duty at the Government Information Service (GIS), Ken Ryan, was bombarded with dozens of calls from reporters. Already a reporter from the *Evening Herald* had learned that the attorney general was taking a flight out of the country and wanted to know the reason for this.

Alerted by Ken Ryan as to unfolding events, Pádraig Ó hUiginn, a senior adviser to Haughey, rang Dunlop at about 9am to tell him what was going on and to discuss what to do.

They knew that Connolly was already on his way to London that morning and was then bound for New York. Dunlop knew immediately how serious the situation was. However, he and Pádraig Ó hUiginn were reluctant to ring Haughey. For one, it would be hard to contact him on his remote island with the poor phone line that had to go through an operator. Secondly, instantaneous reaction to a major breaking story was not expected of politicians in 1982. Dunlop recalled that senior officials eventually agreed to allow the situation rest until Haughey arrived back in Dublin on Monday for a scheduled meeting with trade unions.

"We were not storming the island to get hold of him," Dunlop later wrote in his 2004 memoir, *Yes, Taoiseach*. "It was before the era of 24-hour news and satellite communication and the idea of letting a night go by without speaking to the key player in a major political story was not so shocking."

But that approach was quickly being overtaken by events. As the volume of calls intensified, including from the international media, it became apparent to Dunlop and to others that the holding position could not be sustained. They were already on the back foot. The media, one step ahead of them since early morning, were contacting the Government Information Service demanding to know why Connolly was "fleeing" the country. Not until mid-morning on Saturday were government officials aware that Connolly had actually phoned Haughey the night before. Reporters were also floating various conspiracy theories to the beleaguered Ken Ryan, the GIS duty officer that weekend. The unfortunate Ryan had no information to share with the press, except "no comment".

By 9.30am, Haughey's private secretary, Sean Aylward, also briefed by Ken Ryan, began to try to contact Haughey through the antiquated manual exchanges in west Kerry. Senior figures in government were also being contacted to let them know about the developing situation. When Bertie Ahern heard about it shortly after 10am, he immediately knew that this could escalate into a political catastrophe. As chief whip, he too needed to get hold of Haughey as soon as he could.

As it happened, Ahern was himself leaving Dublin that very morning on his way to his family's annual holiday in Ballyferriter, west Kerry, the nearest mainland village to Haughey's island bolthole. Ahern tried to reach Inishvickillane by phone before he left Dublin but to no avail. On the journey to Kerry, he stopped off periodically in villages and towns, using public phone boxes to contact the exchange.

"It was very difficult," he said. "People wouldn't understand nowadays. The Ballyferriter exchange used to close down at six o'clock, or at one o'clock on a Saturday. And of course there were no mobile phones."

Ahern finally made contact with Haughey soon after noon and filled him in on events unfolding. Sean Aylward also succeeded in reaching him. By this stage, Aylward had been fully briefed by the gardaí on the circumstances of the arrest, and of Macarthur's connection with Connolly. He told the taoiseach that the suspect for the two murders that had gripped the public that summer was a close friend of Paddy Connolly's and was, in fact, arrested in the attorney general's flat.

For the first time, Haughey also heard that a shotgun had been recovered in the apartment. It was also becoming clear that what Connolly thought the taoiseach had understood from their conversation – that Malcolm Macarthur had been arrested in his flat – and what the taoiseach actually understood, were not one and the same thing. It appeared the taoiseach was under the impression that Macarthur was merely somebody Connolly knew socially, no more than that.

Aylward relayed the available information to a taken-aback Haughey, whose reaction could not have been more different than it was the previous night when he had wished Connolly "bon voyage". When Aylward finished talking, an incredulous Haughey was silent for a moment. He then said: "I don't believe you."

It was an expression of astonishment rather than denial. What had been missed in the conversation with Connolly on Friday night amounted to a brewing catastrophe. Haughey, who thought that Connolly was informing him about Macarthur's arrest out of courtesy, had not thought about it since. This left the Department of the Taoiseach in a position where it only discovered it was caught in the headwinds of a developing political crisis *after* media were all over events. To compound the situation, the media were also implying that Connolly had effectively absconded from the jurisdiction. It was an omnishambles.

The urgent imperative now was to get Connolly home from London, where he was staying overnight. He was due to fly to New York by Concorde on Sunday morning to begin his multi-stop holiday.

By Saturday afternoon, Dunlop was back in Dublin trying to respond to media queries and dampen the salacious theories starting to emerge. One rumour already doing the rounds was that Macarthur and Connolly were having an affair; another was that the government had arranged for Connolly to leave the country in order to cover up some dreadful national scandal.

"All hell was breaking loose," Frank Dunlop says of that day. "Apart altogether from the dreadful murders of Bridie Gargan, and Dónal Dunne in Offaly, the conspiracy theorists got to work. Why would the senior law officer of the government – in whose apartment the suspect had been found – leave Ireland without any interface with the gardaí, or indeed with anybody other than the taoiseach?

"[His actions] began the urban myth that, in fact, there was something to hide, and that Charlie had given him the go ahead to go on his holiday, and things would be covered up. You can imagine the pages and pages that were devoted to this. It was international news."

For Charles Haughey and Patrick Connolly, their respective roles of the previous 24 hours were reversed. By late afternoon, and having been fully briefed by Aylward and Ahern, Haughey was now trying, without success, to track down Connolly in London.

Connolly had taken a mid-morning Aer Lingus flight to London where he was met at Heathrow by an official from the Irish embassy – a courtesy extended to all cabinet members. He was brought by the embassy car to his hotel, The Cavendish, at 81 Jermyn Street, just off Piccadilly. Tired and sleep-deprived after the shocking news of the night before, he had rested in his hotel for a few hours. He then went out for an afternoon meal and was out of contact for several hours. Aylward spent most of the afternoon calling the hotel and leaving messages. It was late that evening when Haughey eventually spoke to his attorney general. Paddy spoke with his brother Tony each day, and he rang him on that Saturday evening to update him on his progress. Aylward had called Tony earlier to convey a message to Paddy that the taoiseach wanted to talk to him urgently. Paddy Connolly rang Haughey as soon as his call with his brother had ended.

Haughey tried to persuade Connolly to return to Dublin, but he refused. It is not known if the call was courteous or curt. Connolly's diary entry for that day merely states that when Haughey made the request he "demurred". The attorney general insisted he would continue his holiday and fly to New York the following morning. As a concession, he agreed that he and Haughey would speak further after he arrived.

For the second time, both men made serious errors of judgement. Connolly displayed political naivety in not appreciating that the scandal had enveloped public discourse in Ireland. And then there was the issue of perceived insensitivity to the grief of the victims' families.

For Haughey's part, his decision not to order Connolly home – perhaps motivated by personal sympathy, but by any standards rash – would quickly rebound on him.

At 10.30am on Sunday, 15 August, Connolly departed Heathrow Airport on the British Airways Concorde flight to New York. His usual thrill from flying this way was in short supply. In a diary entry, he said the service he received on the flight was "superb", but he "didn't enjoy it one bit, completely distracted".

Meanwhile back home, the Sunday newspapers all led with the story. Despite having established that Macarthur had been arrested in the attorney general's flat, there was a reticence at the highest editorial levels of *The Sunday Press* and the *Sunday Independent* about reporting that fact. Both papers confined their reports to coverage of the brief court appearance in Dún Laoghaire the previous day. When it came to the kernel of the crisis, the newspapers tip-toed around the very large elephant in the room – that the attorney general was caught up in the scandal. "Man on Double Murder Charge", read the headline in the *Sunday Independent*. RTÉ's coverage was even more insipid, hardly referring to the attorney general in its reports over the weekend, and never in the same sentence as Macarthur.

For the *Sunday Tribune*, however, there was no such trepidation. It was a new publication and had a reputation for being less deferential than its more established rivals. Its headline baldly stated: "Double Murder Suspect Held in A-G's Flat". In later editions of the paper that day, it changed its headline to the more dramatic line concerning Connolly's departure: "A-G Flies Out as Murder Suspect Charged".

The floodgates were unleashed. It was open season.

When Connolly arrived in New York on Sunday, he was unaware of the storm Macarthur's arrest had created at home, and of the trap that lay ahead for him.

As Dunlop wryly noted in his memoir, on Connolly's arrival into the JFK Airport arrivals terminal in New York, he was "subjected to a media frenzy that made the Irish reporters look like correspondents for the 'Irish Messenger of the Sacred Heart'."

He was jostled and harried as he tried to make his way to the exit, with reporters firing questions at him indiscriminately. The aggressive tactics were matched by the hyperbole of the headlines. "Irish Biggie Flees Here After Slay Scandal" was the screamer from the *New York Post*. Its rival, the New York *Daily News*, was slightly less declamatory: "Irish Lawman in Shocker", it declared.

"Connolly was confronted by the bear pit of American media," Dunlop told me. "There were questions thrown at him, which, in retrospect, were raw and insulting and difficult for him to handle. That was a foretaste for him of what actually was at the nub of this."

The American reporters had little trepidation in subjecting Connolly to a battery of questions about his exact relationship with Malcolm Macarthur, dropping heavy innuendoes that it may have been sexual. This was the most salacious of the conspiracy theories that instantly cropped up following Connolly's departure. It would become the most enduring – and unquenchable – of all the myths that surrounded the scandal.

In Britain, the tabloid newspapers were hinting heavily at this with a nod-and-a-wink use of adjectives to imply the attorney general's perceived sexuality. The *Daily Star* described Connolly as "vivacious and debonair". *The Sun*, on its front page, described him as "ballet-loving", while the *Daily Express* also chose to describe him as "debonair". All were codes of the era for gay.

*

As tensions mounted around events that Sunday, 15 August, Haughey became resolute: Connolly must come home from the US immediately. The diplomat from the Irish embassy in New York who had met the attorney general at JFK Airport was now instructed to get Connolly to the nearest phone. When Connolly spoke with Haughey this time, there was no ambiguity to the taoiseach's instruction that he return to Ireland forthwith.

Connolly knew by this stage that there was little choice in the matter. His bruising encounter with the American reporters had brought home the seriousness of the situation facing him. He had been treated on his arrival in the United States as if he were a fugitive from justice. Exhausted and shattered by the unreal events of the preceding 48 hours, he readily agreed to return.

Arrangements were made for his flight back. Despite its outrageous expense, officials determined the quickest way to return home would be by Concorde. The following morning, Monday, 16 August, Patrick Connolly was driven to JFK Airport to board a Concorde and take his second transatlantic flight in two days. In London, a state plane would be waiting to take him to Dublin and on to Abbeville, to face an uncertain fate.

# 30

## AN ATTORNEY
## GENERAL RESIGNED

"I'm innocent. I'm an innocent man. The circumstances are extraordinary, I admit." Paddy Connolly, attorney general

For the harangued Government Information Service (GIS), events were complicated further by its own shortcomings. While doing its best in dire circumstances, it was relaying contradictory information that only compounded the general confusion and fuelled already mounting speculation. Reporters were told that Haughey was first contacted in Inishvickillane on Saturday. When the Friday night call from Paddy Connolly became clear, it made GIS look inept. In addition, the GIS told callers that Haughey would not return to Dublin until Monday when, in fact, he arrived back in the capital on Sunday evening, the better to be ready for the return of the attorney general, who would promptly be summoned for a visit to the stately home of his boss.

Meanwhile, a downcast Paddy Connolly made his return flight across the Atlantic. Over the course of it, he requested a pen and paper. He wrote out a statement setting out his relationship with Macarthur and defending his decision to leave the country on holidays.

The text was barristerial in tone but gave a full explanation.

*I feel that I should now issue a statement to the public to explain the facts in order to allay any public disquiet which may have arisen.*

*I have known the accused for some years. I have been acquainted with his fiancée and members of her family for many years. So far as I am aware from conversations, the accused holds a postgraduate degree in Science from Cambridge University and a degree in Economics from the University of South California.*

*Since last May he has been resident in Tenerife with his fiancée and their child. I understand that it had been his intention to reside there for a few months.*

*On the evening of the 4th of August, he arrived at my flat. He intimated to me that he had been in London and Belgium dealing with financial matters and that he would be some few days in Ireland dealing with his financial affairs. I told him he could stay in my flat if he wished and he accepted.*

*At no time did I have any knowledge whatsoever of the fact that the gardaí were trying to find him in relation to the offences with which he now stands charged.*

*At no time did I entertain any such suspicion. The events which have taken place have taken me wholly by surprise and came as a very great personal shock to me. The holiday on which I embarked on Saturday had been arranged by me for almost two months. Having told the gardaí of my arrangement, I was informed it was in order for me to depart. I had already furnished them with all the information I had concerning Mr Macarthur's presence in my home.*

*I proceeded to London en route to New York on Saturday, August 14th. The Taoiseach contacted me in London and suggested I should return. I informed him I would prefer to discuss the matter from New York and that any arrangements could be made from there. When I arrived in New York the Taoiseach again contacted me and asked me to return to Dublin to discuss the situation that had arisen.*

An Air Corps plane had flown from its base in Baldonnel, County Dublin, to Heathrow on the Monday afternoon of his return. It was now parked on an apron close to where the Concorde would taxi in. The inward jet from New York arrived at 8.30pm.

Half a dozen TV crews and a large number of reporters were at Heathrow terminal to record the jet arriving. They saw Connolly being ushered across the tarmac to the waiting Air Corps Beechcraft aeroplane.

The attorney general arrived back at the defence forces airbase at Baldonnel just before 10pm on Monday evening. His state car was waiting for him. The driver, a garda, had been instructed to bring him straight to Charlie Haughey's Kinsealy home of Abbeville. Haughey, back in Dublin since the previous night, also summoned Frank Dunlop to his home.

Connolly's brother Tony desperately tried to contact him before he reached Haughey's home. He was concerned about Paddy's political naivety and wanted him to be well prepared for his encounter with the taoiseach. He asked gardaí to make contact with the driver via his car radio, but his request was turned down. From his long experience of management in the semi-state sector, Tony knew that there could only be one outcome to the meeting and his instincts told him – correctly – that Paddy was unaware of this.

Dunlop was the first to arrive at Abbeville. As he approached the gate in his Fiat Mirafiori, he saw there was a substantial media presence clustered. "The place was absolutely crawling, mostly photographers. And I just waved at them and went in because I had nothing to say, I had nothing to add," he said.

Dunlop parked his car at the side of the palatial home and entered. Haughey was in the house alone, pacing up and down the darkened hallway. "He did not seem to me to be overly concerned about his meeting with Paddy Connolly," Dunlop recalled. "He was alone in the house and giving out yards that he hadn't had anything to eat that day."

The meeting took place in the office, which was to the left of the hallway. Haughey told Dunlop: "I want you nearby. You can't be in the room but I want you nearby." It was clear to Dunlop that the attorney general was not to be aware of his presence.

Dunlop agreed, although he was unsure if Haughey expected any difficulty during his meeting with Connolly. The door of the room was left ajar so that Dunlop could hear the gist of the conversation. He stayed unseen in a back room when Connolly arrived.

As soon as the attorney general stepped into the hallway, he handed Haughey the statement he had written during his flight home on the Concorde. Haughey glanced at it and left it aside. The scene was already set for what was plainly a whiskey-and-revolver scenario. Dunlop listened from outside to the early exchanges. Then, without much preliminaries, Haughey got to the point and told Connolly he would have to step down. "There is only one other option and that is you will be fired. So the most gentlemanly way of dealing with the matter is to resign."

Dunlop, standing outside the door, could hear Connolly protest: 'I'm innocent. I'm an innocent man. The circumstances are extraordinary, I admit. But I mean, I didn't murder anyone. I wasn't knowingly harbouring a criminal, or somebody suspected to have caused a criminal act."

Dunlop knew the writing was on the wall. "This was where the tectonic plates had to move. This was the interface between politics and the law, and between politics and the extraordinary circumstances of this case. Politics in these circumstances always wins."

Connolly soon ceded. From the shadows, Dunlop watched the doomed attorney general as he left the room, walked slowly down the hall and out the front door. "He was a beaten man. He looked as if somebody had hit him with a sledge hammer. He was just completely dejected."

Haughey gave Dunlop Connolly's statement and Dunlop retreated to the office at the back of the house, where Haughey's secretary worked. On a typewriter, he transcribed the notes and then appended a few of his own paragraphs to the end. What had been a statement of explanation had now become a resignation letter.

The last three paragraphs now read:

*Although my involvement in this case is entirely innocent, I have to have responsible regard to the unique situation and duties attaching under the Constitution and law to the office of the Attorney General.*

*I must also have regard to the embarrassment which, however unwittingly, must inevitably be caused to the Government by these events.*

*Accordingly, I have come to the conclusion with much regret that it is my public duty to tender my resignation from the office. I have therefore tendered my resignation to the Taoiseach which he has this day accepted.*

As the red lights of Connolly's state car receded down the avenue, Haughey's attention turned to more prosaic matters. He was trapped in the estate, the entrance of which was effectively blocked by a swarm of reporters, photographers and TV cameras. And he was now very hungry. He waited in the grand hallway for his press secretary to finish typing up the statement and to make carbon copies.

When Dunlop had finished typing the statement, and making carbon copies, he asked one of the gardaí on duty near the house to distribute it to the reporters at the front gate, a quarter of a mile away down the tree-flanked avenue.

Haughey told Dunlop to get his own car. He needed a lift to the home of his nearby friend, Pat O'Connor. Dunlop's

Mirafiori had seen better days and was filled with the detritus that comes with having a young family. It was a step-down for Haughey from the Mercedes and Daimlers he favoured. Haughey sat into the passenger seat and crouched so the photographers would not spot them as they approached the exit. Dunlop put the boot down as soon as he reached the gate and drove off towards Malahide at speed. Some photographers spotted Haughey in the passenger seat, jumped in their cars and gave chase.

Outside Pat O'Connor's house, still well ahead of the posse, Dunlop stopped the car. Haughey jumped out with an agility that surprised his press secretary. Dunlop quickly drove on. Haughey hid behind a tree until the chasing cars had passed. He then sauntered up the driveway of his friend's house.

Dunlop continued driving into Malahide and parked up outside Gibney's pub in the town centre. The photographers caught up with him as he entered it. When they asked where Haughey was, Dunlop flashed a "don't know" smile with pressed lips and spread his hands. "They knew I had deposited him somewhere but could not work out where."

Meanwhile, a melancholy Paddy Connolly was returning to the other side of the city, utterly shattered. He arrived back in Pilot View late on Monday night. In the 72 hours since Macarthur's arrest in his home, Connolly had flown to London and New York and back again. His holiday had been aborted. He had just resigned as attorney general. He was exhausted, still reeling from the revelation that his houseguest, and friend of eight years, was a suspected double murderer.

As he arrived at the steps of his apartment, he was

confronted by a small huddle of reporters who immediately started barraging him with questions.

"Would you ever fuck off," he roared at them, before going in through the door. His unexpected dropping of an f-bomb silenced the baying mob.

"He derived a fair degree of pleasure out of that moment," his nephew Stephen recalls. Indeed, it was the only sliver of pleasure that Paddy had during the most traumatic three days of his life.

# 31

# THE MEDIA AND
# THE TAOISEACH

"I think perhaps the only relationship one could have had with Charles Haughey as a journalist was either to be regarded by him as a critic and an opponent, or else to be a total lap dog." Olivia O'Leary, journalist and broadcaster

There is a grainy black and white news clip from the late 1960s showing a press conference with Charles Haughey. A reporter asks how he acquired his wealth. It is a brave question. Haughey takes great exception to the impertinence of the questioner, saying it's an intrusion on his private life. There is a cringy silence. Haughey, with his hooded eagle brow, stares at the reporters. Now and again, his pupils dart quickly from side to side in a furtive manner before zeroing in on an unseen prey, out of camera shot.

"What are you smirking at?" he barks at an offending

reporter in an intimidatory fashion. The reporter makes no reply. There is no question as to who is in control here: the state has the whip hand over the so-called fourth estate.

This was before the 1970s, when the media was largely deferential to politicians and the ruling class and reported on what was said as writ. The concept of speaking truth to power, or holding powerful institutions or political leaders to account, was not rooted in Irish journalism. Newspapers still divided into whichever Irish Civil War camp they came from.

In 1973, that relationship was to change, on the back of the Watergate affair that forced the resignation of President Richard Nixon. Although the true inspiration for emerging journalists in the mid-1970s might not so much have been the real-life cover-up that brought Nixon down, as its derivative: the classic movie based on those events, *All the President's Men*.

The extraordinary portrayal of the two *Washington Post* investigative reporters, Carl Bernstein and Bob Woodward, by Dustin Hoffman and Robert Redford, fired a new generation of young journalists with idealistic fervour. Journalism had found a new purpose and that was to hold powerful people, and institutions, to account.

This new wave openly challenged the status quo. In Ireland, *Magill* magazine, founded and edited by another driven journalist, Vincent Browne, conducted in-depth investigations and long reads, written in prose that pulsed with energy. It pioneered forms of writing and investigation unknown in Ireland until then.

News journalism was almost exclusively male until that time. In the vanguard of exceptional journalists that emerged in Ireland during the 1970s, there was now a trailblazing group of women, including Nell McCafferty, Olivia O'Leary and Geraldine Kennedy.

Peter Murtagh reflects on the era and how it is judged today. "People look back now with the benefit of hindsight and ask where the journalists were, they weren't asking questions. That's not true. Journalists were asking questions.

"Everybody wondered, how come this man [Haughey], born in the poor circumstances we know, was now living in a Gandon-designed mansion in North County Dublin and living high on the hog? Where was the money coming from? Whenever you asked those questions, you were firmly slapped down by Haughey and those around him, who said that it was none of your business, you had no right to be asking these sorts of questions . . .

"The notion of transparency has become an absolute cornerstone of politics, and a politician must account for his or her income and wealth . . . That notion was not widely accepted 40 years ago, and it certainly wasn't accepted by Charles Haughey, for reasons we now know."

Murtagh was of course referring to the point-blank refusal of Haughey to talk about the source of his wealth, which many years later was found to have been obtained by corrupt means.

Haughey's resentment to such questions, however legitimate, formed part of his sour relationship with journalists. It also derived from the events of the 1970 Arms Trial, where he was accused of being part of an illicit ministerial plot to import arms for the IRA. Despite being acquitted in the 1970 trial, Haughey was nonetheless fired from government, and spent most of the next decade in the political wilderness. Added to this, Haughey's constant plotting against Jack Lynch's leadership had created enemies in the media, as had his dismissive, almost sneering, disregard for the journalists who were known to favour Lynch.

If some parts of the media were suspicious of Haughey, his mercurial nature meant that they were always fascinated by him: simply put, Charlie Haughey made headlines.

As the Gargan and Dunne murder hunts of the summer of 1982 came to their astonishing denouement, the media bayed for answers to the relationship between a double killer and the most senior political figures in the land. It would strain the fractious relationship between taoiseach and media to breaking point.

Normally in the face of controversial events in politics, the resignation of a senior cabinet figure such as Paddy Connolly would lance the ensuing boil. Having offered a sacrificial head on a plate, the government would brush itself off and move to regain control of the agenda.

Not so here. The day after Connolly's resignation, the wound created by the Macarthur scandal was showing no signs of healing. On the contrary, as the morning of Tuesday, 17 August wore on, the media frenzy continued to grow. Government press secretary Frank Dunlop was back in Government Buildings trying his best to deal with the monsoon of calls raining down on him.

"It was unbelievable," he said. "You put the phone down, it rang immediately. You lifted the phone, talked, hung it up, it rang, and you lifted the phone again. You could almost not take a breath."

He recalled the questions being put to him: "One theory was worse than the other. And I kept saying to them, 'Look, it's a garda matter. We cannot discuss this issue. I can discuss the political aspect of it in the context of Charlie Haughey ordering the attorney general back to Dublin, but that's all.'"

Over 50 international reporters and dozens of TV crews had by now converged on Dublin. That events in Ireland were now featuring on the front pages of the British press underlined the far-reaching scale of the scandal. Haughey had few sympathisers in the British media. The memory of his contrarian stance on the Falklands War was still fresh, and added greatly to the schadenfreude on display in reports of the Macarthur crisis.

The London *Times* focused on the close friendship between Haughey and Connolly. "The scandal is a further embarrassment to Mr Haughey because the Attorney General is not only the highest-ranking law officer in the Republic, but is also one of his closest personal friends," its leader stated.

In the wider political sphere, already a full-blooded political hue and cry had started. The Fine Gael leader, Garret FitzGerald, was cutting short his month-long holiday in France and would return the following day to chair a front-bench meeting of the main opposition party. Fine Gael had already issued a statement demanding a full explanation from the government. It read:

*The fact that a man charged with two murders was arrested in, and gave his address as, the home of the Attorney General has led to unprecedented public disquiet. The puzzling sequence of events involving the Attorney General requires urgent clarification by the Government. Has the matter been considered by the Government as a whole? Can it explain the appropriateness of the Attorney General leaving the country when he did?*

The Labour leader Michael O'Leary called on Haughey to recall the Dáil from its summer recess. He wanted an emergency sitting and a full explanation from Haughey of all the events surrounding Macarthur's arrest and Connolly's decision to take flight.

"At this stage," O'Leary said in a statement, "it is the only course which will allay the public disquiet which has arisen over the entire affair."

In 1982, the public's right to know was not a concept that had fully percolated to the top levels of government. Reporters seeking information on the extraordinary events of the weekend were becoming increasingly frustrated by the dearth of information being shared by the Government Information Service. To compound matters, the little that trickled out was confusing and contradictory.

Something had to give. Dunlop decided the only way the matter could be dealt with properly was by holding a full, no-holds-barred press conference later that same Tuesday, 17 August, where Haughey could take on all comers. Dunlop wasn't without trepidation, however. "Charlie hated press conferences, couldn't abide them," he confessed. "Haughey felt that they were gang-ups against him."

So it was to his surprise when the taoiseach readily agreed. By this stage, Haughey was acutely aware of the gravity of the situation, the stories doing the rounds, and the potential damage it could all cause to his unsteady government.

Temperatures rose as arrangements were hastily put in place for a press conference in the largest available space to accommodate the unprecedented media interest: the Fianna Fáil party room on the fifth floor of Leinster House.

# 32

# THE BIRTH OF GUBU

"Under Haughey, stunts have followed on happenings, and happenings on stunts. The stunts have misfired and the happenings have been mishandled." Conor Cruise O'Brien in *The Irish Times*

In addition to a large contingent of Irish media, over 40 foreign journalists crammed into the Fianna Fáil room for the press conference that afternoon. They stood on chairs and tables behind a bank of cameras. Despite the large sash windows being raised to their fullest, the room was stiflingly warm and uncomfortable.

Haughey arrived, true to form, in an impeccably sharp suit, and walked to the top table in his distinctive slow, courtly style. He was accompanied by Minister for Labour, Gene Fitzgerald, and two senior government officials. Dunlop stood at the corner of the table looking out at the phalanx of reporters facing them. Reading the room, he could sense the hostility. He knew that this was going to be one of the most difficult 20 minutes in Haughey's career.

The opening minutes were a limp affair with local journalists politely asking pro forma questions about a pay deal that had been struck with trade unions that day. After about ten minutes, a British reporter finally lost patience and directly broached the subject.

"Do you understand the widespread concern that has been expressed about what's happened in the last few days in relation to the attorney general?" he boomed.

Haughey sounded prepared for the question. "Yes, I understand that this is an *unprecedented* situation," he intoned. "And one that came as a shock to many people, including myself. It's a tragic situation. Apart from anything else, it has deprived us of the services of a very competent and excellent attorney general. It is an almost *unbelievable* mischance."

Newspapers had reported for the first time on Monday, the day before the press conference, that the attorney general had phoned Haughey in Inishvickillane the previous Friday night. But Haughey was careful not to dwell on that fateful Friday-night phone call with Connolly, where he failed to appreciate the enormous ramifications of what he was being told. Instead, Haughey explained that once he became fully aware of the facts on the Saturday, he suggested to Connolly he should return from London, but by Sunday he directly requested his attorney general, who was by then in New York, to come home. What he learned on Saturday, Haughey said, was that a sawn-off shotgun was found in the attorney general's flat. That prompted him to recall Connolly.

Some of the journalists asked multi-clause questions that allowed Haughey to pick and choose how he might respond. Peter Murtagh for *The Irish Times*, positioned near the front of the media scrum, now dived in and asked a series of rapid-fire questions in succession.

Murtagh pressed Haughey on why he did not make the direct request for Connolly to return on Saturday. Haughey responded that it seemed to him on Saturday that Connolly was thinking of resigning but needed time to think it over and, by travelling on to New York, he would have the space and time. Murtagh reminded him that the conversation they had on Sunday was the third they'd had in three days.

"When were you aware that a gun had been found in the flat?" asked Murtagh.

"Sometime on Saturday," replied Haughey.

"Before he [Connolly] left the country?"

"No, no, no."

"What do you make of Mr Connolly's judgment in leaving the country?"

"Mr Connolly has given his own statement on that. And I wouldn't like to comment any further as Mr Connolly has now resigned."

"Having been appointed by you."

"Yes, and at the time I was quite satisfied that he was an entirely eminent lawyer suitable for the appointment."

"Do you think he made a miscalculation by leaving the country?"

"Well, that's not for me to say at this stage. Mr Connolly has resigned and you can draw your own conclusions from that."

Other reporters asked him if he should have ordered Mr Connolly to remain after being contacted on Friday night.

"I think it's very easy now to have hindsight about this," Haughey said. "But this was, as I say, a *grotesque* situation, one that none of us have ever experienced before. I don't think anyone in this room has ever had such an experience and it's such an unprecedented situation."

Haughey repeated that the most salient new fact he had not been appraised of on Friday, but learned of on Saturday, was that a gun had been found in the flat. Murtagh and others then pressed him on whether Connolly should have informed him about that on Friday night. He replied he did not want the conference to turn into an inquisition on the role of the attorney general. He suggested that even on Saturday everybody was still thrown, and dazed, by what had happened.

"Even at that stage, it was hard to credit that such *bizarre* happenings had taken place," he explained.

Invited to congratulate the gardaí by a reporter, Haughey said: "I think it was a very good piece of police work, slow, painstaking, putting the whole thing together and eventually finding the right man."

There was a long silence. In the recording of the full press conference preserved in the RTÉ archive, a journalist can be heard exclaiming incredulously in the background, "Finding the right man?"

Dunlop picked up on the import of the throwaway comment immediately. It had the potential to prejudice a criminal trial by dint of the fact that the taoiseach of the day could be seen to have prejudged its outcome. "I knew instinctively that that was wrong. And I can visualise the look on Peter Murtagh's face. He looked at me and sort of questioned me."

Dunlop could not intervene. "There was one rule when you were dealing with Charlie and press conferences," he observed. "You didn't interrupt him."

The persistent Murtagh kept returning to the issue of the gun found in the apartment. He peppered Haughey with questions, asking him who had told him about the shotgun. The taoiseach told Murtagh he would not respond to any further questions from him: "You have asked me about 20 questions and I have answered them all as fully as I can," he said tetchily.

Towards the end of the conference, Haughey was asked if he would resign, and he said no. When asked by a journalist to respond to Labour leader Michael O'Leary's demand for the Dáil to be recalled during the summer recess, he aimed a pot-shot at him.

"I think Mr O'Leary is just huffing and puffing a bit. Mr O'Leary is one of these people who is the first one to call for the Dáil to be adjourned and no sooner is it adjourned he finds a variety of reasons for having it recalled."

As the conference drew to an end, it looked like nobody would broach the wild and salacious rumours that were circulating around Dublin, until an English reporter piped up. "Are you satisfied that there was nothing improper in the relationship between Mr Connolly and Mr Macarthur?"

Haughey appeared taken aback. "I wouldn't comment on that at all," he replied guardedly. "I wouldn't. I wouldn't."

After a pause, he responded more emphatically. "I wouldn't accept that question. I can't accept that question. I can't accept that," he repeated for emphasis.

And thus a twenty-minute press conference of intense exchanges drew to a close. Many of the reporters' shirts were soaked through with perspiration. As Haughey left the room with his small entourage, he seemed satisfied with his performance. One look at Dunlop, however, and he knew this was not the case. His press secretary broke it to him that he had said the gardaí had found the "right man".

"Oh God, I didn't, did I?" he groaned.

Dunlop spent most of the rest of the day briefing journalists that Haughey had made the comment inadvertently, that it was a slip of the tongue. It did not prevent newspapers the following day from suggesting the remark could be in contempt. In the conspiratorial fervour that was now surrounding the case, some even believed Haughey had made the comment deliberately, essentially to nobble the case against Macarthur.

"Gun Caused A-G's Recall" ran the front-page headline in *The Irish Press* the following day, with the strapline, "Taoiseach Not Told Until Saturday of Find in Flat". Elsewhere was a headline which picked up on a phrase that Haughey had used a few times in the conference: "Grotesque Mischance".

It was later in the week when journalist Conor Cruise O'Brien – a former Labour Party minister whose visceral hatred for Haughey was well established – seized on the leader's phraseology in an *Irish Times* column, producing an acronym that came to define an era. Using four adjectives Haughey had used at the press conference – grotesque, unbelievable, bizarre and unprecedented, or GUBU for short – O'Brien eviscerated his former political opponent.

"Those, remember, are the adjectives that sprang to his own

lips, at that press conference of his last Tuesday, to characterise 'the situation which had arisen' in and around the flat of the Attorney General," wrote O'Brien.

The column amounted to a vicious attack on the leader. For O'Brien, even given the extreme nature of events, there was only one true villain of the piece, and that was Charles Haughey.

"You see, the worse the situation that had arisen was the better Mr Haughey looked, in his own estimation. If the situation was GUBU then the greater the credit due to Mr Haughey, for dealing with it. The more heads the Hydra had, and the more fangs they bore, the more highly we think of Hercules."

No shortage of venom was pumped under O'Brien's enemy's skin. He accused Haughey of bringing the state to financial ruin, damaging relations irreparably with Britain, and bringing industrial relations to their lowest point in the history of the state. The government had to be collapsed, he concluded, because it was "clearly unsafe at any speed".

With astonishing alacrity, the GUBU acronym stuck. It was picked up on the airwaves and by other newspapers. Within days its use was widespread to describe the incredulous events of that August weekend. The fact that it had been coined by his arch-enemy Conor Cruise O'Brien stuck in Haughey's craw, as those close to him knew he could not abide even a mention of his name.

GUBU quickly became part of the political lexicon, as a shorthand for Haughey's style of leadership. As Peter Murtagh observed: "It was a GUBU situation and Haughey was right in the middle of it. No politician likes exploding landmines.

They like to feel that they're in control and that they're on top of things. And clearly, Haughey was not in control of the situation. He was doing, in fairness to him, the best he could under the circumstances. But there were so many questions arising from this."

The press conference that had been designed to contain the wildfires had instead fanned the flames. In the weeks and months that followed, fanciful rumours continued to do the rounds, of a state cover-up, an elite plot, a nefarious homosexual circle at the heart of power being protected by the establishment.

And now there was a newly minted word for this elaborate and fantastical political conspiracy, with Charles Haughey at its centre. Move over Watergate, GUBU had entered the scene.

# 33

## GAY CONSPIRACY

"Given Macarthur's demeanour and appearance and his dicky bow, you might as well hang a sign around your neck in Dublin at the time." Brenda Power, journalist and barrister

In 1968, the American actor Rock Hudson came to Ireland for several months. He was starring in a First World War film, *Darling Lili*, which co-starred Julie Andrews.

Every night Hudson, whose sexuality was a badly kept secret in Hollywood, socialised in Bartley Dunne's pub on Stephen's Street. The historian, writer and former unionist politician Jeff Dudgeon was a student in Trinity College Dublin at the time. He remembered there was a kerfuffle in the bar every time Hudson arrived in. Hudson invariably headed to the gay section at the front.

"Bartley Dunne's was divided into two parts. The back

was straight. The front with the little snugs and cubicles was entirely gay," recalled Dudgeon. "The whole thing was decked out like a French brothel with candles and red velvet. It was about as exotic as you could get in the 1960s.

"At the end of the night, Bartley always spoke in French over the PA system. He would say, '*Messieurs et Mesdames, on y va*, it is time to leave.' Some exoticism was always maintained."

Although the pub was a known meeting place for gay men from the late 1950s, gay nightlife in Ireland did not even officially exist in the 1980s even though it was happening in reality. Indeed, it would be two and a half decades on from Hudson's visits to Bartley Dunne's before homosexuality was finally decriminalised, in 1993.

"It was the grand old dame of gay bars in Dublin," said documentary maker Bill Hughes. "It was very funny because the two owners were behind the bar every night and denied that it was a gay bar. They were serving drink to an almost exclusively male clientele. They prided themselves on having every possible spirit behind the bar, and they mixed the most exotic cocktails for people. How they could deny that it was a gay bar was always kind of a joke to me. But that was their way of running their business."

The straight part of the premises at the back had a mix of arty types and buttoned-up professionals, savouring its bohemian atmosphere. A number of criminals drank there including John Traynor, who operated as a fence – a receiver of stolen goods – for criminal gangs.

The presence of criminals also meant the presence of cops. Detectives from the Central Detective Unit were regularly assigned to spend afternoons in Bartley Dunne's back bar, watching the criminals and their associates.

Brian Sherry was one such detective. He remembers that in the late afternoon, the 'kite men' would arrive in with their booty. These were con artists who typically arrived into a shop a few minutes before closing and offered to buy an expensive item such as a camera or a watch with a cheque. By this stage of the evening the banks were closed, so the retailer ran the risk of being conned or losing a big sale. The purchasers were confidence tricksters, well-dressed and plausible in manner, but involved in cheque-kiting. The cheques would bounce and the kite men would repair to pubs like Bartley Dunne's to sell on their items.

Within a day of Malcolm Macarthur's arrest, media became aware that the accused and Paddy Connolly, along with Brenda Little, had socialised frequently in Bartley Dunne's and another gay-friendly Dublin pub, The Bailey, in the mid-1970s.

Connolly's nephew Stephen recalled how at the time of Macarthur's arrest, he and his father Tony quickly understood the inferences likely to come out after the connection of both men to Bartley Dunne's pub in the 1970s was made public: that their present-day connection was a secret, romantic one.

"My father and I would have copped on before there were any rumours," Stephen said. "You had the chief legal officer and this eccentric companion sharing a house. There was no basis to it [that the two were having an affair], but the public were not going to see that. What they saw was a dandy figure, Bartley Dunne's, and all that type of stuff. It was obvious that the rumours were going to happen."

Neither man was gay, but rumours did indeed spread.

Connolly was a well-to-do single man in his 50s. Macarthur dressed and comported himself in a way that suggested he was comfortable being different. Brenda Power, a reporter with *The Irish Press*, remembered how the connections between an "elderly lawyer type" and Macarthur were made.

"Many people were surprised to discover that Malcolm Macarthur had a female partner and a child," she said. "Given Macarthur's demeanour and appearance and his dicky bow, you might as well hang a sign around your neck in Dublin at the time."

Rumours may have been swirling around but the Irish media showed a reticence to repeat them. There was less reluctance on the part of the British media. Every time Paddy Connolly was mentioned it was accompanied by a typical euphemism of the era to denote homosexuality, such as "confirmed bachelor" and "debonair".

It so happened that gardaí had seriously canvassed the possibility of a homosexual dimension to the murders for a short period. This happened after they spoke to Harry Bieling in the aftermath of Macarthur's attempted robbery at his home, and after they established a possible connection between the suspect and Paddy Connolly, a single man living alone.

Macarthur had gained entry to Bieling's home, Camelot, after saying that he'd been to parties there years ago. Bieling was an openly gay man and the assumption was made by gardaí that most of those who attended his parties were also gay. During his long interview on the eve of Macarthur's arrest, gardaí had pursued this line of enquiry, asking him about Pilot View and whether he knew the attorney general.

Bridie Gargan and Dónal Dunne were mentioned. Had he encountered them? Had they been to his parties?

Part of the basis for this line of enquiry was another murder, yet unsolved, which had occurred in Dublin earlier in 1982. In the early hours of 21 January, a 32-year-old Scotsman, Charles Self, had been mercilessly attacked in his own home. Self, a gay man, had lived in Ireland for a decade and worked as a set designer for RTÉ. He was an outgoing man with a colourful dress sense, who frequently socialised in bars like Bartley Dunne's and The Bailey. He lived in a mews house in Monkstown, a well-to-do Dublin suburb not far from Dalkey.

On Wednesday, 20 January 1982, Self had been socialising in city-centre gay bars for most of the evening. Sometime after midnight he was spotted near the public toilets at Burgh Quay, which was then a cruising spot for gay men. Soon after, he called into a late-night fast-food outlet nearby. He was a regular there and staff recognised him.

In that short period, he met a man on the street who agreed to accompany him home. A taxi driver who brought the two men back to Monkstown gave a very accurate description of the passenger. He was in his mid-20s, wearing a dark suit, with fair, collar-length hair. He was quite drunk and urinated against a wall as soon as he got out of the taxi.

On the night Self arrived back with the mystery man, there was a guest staying in the spare room, a designer colleague from RTÉ, 67-year-old Bertie Tyrer. Originally from England, Tyrer lived in Wicklow but occasionally stayed over if the weather was bad, or if there was a social event in Dublin.

Tyrer told gardaí he went to sleep sometime after midnight

but was awoken at around 2am by loud conversation downstairs. He presumed Self had company. A short time later he was again disturbed when somebody opened his bedroom door. He looked up and caught a glimpse of a young man whom he thought had dark hair.

"Sorry, wrong room," the man said in what Tyrer remembers as a clipped, mannerly accent, possibly English. He went back to sleep.

The following morning Tyrer woke to mayhem and chaos. He found Self's lifeless body slumped at the foot of the stairs surrounded by pools of blood. He had been stabbed repeatedly in a ferocious attack. The knife had entered his chest with such violent force that there were exit wounds on his back. The attacker had also tried to strangle him with a cord taken from a dressing gown. In the sitting room a record was still playing on the stereo deck.

Items were strewn everywhere and the murder weapon, a kitchen knife, had been abandoned there. There were clear shoe prints left in the congealing blood. It seemed that the killer had escaped through a window in the kitchen.

Tyrer tried to ring the police from the house phone, but the line was dead because Self had not paid the bill. He ran to a nearby house, where he phoned the gardaí. Although there were some raised eyebrows among investigating gardaí as to how Tyrer could have slept through it all, he was never considered a suspect.

The murder triggered a long – and ultimately fruitless – investigation. Now, several months on and with the Self murderer still at large, for a short while gardaí countenanced the possibility that Macarthur could be the missing link, and that somehow the brutal killing of the two young people that summer could also be connected.

Macarthur was still in Dublin at the time of Charles Self's murder in January 1982, but he had long exited Dublin's alternative scene by then. Nor did he resemble the detailed description given by the taxi driver of the man who accompanied Self in his cab. Gardaí weren't long dismissing the theory.

On 18 August, the question of a connection between Macarthur and the Self murder was directly broached with DSI Hubert Reynolds, who was leading the Self investigation. *The Irish Press* reported:

> He dismissed speculation that there was a connection between the two murders and that of RTE designer Charles Self.
>
> "We are still investigating the Self murder, but our investigation has not been intensified following the break in the other cases," he said.
>
> He added there were a lot of rumours circulating following the arrest of Malcolm Macarthur but he could not comment as these matters were sub judice.
>
> Asked about reports that Macarthur was questioned about the death of Self, he said no.

In the same *Irish Press* report, Supt Reynolds responded to a question by saying categorically that Dónal Dunne was *not* one of the hundreds of men interviewed during the Charles Self investigation. By now, both the murdered farmer and Bridie Gargan were getting dragged into the wild conspiracies.

Elsewhere, speculation on an affair between the suspect and the attorney general continued full tilt. On 16 August, editor Vincent Browne wrote about it in the current affairs magazine *Magill*: "The spate of rumours which this affair has given rise to has been truly fantastic. No matter if there isn't a titter of evidence to support a single one of them, they are still given a currency, and inexplicably a credence, which swiftly established them as 'well known facts'."

Of all the myths that grew up around the case, the one that stuck most was that the system was somehow protecting a shadowy homosexual ring which involved leading members of the establishment. All the extraordinary happenings surrounding Malcolm Macarthur, Paddy Connolly and Charles Haughey were part of an elaborate cover-up, so the conspiracies went.

How much Malcolm Macarthur was aware of such speculation is not known. Locked away in his prison cell, he was in the eye of a bigger storm, the ravages of which spelled an end to the lifestyle he'd shown he'd go to any lengths to protect. But if his life was unravelling in those early days of incarceration, his next act would show that both his detachment from reality and his heightened sense of self-regard were as intact as ever.

# 34

## DEAR MR HAUGHEY

"My good friend, Mr Patrick Connolly, Attorney, had no
knowledge whatsoever of any wrongdoings of mine."
Malcolm Macarthur

The basement of B Wing in Mountjoy Prison was known as
the Base. This area, darker than the rest of the prison, was
reached by a steep spiral staircase. The cell windows were
near the ceiling and afforded no real view other than passing
feet in the yard.

This was the place prisoners who needed to be protected
from other prisoners were put. Malcolm Macarthur was one
such case – his safety was considered to be in jeopardy if left
among the general prison population. Unlike other inmates,
remand prisoners were not required to work.

Mountjoy was a Victorian jail and the conditions in the
1980s had not improved much over a century. There were

no individual toilets in cells and prisoners were required to 'slop out', or empty their potties, each day. Many of the cells in the Base were communal cells, with up to six prisoners sharing small, cramped spaces. Macarthur was a high security prisoner and because of that – and for his own safety – he was placed in an individual cell.

That meant long periods of being locked in his cell with little to do, other than an hour of recreation. On his first weekend in the jail, he requested writing paper, an envelope, and a pen. From his prison cell, he wrote a letter to the taoiseach, Charles Haughey.

*Dear Sir,*

*I have already stated to the police and now wish to state to you also, that my good friend, Mr Patrick Connolly, Attorney, had no knowledge whatsoever of any wrongdoings of mine and must be considered to be utterly blameless. I earnestly hope that the career and happiness of this splendid man shall not be adversely affected.*

*Yours sincerely,*
*Malcolm Macarthur.*

It was a breath-taking act of audacity, to think that it was either appropriate to write to the taoiseach in such circumstances, or that his letter would carry any weight. But it was perfectly in keeping with Macarthur's character. Perhaps more surprising was that it actually arrived at its destination. Macarthur sent it on Monday morning, and it was received in Haughey's private office that afternoon. It was read by the taoiseach himself, then quickly passed on to the Garda Síochána, who pored over it with the Director of Public Prosecutions.

There was general astonishment at its temerity: the anachronistic tone – like the honourable confession of a gentleman killer from a 1940s British whodunnit; the underlying assumption of standing or entitlement, all of it emphasising the delusions of grandeur so characteristic of the man who appeared to be presenting himself as if in a bit of a pickle from which he could somehow extricate himself in due course.

The gardaí inquired of the prison authorities if Macarthur had fired off any other missives from his cell. They were told he had also written a letter apologising to Paddy Connolly for involving him in events but it had not yet been sent. The letter was immediately seized by prison staff and never reached its intended recipient.

On Wednesday, 18 August, four days after his first court appearance in Dún Laoghaire, Macarthur got his first proper bite of a reality sandwich. He was brought before the Bridewell Court, behind the Four Courts in Dublin city centre, for a remand hearing. This was the morning after Charlie Haughey's GUBU press conference and – as far as the media and public were concerned – little else existed in the universe.

A large number of reporters and curious members of the public were crammed into the small Victorian-era courtroom, to witness Macarthur's arrival from an underground cell into Court Number 6, just after 10.30am.

Flanked by two detectives for the short hearing, he was wearing a large grey bow tie, a white waistcoat, a white shirt, and the same corduroy fawn jacket he wore the previous Saturday. A distinctive saffron handkerchief protruded raffishly from his top pocket. A pallid Macarthur stared straight ahead, paying no attention to the large crowd, catching no one's eye.

The hearing itself was procedural and the judge granted the application of the state solicitor for a three-week remand in custody. Det Inspector Noel Conroy told the court an additional charge of possession of a shotgun with intent to rob (at Harry Bieling's house in Killiney) had been laid against the accused. Conroy told the court that when the charge was put to him, Macarthur replied: "I won't say anything."

Proceedings were quickly wrapped up and as the two detectives led the accused from the court, Macarthur removed his jacket to cover his head and shoulders before they hit the street.

Just as with his first court appearance the previous Saturday, a large crowd had gathered outside, and as Macarthur emerged at the doorway of the Bridewell, the situation quickly descended into mayhem.

People surged forward and there were yells of "murderer", "toerag", "scum". One woman broke through the detectives and, screaming abuse at the top of her voice, whacked Macarthur over the head with her handbag. Another man lunged forward and landed a punch into the side of his face.

From within the Bridewell, prisoners waiting in holding cells for their cases to be called cat-whistled and shouted through the windows. For a fraught moment or two, the situation looked like it would get out of hand, as the crowd continued to swell around the moving scrum of gardaí, some shouting at them to reveal the face of the killer.

With some difficulty, Detectives Conroy, Hickey and their colleagues managed to open the door of an unmarked blue Talbot Solara and bundle Macarthur into the back seat. The car raced away from the courthouse, as the *Evening Press* put it, "pursued by photographers and youths".

Later on the Wednesday of his Bridewell Court appearance, Irene Macarthur arrived at the prison, wearing dark glasses and a low-brimmed hat to avoid the attention of any press photographers who might be hanging around the front gates with a view to getting a picture of Macarthur's visitors.

It was the first meeting of mother and son since their strange encounter the previous week at the hotel in Mullingar, when in a bizarre aside, he had told her not to be surprised if the Italian police contacted her to ask questions about him.

Irene was in her early 60s at the time, an imposing woman with shoulder-length grey hair, who wore Barbour jackets and practical boots, and was seldom seen without her dogs. Her outward appearance was of a buttoned-up, no-nonsense country landowner. In person, however, she was warmer and less flinty than appearances suggested.

After separating from Malcolm's father, Daniel, Irene had lived in an apartment in the grand house of Freffans in County Meath during the 1970s, but in recent years had moved to a modest suburban home in Mullingar, County Westmeath.

She had found out about Malcolm's arrest indirectly from Paddy Connolly on the morning of Saturday, 14 August.

Brenda Little had given Connolly a number for a friend of Irene's with whom she thought she was staying. As it happened, Irene was not a guest at the house that night but the woman contacted her the following day and passed on Connolly's message.

The day after her first prison visit on 18 August, Irene spoke from her County Westmeath home to Gregg Ryan, a reporter from *The Irish Press*. She was still struggling to make sense of it all. She tried to articulate the conflict between her personal response to the terrible events and her discovery that her son may have been responsible for them.

"My first sympathy must be with those who have suffered, but my sympathy must also be with my son who stands accused. As a Christian mother I must have such feelings," she said.

She described her son as a gentle person. "He's the sort of person who would take an insect out of a bathtub before filling it. Malcolm is an academic, a kindly person who lived for his books, his girlfriend and child."

That week, media organisations had essentially cleared the desk to gather every possible screed of information relating to the case. The new owners of Breemount had a steady stream of reporters calling to the door. The family had only recently moved to the area and were of little help. However, around Trim and Laracor, others who knew the Macarthurs were willing to share what they knew.

Already stories had been published, for example, about the distant relationship she and her late husband had with Malcolm when he was a child. In *The Irish Press* interview, Irene contested that assertion vigorously: "We are very close as mother and son and anyone who says otherwise does not know us," she retorted.

She relayed to the reporter that her son had been at King's College Cambridge for three years and was a member of staff who had interviewed prospective students. Like so many others who knew Malcolm, even his own mother believed this fallacy to be true.

Irene finished the interview with a plaintive plea. "Please do not hound me. I have nothing further that I can add."

As it turned out, there was far more that she could add, and it would not be long before she did. In an interview with RTÉ's David Hanly some months later, Irene recalled her experience of the visits while her son was on remand. Hanly mentioned to her that she visited him several times in prison during his pre-trial incarceration and asked how he had reacted to her. She replied that, initially, Malcolm seemed contrite.

"The first time I went in, which was just a few days after the arrest, he apologised to me. And he apologised to any relations we had and friends for any distress that he had caused."

In September, the *Evening Press* quoted Malcolm as telling a friend from prison the trial would be "only a banal affair, quite banal" and nothing to be too concerned about.

For Macarthur's partner Brenda Little, the appalling news she had heard when Paddy Connolly spoke to her on Friday night, 13 August, had been beyond distressing. Now, she had to arrange a hasty flight home, and confront the unthinkable reality that her partner of eight years could be a killer.

Soon after arriving back in Dublin on Monday, 16 August, she was interviewed by murder squad detectives. They quickly established she had no inkling of what Macarthur intended to do on his return to Ireland. Brenda and Colin, who was six years old, moved into a house in Swords. Because she and Macarthur were not married, it took some time for her to be allowed to visit him in prison. Supported by her large family during a deeply traumatic period in her life, she consciously shunned the media. She gave no interviews and did not appear at her partner's remand hearings, nor did she appear in public. There were no photographs. Indeed, she was far more effective at disappearing than her partner's bumbling efforts to go incognito. Once Brenda Little disappeared from public view, she would never resurface.

# 35

## IRELAND'S MOST CELEBRATED LAWYER

"McEntee would have to understand what made Malcolm Macarthur tick." *Magill* magazine

In his first remand hearing on Saturday, 14 August, the solicitor assigned to Macarthur by the state's free legal aid system was Roger Sweetman, a well-regarded criminal specialist.

Given the high-profile nature of the case, Sweetman wanted to assemble a formidable team. The senior partner in his law firm was John Jay, who also represented David Norris in his long-standing legal battle to decriminalise homosexuality. Jay rang Senior Counsel Patrick McEntee – Ireland's most celebrated criminal barrister – early the following week to ask would he take the brief. He readily agreed. Michael McDowell, a young up-and-coming barrister and future politician, was the junior counsel in the case.

Patrick McEntee was a flamboyant character, rarely seen

without a fat cigar in his hands. He had thick silver hair and looked a little like the actor John Forsythe, who played the patriarch Blake Carrington in *Dynasty*. Born in Monaghan, McEntee first came to prominence as a talented actor in UCD's dramatic society in the 1960s, a skill he put to good use during a long career as a barrister.

He defended many of the major paramilitary cases in the non-jury Special Criminal Court during the 1970s. A polished courtroom advocate, he could rely on instant recall of arcane details of fact and law when on his feet, alongside being a master at turning a memorable and witty phrase. It was he who coined the term "heavy gang" to describe a group of gardaí, led by DSI John Courtney – the detective in charge of the Macarthur investigation – who had used physical tactics to extract confessions from republican suspects during the 1970s. McEntee's cross-examinations – delivered in a rich border burr – left no stone unturned.

In criminal cases, senior counsel rarely became involved in proceedings until many months after the charge, often stepping in just as the trial itself was looming. The Macarthur case was different. The accused had already made an inculpatory 20-page confession. Even as the gardaí began assembling their case that week, the evidence against Macarthur was overwhelming. Scores of eye witnesses would be lined up, including the gardener, Paddy Byrne, who saw first-hand Macarthur's savage attack on Bridie Gargan; and Harry Bieling, the American whom he might have killed at his home. There was also slam-dunk forensic evidence: Macarthur's fingerprints on the plastic wrapped around the shovel which he abandoned in the Phoenix Park; and those from the milk carton he had discarded in a bin in Edenderry, County Offaly, hours before he shot Dónal Dunne.

The battle for the defence team would not revolve around the facts of this open and shut case. Instead, McEntee was keen to explore the limited number of alternatives that were open to him. Principally, they were a plea of guilty but insane; or a plea of manslaughter on the grounds of diminished responsibility.

"It was felt that McEntee would have to understand what made Malcolm Macarthur tick," *Magill* magazine later reported in an article on the pre-trial period. "More importantly, he had to know what kind of impression Macarthur would make on a jury should he ever enter the witness box."

To prove insanity, the defence would have to show the accused had a defect of reason due to disease of the mind so that he did not know what he was doing, or did not know that it was wrong. The accused would also need to be a figure for whom the jury could have sympathy.

In the following weeks, Macarthur was seen by four psychiatrists: two representing the state; two commissioned by the defence. Their full reports would be returned in December.

McEntee had a deep grasp of the criminal law and a talent for choosing particular court strategies to maximise the benefit for his clients. That included knowing instinctively how different scenarios would play out with juries and with the wider public.

But it didn't take a brilliant legal mind to see that if Macarthur was put in front of a jury to give evidence of any kind, he would be putting himself on a hook from which it would not be possible to wriggle free. For one, public sympathy for Macarthur was already at zero; the media portrayal of a spoiled playboy who'd never worked a day in his life had taken a firm hold. What's more, putting the accused, with his cold and superior manner, into the witness box would have only one outcome.

Moreover, the legal team concluded at an early stage that pursuing an insanity defence was a high-risk strategy. No matter how persuasive and compelling the expert evidence was, a jury could still reject outright any arguments of insanity straight off the bat, given the callous nature of the killings and a public perception of an arrogant killer. The only way such a strategy would work is if the state agreed that such a plea was appropriate and did not contest it.

A not guilty plea, or a plea of manslaughter, would also be a perilous route for the defence team. The chances of Macarthur's defence on either succeeding would be minimal, McEntee told his team. The defendant would get no sympathy from a jury. In fact, anything related to his client that had to be put before a jury would be a beaten docket before the off.

By mid-September, the defence team learned that the state would be relying on a total of 300 witnesses. It was the highest number of witnesses ever called for a criminal prosecution in Ireland. If it came to a trial, there would be intense interest in the testimony of Ireland's former attorney general Paddy Connolly, who had been summoned as a witness. Until the Office of the Director of Public Prosecutions had been formed in 1974, it was the attorney general who took criminal prosecutions on behalf of the state. For one to be a key witness would be sensational in the extreme.

A trial of this kind would end up being a circus. There would be an insatiable public appetite for each day's developments. Newspapers and broadcasters would pull out all the stops to cover almost every syllable of evidence.

It would mean testimony lasting weeks on end, with extensive coverage of the details of Bridie Gargan's gruesome fate and Macarthur's execution-style killing of Dónal Dunne.

For McEntee and the defence team, such a scenario had to be avoided at all costs.

# 36

## MURDER IS MURDER

"If the publicity is bothering you, why on earth did you commit the crime?" Irene Macarthur

As the weeks turned into months, the reality of prison life sank in for Macarthur. During his killing spree, he had not thought too much about the consequences of his actions or the price he would have to pay for getting caught. As he realised that he could no longer avoid his fate, and years of incarceration, his initial calm and poise lessened and his mood darkened.

Irene did her best to try and keep her son's spirits up in the face of very bleak prospects. She ensured, for example, that he received *The Irish Times* each day and sent him a copy of the *New Scientist* magazine every week. But despite her best efforts, as time went on, their encounters became increasingly fraught and he was given to angry outbursts.

During a visit in early October, she was at the receiving

end of one of these outbursts, over a family photo that had appeared in a Sunday newspaper in late September. It had unwittingly been handed over by a relative. Malcolm berated her for speaking to reporters about the case and about him. She didn't take it lying down.

"I had to be frank with him," she told reporter Gregg Ryan of *The Irish Press*, in her typically forthright manner. "He said to me he did not want any of this publicity. I replied by saying, 'If the publicity is bothering you, why on earth did you commit the crime? After all, I have to defend myself and I am getting a lot of annoyance as a result of your behaviour. I didn't go into the Phoenix Park and do what you did, now did I?'"

In another interview Irene told David Hanly, "He became fractious. Various people told me people, when they are in prison, become like that. They have a lot of time to think. And they become very irritated. And then whoever visits them, it's quite possible they are attacked."

Seeing that she was upset after visits, the prison authorities allowed Ms Macarthur to start being accompanied by a friend. "It is very difficult to talk to anybody that you visit. In a jail, you can't talk about the mountains and the trees and the lakes and the sea because, after all, you don't even want to bring up the subject of pleasant things that happened outside. You feel you're being very unkind and very cruel."

Irene tended not to bring up her son's case and ignored all reporting on it. With little to talk about, in the cauldron atmosphere of Mountjoy's four walls, outbursts flared quickly. "I always seemed to put my foot right into the middle of it. And the result was that – I don't want to call it 'attacked' – but I was certainly contradicted."

When Irene let slip that she had sent a Mass card to the family of Bridie Gargan, Macarthur reacted in fury, saying she had pre-condemned him. On another occasion, she mentioned that Brenda Little had told her he might be charged with the manslaughter of Bridie Gargan and not her murder. He roared at her: "Murder is Murder is Murder."

Under strain from what she called a "bizarre nightmare", Irene put her foot down.

"Finally one day I walked out. I couldn't take any more of it," she told Hanly. "I think that probably made him realise that many of his friends were going out of their way to go to Dublin and to visit him, and perhaps he was becoming more appreciative. I'm quite sure that if I were put into jail I would have, maybe, behaved much worse. I mean, who are we to say that, because we haven't been there?"

In late August, two weeks after her return from Tenerife, Brenda Little was allowed to visit her partner in prison. Malcolm told her not to speak to the press and she was as good as her word. Several other of Macarthur's friends in Dublin were also allowed to visit, including Victor Melia, the mathematician from Trinity College whom he had palled with during the Bartley Dunne days in the mid-70s.

As weeks passed to months, Malcolm Macarthur had to accept that life in the basement of B Wing would be his lot for the foreseeable future. The best shot for him of freedom before he was an old man was a guilty plea to murder, the most heinous of all crimes.

# 37

# CONFIDENCE TRICK

"That the Fianna Fáil members of Dáil Éireann have no
confidence in Charles J Haughey as Leader and Taoiseach."
Charlie McCreevy, Fianna Fáil TD

Two days after the dramatic GUBU press conference, on 19
August, DSI John Courtney received a call from Garda
Commissioner Patrick McLoughlin. He told him that
Charles Haughey wanted to meet both men at his home in
Kinsealy.

At the time of Macarthur's arrest, Minister for Justice Seán
Doherty had been away on holidays, and Haughey himself
had been the acting minister. Courtney knew that now the
taoiseach would want to know why he had not been contacted
in advance of Macarthur being arrested in the attorney
general's flat. He was essentially being summoned to
Haughey's mansion to explain himself.

Haughey was waiting for the two men in the drawing room when they arrived. He asked Courtney were there any circumstances in which he could have kept him in the loop before gardaí moved in to Pilot View. Courtney was blunt. He said no. He went through the events of that Friday and argued that things were moving too quickly. His priority was to capture a dangerous suspect. "We would do the same again," he insisted.

Haughey listened intently and made no response. He went over to the bar and poured drinks for the three men. Then he started talking about west Kerry. He knew that Courtney was from Annascaul, close to Dingle.

Haughey talked about his holiday island of Inishvickillane and chatted amiably about his fondness for the Blasket Islands. Courtney shared memories from boyhood of the island men, who were instantly recognisable in Dingle by how they walked in single file along the streets. The reason for that, he explained, was that the rutted paths on the island were too narrow to allow islanders walk side-by-side. The meeting continued in an amiable fashion and it seemed to Courtney that Haughey just wanted to put the whole episode behind him. The men left on good terms.

It would be a long time, however, before Haughey could put the episode behind him. In the days and weeks to come, the phrase concocted by his arch enemy Conor Cruise O'Brien refused to go away. GUBU had succeeded in tethering together the narratives of Macarthur and Haughey in a way that would not be untangled.

On 1 September, Haughey's inadvertent comment during the by now famed press conference, where he congratulated the gardaí for "eventually finding the right man", came back to bite. Macarthur's defence team made an effort to attach him before the court for contempt on the basis that he had inferred that the suspect of a sub judice case was the clear perpetrator. In the High Court, Mr Justice Declan Costello rejected the application, saying Haughey's inadvertent comment would not prejudice the upcoming trial.

Meanwhile, the British press continued to hammer Haughey.

"How can Britain trust a man like Haughey?" the Irish-based journalist Patrick Cosgrave wrote in *The Daily Telegraph* in early September.

"The depth of Mr Haughey's incompetence and would-be clever deviousness is so great and so well documented that one wonders whether it would be possible for any government, and particularly the British government, to have any faith in the man's ability to discharge the ordinary duties of his job."

This was no skin off Haughey's nose. For an Irish republican, getting hounded by the right-wing British media was, in one sense, a back-handed compliment.

There was, nonetheless, more perilous political trouble on the horizon. On 1 October, a week after the Dáil resumed, a courier arrived with a letter to Kinsealy. Haughey was about to depart by helicopter for a commemorative event in Rockwell College in County Tipperary.

The sender was Charlie McCreevy, a back bench TD from County Kildare. He informed the taoiseach that he was submitting a motion to the chief whip, Bertie Ahern, for the meeting of the parliamentary party the following Wednesday.

It read: "That the Fianna Fáil members of Dáil Éireann have no confidence in Charles J Haughey as Leader and Taoiseach."

McCreevy was a bit of an outlier within Fianna Fáil. He had an independent cast of mind, strong views, and tended to be outspoken. The 33-year old was a successful accountant, with a consuming interest, like Haughey, in horses and the GAA. He also shared Haughey's republican views, and indeed had been a fervent supporter at the time of the party's leadership change.

McCreevy's disillusionment with Haughey grew during 1981 when the taoiseach failed to live up to his tough rhetoric in the televised 'Address to the Nation' in January 1980. Then Haughey had promised stringent cutbacks due to the bleak economic situation. "As a community we are living way beyond our means," he said in a phrase that became infamous. From McCreevy's perspective, Haughey had bottled it when it came to taking tough decisions on the nation's finances in the period to follow. Ever since, McCreevy had been a persistent critic and had, for a while, lost the parliamentary whip.

Paradoxically, the no-confidence challenge came half-way through preparation of the government's long-term economic plan, *The Way Forward*. It proposed a new social partnership model to move away from the poisonous atmosphere of industrial relations. Much of 1982 had been pockmarked by strikes and disputes of one kind or another. The plan also provided for the most swingeing cuts ever announced by a Fianna Fáil government.

McCreevy was not impressed, believing Haughey did not

have the courage of his convictions to see it through. Nonetheless, his motion caught many of his parliamentary colleagues by surprise, including the leading dissident, Desmond O'Malley, who was returning from holidays in France.

The reason McCreevy had kept it tight was that he was determined that Haughey's leadership would be put to the vote this time. He had been crestfallen with the abandonment of the leadership heave just after the February election.

The young deputy was not acting in isolation. The dissidents from February had not gone away. And some of the party's new intake of TDs were no fans of Haughey. The economy was in freefall, unemployment was high. Unpopular cuts in services had been announced at the end of July. On the day before McCreevy's letter was sent, the price of petrol had gone up another five pence.

McCreevy was confident he had the numbers, that there was a majority who opposed the "deals" and "convulsion politics" that characterised the government. He calculated that, for them, the GUBU incident was the latest in a series of scandals and morale-sapping setbacks that could not continue.

With only five days to go to the meeting, that weekend both sides hit the airwaves. The campaign teams began contacting parliamentary party colleagues to cajole them into voting for their side. Hard-chaw tactics were used. In a radio interview, Haughey said he would be calling on all the cabinet members to pledge their loyalty. It was a demand that had predictable consequences. While the majority of the cabinet were Haughey loyalists, there was a residue of ministers who had been Jack Lynch supporters and now served in Haughey's government under sufferance. Chief among them was O'Malley, and Minister for Education Martin O'Donoghue, both of whom resigned rather than pledge loyalty to Haughey.

In the days leading up to the vote, both camps bickered over the question of a secret ballot. It became a proxy for the leadership question. Given the adulation in which the taoiseach was held by the grass-roots party members, the anti-Haugheyites believed that TDs would not be able to freely cast their votes in an open vote for fear of repercussions, including deselection from their local constituency organisations. As it was, TDs were deluged with telephone calls and letters. The known dissidents were subjected to threats and abuse, much of it coming from anonymous callers and poison-pen writers. Some too were obscene. David Andrews from Dún Laoghaire, Hugh Byrne from Wexford, and Séamus Brennan from Dublin South all confirmed they had received abusive calls. Mary Harney's family received crank calls with outrageous falsehoods about her personal life.

The parliamentary party meeting on 6 October was a highly charged affair that lasted for over 12 hours. Practically all 80 deputies participated, and many spoke their minds in public for the first time. It might have been cathartic were it not for the entrenched views on both sides. Some Haugheyites accused the dissidents in the party of being swayed and manipulated by the anti-Fianna Fáil media, and by sinister forces: British anti-national interests, in other words.

One of Haughey' supporters, Paddy Power, mused aloud that the party would be in much better standing, and unified, if all the rebels were expelled. From the other side, McCreevy and George Colley told Haughey that his real enemies were among his own so-called supporters who privately wanted him to go. Galway West TD Bobby Molloy openly accused Haughey of being a divisive figure and said he should resign, otherwise the party would be split. A number of newly elected deputies – in the door only since February – stood up and surprised colleagues when they spoke trenchantly against Haughey.

Those interventions buoyed the dissidents. For a while, they believed they could sway the vote, but as the evening wore on, more and more TDs declared for Haughey. The first vote decided if the substantive matter would be decided by secret ballot. TDs rejected it by a majority of 50 to 27, with three abstaining. In the open roll call that followed, Haughey won the contest comfortably with 58 votes for, and 22 against.

It was now late in the evening, and as the TDs filtered down from the Fianna Fáil room on the fifth floor of Leinster House to break the news, they were mobbed by reporters, and also a large crowd of Haughey supporters on the ground.

The 'Club of 22', as the dissidents became known, were happy to do interviews. Haughey did a short press conference in which he said he looked forward to resuming the normal business of government.

The cordial atmosphere quickly evaporated as a mob situation developed. Drunken Haughey supporters, who had spent the day in the Dáil bar, began taunting dissident TDs as they emerged, first with verbal abuse and then jostling and pushing them. Jim Gibbons was struck and fell to the ground. Mary Harney was also verbally abused. The mob reserved the most bile for Charlie McCreevy. He insisted on leaving by the front door. In the event, he needed an escort of gardaí and Oireachtas ushers to get to his car. Amid all the pushing and shoving, he was called a "bastard", a "Judas", a "traitor" and a "Blueshirt". Gibbons later denounced the mob, claiming there was now a "Nazi fascist element in Fianna Fáil".

When the dust had settled, Haughey could bask in a decisive winning margin over his internal rivals. As time would tell, the victory would prove to be Pyrrhic.

The GUBU scandals and mishaps had already widened the cracks. The state was in recession and unemployment figures were rising. The government's new economic plan was not a crowd-pleaser. With support waning from the independents on which his minority government relied, Haughey's administration was beginning to totter.

# 38

## A SERIES OF
## UNFORTUNATE EVENTS

"If Charlie had ducks, they would drown." John Healy,
political columnist, *The Irish Times*

For Haughey, 1982 was a year pockmarked by controversy,
scandal, political strokes, and two leadership heaves which he
managed to see off. Even his few victories were what boxing
people would call split decisions: the February election, the
Galway by-election, his success in seeing off internal opponents.

There was no shortage of situations to which the phrase
GUBU could be applied and the media used it at every turn
as it came to symbolise far more than the gruesome Macarthur
case.

"It really annoyed Haughey that Conor Cruise O'Brien, who
he had beaten comprehensively in a whole series of elections,
would have coined the phrase GUBU," observed Haughey's

biographer, Gary Murphy. "In many ways, it haunted Haughey like Banquo's ghost. He couldn't shake it off."

Haughey's success in seeing off the internal October putsch was short-lived. The minority Fianna Fáil government was in a precarious parliamentary position to begin with. Already it relied on four left-wing TDs to keep it afloat. If it were to lose more than one vote, it would no longer have a majority in the 166-seat Dáil.

On 18 October, a series of events precipitated the end. The veteran Fianna Fáil TD for Clare, Dr Bill Loughnane, died of a heart attack. He had been a loyal Haughey supporter. The following day, another Fianna Fáil TD, Jim Gibbons, himself suffered a severe heart attack. Gibbons was a leading dissident whose dislike for Haughey went back to the Arms Trial in 1970, where there was a clear conflict between their respective accounts of how the illegal arms came to be imported into the state.

Those close to Gibbons believed the way in which he had been manhandled and struck by Haughey supporters in the Leinster House car park after the leadership vote on 6 October contributed to his medical episode. Gibbons suffered a second heart attack in the following days and was kept in hospital. If his vote was needed if a motion of no-confidence in the government was tabled, he would have to be stretchered from hospital. That was never realistic. He was too ill. Besides, he and Haughey were implacable foes.

The government was atomising. The economic plan it had spent the autumn devising, *The Way Forward*, was immediately met with a hostile response from the mandarins at the Department of Finance, who quickly dubbed it *The Way Backwards*.

Nor did the plan go down well with the three TDs from The Workers' Party or with the independent, Tony Gregory. They recoiled at the austere cuts that were being proposed for public expenditure and for social welfare, on top of unpopular health cuts already in place.

The breaking point happened on 4 November. Fine Gael tabled a motion of no-confidence in Charles Haughey's government. Despite the efforts of Haughey's chief whip Bertie Ahern to keep them on board, the three Workers' Party TDs voted against the government in the motion.

It was a disaster for Fianna Fáil. Its shambolic government had lasted only eight months, embroiled itself in multiple crises, and had ultimately achieved very little. Haughey had not been a lucky general.

"If Charlie had ducks, they would drown," the columnist John Healy wrote during the height of the GUBU autumn of '82.

A general election was called, the third in eighteen months. It was a lacklustre campaign. Despite the economy tanking, the big issue of contention was policy on Northern Ireland. Haughey accused Fine Gael leader Garret FitzGerald of essentially colluding with a "trained British spy", the duke of Norfolk. During the campaign, FitzGerald also proposed an ill-thought-out idea for a "border police force", separate to the forces in each jurisdiction. Fianna Fáil was able to recover some ground, but not enough, by playing the green card and raising the threat of Royal Ulster Constabulary (RUC) members policing within the Republic.

Lack of public trust was a huge issue for Haughey. There had been too many mishaps and scandals, too many fast ones pulled, too much patronage, too much incompetence, and too many failures. Polling day was 24 November. When the results came in, Fianna Fáil had lost six seats. Fine Gael had added four and was able to form a coalition with Labour.

Haughey was out of power. He had to brace himself for another five years in the wilderness. The government had been done for by the GUBU factor. But the series of unfortunate events was not behind it yet. Nobody could have foreseen the consequences of what was yet to come.

# 39

# HOW TO KILL A MOTHER

"Put her prints on the letter and the envelope, giving my
address and telephone number for a certain length of time."
Malcolm Macarthur

The follow-up search of Paddy Connolly's home after Malcolm
Macarthur's arrest led to rich pickings for the garda
investigation. In the spare bedroom they came across
Macarthur's suitcase and the blue hold-all bag. There were
a few neatly folded items of clothing as well as accessories
that included silk cravats, silk bow ties, and a battered
Panama hat.

Among other items recovered were: lengths of rope, a phase
tester (an electrical testing device used to detect the presence
of voltage), vinyl gloves, and an Ordnance Survey map of
County Meath. The suitcase also contained two books, one of
which was a thick primer on forensic medicine. When

detectives leafed through the pages, they came across two sheets of paper inserted between them.

The writing on the sheets was done in a feverish scrawl, with a jumble of additional notes squeezed into the margins and at the bottom of the pages.

From the very first sentence, it was jolting. At the top of the page were written the chilling words: "Wait for a while to ensure that death is final."

By 9 October, the book of evidence in the Macarthur case had been completed. It ran to a few hundred pages. And with 300 witnesses, in the event it ever made it to trial it would be by far the biggest and most anticipated case in Irish legal history. Since Macarthur's arrest two months beforehand, there had been little let-up in media and public interest. At each of his five remand hearings, the public gallery and the press benches had been packed to capacity.

Although a full trial was the last thing that Paddy McEntee and his defence team wanted, it was still too early to set out to the opposite side the plea bargain sought for Macarthur – to plead guilty for the Bridie Gargan murder in exchange for some mitigation deal on the Dónal Dunne murder. For now, lawyers on both sides proceeded as if they were preparing for a full case that would last many weeks.

However, as the *Magill* magazine investigation into the behind-the-scenes machinations observed, there was no way McEntee could run a full trial. The evidence against Macarthur was overwhelming and incontrovertible. For the defence lawyer, it would be like watching a tidal wave quickly advancing towards him as he sat in a rowing boat with one broken oar.

From early October onwards, Macarthur's legal team let it be known they wanted an early trial, and complained when there were delays from the Director of Public Prosecution's (DPP's) side. At the remand hearing on the 9th, the trial date was set, with hearings to commence on 11 January 1983.

From then until December, the defence examined all possible scenarios. In none of them would Macarthur be walking out of court a free man. All were geared towards cutting his losses and his time in detention. One possibility was to try and get the charge for both killings changed from murder to manslaughter, with Macarthur pleading guilty to both. Unsurprisingly, it was rejected out of hand by the DPP.

As they awaited the psychiatrist reports, the defence team invested most effort in trying to broker some form of insanity plea that would be agreeable to the prosecution. McEntee looked at using a defence that was extremely rare in Irish law, "automatism". The hypothesis floated was that Macarthur was essentially in a trance, or had some form of sleepwalking malaise, for the entirety of his time back in Ireland after returning from Tenerife on 8 July. He urged the psychiatrists being used for the defence to consider the possibility and to share their findings with their colleagues who examined Macarthur on behalf of the state.

In the meantime, other options were explored and floated with the DPP, with prosecuting barrister Harry Hill acting as conduit. One was that Macarthur would plead guilty for the murder of Bridie Gargan and also plead guilty for the manslaughter of Dónal Dunne. McEntee also suggested a guilty plea for Bridie Gargan's murder with the other charge being dropped completely.

In legal terms, that was a *nolle prosequi*, where no prosecution would be pursued in relation to the Dónal Dunne charge.

McEntee argued there was a case for allowing this, as the evidence in the Dunne killing was more circumstantial than the first killing. Unlike the Gargan killing, there had been no witnesses. Nor had Macarthur explicitly admitted to murder in his statement. He claimed the young farmer had tried to grab the gun and he had pulled back and pulled the trigger while doing so. That could be interpreted in several ways but it did, at least, open up marginal grounds of self-defence.

It was a thin argument, however. Macarthur had admitted in his statement that he desperately required a gun, and subsequently used the gun in an attempted armed robbery, and had the shotgun in his possession when he was arrested by gardaí.

A slightly more persuasive argument was that the welter of pre-trial publicity was such that it would hopelessly prejudice a fair trial. Indeed, the contempt of court case taken by the defence team against Haughey on 1 September for his throwaway remark at the press conference put huge emphasis on the mass coverage of the case and how it would compromise Macarthur's defence.

The psychiatrists' reports came back in December. They were, on the face of it, favourable for Macarthur. The two defence psychiatrists had come to the conclusion that his actions, behaviour, and absence of any display of emotion in those weeks lent themselves to a diagnosis of automatism.

"They were basically saying that everything he did that summer, he was doing it on automatic pilot," said a senior source who was privy to the discussions and negotiations taking place behind the scenes.

What's more, the two state psychiatrists were also now leaning to the same view: that Macarthur had been an automaton and had been in a "fugue state" when he fatally attacked Bridie Gargan and Dónal Dunne.

Automatism describes how a person committed an offence involuntarily, without volition, without any intention to do it, without any conscious thought. There are examples in case law of diabetics going into an involuntary trance because of hypoglycaemia (low blood sugar levels) or hyperglycaemia (high blood sugar levels). Crimes committed during "sleep terror" or "sleep walking" have also fallen under the category of automatism.

In Macarthur's case, the argument put forward was that his automatism had been induced by extreme anxiety. In other words, he had been effectively zombified by what is known nowadays as post-traumatic stress disorder, triggered by his "obsessive" worry about running out of funds.

In legal terms, automatism implied that the crime itself, the *actus reus*, occurred. However, the motive or premeditation to commit the crimes, or *mens rea*, was absent because the person was not the master of their own volition.

None of the gardaí had heard of this defence before and for many of them "automatism" was a new word. If the prosecution and defence agreed on a plea of this form of defence, the facts of the case would be accepted – the two killings. It would still require a jury verdict. What would be put to the jury would be a verdict of guilty by reason of insanity in accordance with the evidence. There was always a chance that the jury would reject the evidence agreed by all sides and deliver a rogue verdict. However, if that were to happen, it would be likely overturned on appeal.

If a verdict of guilty by reason of insanity was returned, Macarthur would be detained as a patient in Ireland's Central Mental Hospital but would be entitled to be released upon a formal diagnosis of sanity. That could happen within a relatively short time, a decade or less.

Within senior garda ranks, there was mounting apprehension. As far as they were concerned, Macarthur had committed two murders. They were firmly opposed to any arrangement that would let him off lightly.

However, investigating gardaí had an ace up their sleeve. It came in the form of the hand-written memo in Macarthur's scrawl that gardaí had uncovered during their search of the attorney general's home, in the aftermath of the arrest – the one containing the chilling line, "Wait a while to ensure death is final." By mid-December, as the trial date loomed, the detectives involved in the case had known its significance from the start. But, for some reason, it appeared to have been lost on the lawyers.

The two sheets of paper of Macarthur's found by gardaí in Pilot View were later reproduced in full by Stephen Rae in his book on Irish murders, *Killers*. The hand-writing was spidery but mostly legible.

What they revealed was a highly elaborate murder plan. The first sheet set out, in considerable detail, how the victim could be stunned with a "shock gadget". Then, when unconscious, the person could be electrocuted to death by a form of electrified straitjacket. The equipment would involve a heavy fuse "to be temporarily installed and then removed"; four leather straps to bind the victim but each containing electrodes; a gag; a blindfold; a screwdriver; pliers; a phase tester; rope for tying the victim; and two black bags for taking all the equipment away.

Further down on the first sheet were notes intended to be aide memoires for the author: reminders to wear rubber gloves and ensure "none of my finger prints" are left at the scene.

"Make sure her fingerprints are on handle [of electric fire]," the notes added.

The planned scenario was for the killer to electrocute the victim with electrified straps, and then pass off the death as having been caused by an electric fire with a faulty plug attached.

On the other sheet of paper, there was another full page of writing, this even more macabre. In a style redolent of a memo, it revealed that Macarthur's intended victim was none other than his own mother, Irene. His "wait for a while to ensure death is final" was a matricidal vigil.

*During this time, take a few very important items (certain small photos into my possession). Make an inventory of other important items so I can check on their presence when I arrive for the funeral.*

*Letter(s) from me left in a prominent place, on the table or in, or beside, her address book, or telephone directory (in an envelope then tear out the stamp). Put her prints on the letter and the envelope, giving my address and telephone number for a certain length of time. Return to that address, wait for message, or if necessary, ring up on a pretext.*

*Then give instructions to R. Ballesty [a family acquaintance] and hurry over to take charge.*

A number of things that need to be arranged are written out in Macarthur's letter. They include a death certificate; a new suit for him; a notice in the newspaper (*The Irish Times*); an undertaker; flowers: and a "cleric at grave".

The notes then listed the names of three friends to be informed, two of which are illegible, the other the initials M.B. It concluded with the banal lines:

*Then on with the job. Shaw and O'Reilly? Sell car and furniture etc, right away.*

This was likely a reference to local undertakers and solicitors.

Was Macarthur's strange meeting with his mother in Mullingar three days before his arrest in August connected with the plot outlined in the note? During the course of that short meeting, from which he uncharacteristically walked away without as much as asking her for desperately needed funds, Macarthur did ask Irene if he could use her home as a forwarding address.

The hand-written note referred to leaving letters and envelopes from him in a prominent place in her home. Would that give Macarthur a legitimate reason to call around to the house to collect his letters, *mar dhea,* and discover the body after the deed had been done?

Whatever his motives for meeting Irene in Mullingar that day, the note was a damning piece of evidence. But for some reason, in the four months since Macarthur's arrest, it had fallen by the wayside. In its absence, the prospect of an unanticipated verdict was now beginning to rise.

# 40

## SCANDAL DOWN THE LINE

"I don't think any politician himself should initiate [phone bugging]. That would be an abuse." Charles J Haughey

As both sides counted down the days towards the most keenly awaited trial in Irish history, further trouble was brewing for a troubled Fianna Fáil party. On Tuesday, 14 December, a new Fine Gael-led government was formed, to replace the buckled Fianna Fáil administration.

The new taoiseach was Garret FitzGerald, Haughey's long-time political rival. That afternoon, FitzGerald summoned senior Fine Gael TDs to his office. These would be the politicians who would form his cabinet.

The biggest surprise was his choice as minister for justice. Michael Noonan was a 39-year-old TD from Limerick who had been elected to the Dáil for the first time only a year earlier. Nobody had predicted the promotion of such an inexperienced politician to a senior ministry, let alone the pivotal role of Justice.

No sooner had FitzGerald told a stunned Noonan about his appointment than he dropped another bombshell. The taoiseach had received information that the phones of two journalists had been tapped by gardaí. The two were Geraldine Kennedy of the *Sunday Tribune* and Bruce Arnold of the *Irish Independent*, both of whom had high national profiles.

Separately, the two journalists had reported extensively during 1982 on the internecine strife within Fianna Fáil, often from the perspective of Haughey's enemies within the party. The precision of their reporting on the government's activities suggested their sources were at the highest level of cabinet. It was well known that Haughey was incensed at the leaks and believed they stemmed from his enemies.

Noonan was astonished to hear what FitzGerald told him and was initially dismissive of it. But the Fine Gael leader's sources were high up in the Department of Justice and were watertight. When Noonan met the secretary general of the department, the intelligence was confirmed.

Despite his inexperience as a politician, Noonan was a canny and intuitive operator. His actions on the back of this alarming discovery would within weeks leave former taoiseach Charles Haughey once again fighting for his political life.

Noonan launched an immediate investigation to find out who had authorised the tappings: had it been the garda commissioner or Noonan's Fianna Fáil predecessor in Justice, Seán Doherty?

Later that same afternoon, he met *The Irish Times* security correspondent Peter Murtagh in Leinster House. Murtagh asked Noonan about rumoured tappings and specifically mentioned Kennedy and Arnold. The new minister was astounded and wondered how many people were aware of this information he had learned less than an hour previously.

Within a week, Murtagh had confirmed the rumour and reported about the phone-tapping on the front page of *The Irish Times*. The journalists whose phones were tapped, Arnold and Kennedy, were both named. It led to a media frenzy in the run-up to Christmas. In a long interview with RTÉ radio on the last Sunday before the Christmas break, Haughey tried to distance himself from what he knew was a coming storm.

Asked about who was responsible for ordering a phone tap, he told Gerald Barry on *This Week*: "I don't think any politician himself should initiate [phone bugging]. That would be an abuse."

In early January, a senior garda began an investigation to identify which gardaí had authorised the taps, and on the instructions of whom. It was quickly established that the phone-tapping had been authorised on foot of requests from Seán Doherty, who wanted to identify the 'Judas' within the Fianna Fáil cabinet who was leaking information to Kennedy and Arnold, that was damaging and embarrassing to the government and Haughey.

The big question on everyone's lips was: was Doherty acting alone, or under instruction from his boss?

# 41

## THE EIGHT-MINUTE TRIAL

"I must now impose on you: penal servitude for life." James McMahon, trial judge

Malcolm Macarthur's first Christmas in prison came and went as his trial date loomed ever closer. There was growing optimism among the defence team that a successful plea on the grounds of automatism was feasible.

On Thursday, 6 January, five days before the trial was due to begin, the senior barrister for the state, Harry Hill, held a case conference in the Law Library to assess the strength of the prosecution case and to discuss strategy. The meeting was attended by lawyers and by senior gardaí involved in the investigation.

The garda file ran to hundreds of pages. There was a clear reference in it to the matricidal murder plan note and what it signified. The two sheets of writing were physically attached at the end, as part of an index to the file.

According to my source who was privy to discussions, at some stage during the meeting, Harry Hill referred to the hand-written sheets he had seen at the back of the file and said he could not grasp what they were. He said he had been unable to decipher the writing.

The gardaí present were flabbergasted at this admission. They explained the sheets were found among Macarthur's belongings in Pilot View. The notes pointed to a plan by Macarthur to kill his mother. The gist of what was written in the note was set out in the garda file itself but, somehow, its significance had never been picked up by the lawyers.

The lawyer leading the state's case was taken aback. There was a stunned silence in the room, as Hill looked around in astonishment.

"My God, I did not know that," he said. He asked if the notes could be photographed and enlarged so they could be more easily read.

The new revelation prompted an immediate change of tack on Hill's part.

"Hill said that the note had never been brought to the attention of the four psychiatrists and it needed to be now," my source explained. "He said if Macarthur had been able to formulate a plan like that, his view was he was clearly not operating on automatic pilot."

The following day, Friday, 7 January, the blown-up photos of Macarthur's scrawl were made available to prosecution lawyers. Overnight, the two psychiatrists appearing for the state had changed their diagnoses on foot of the new information. They would no longer agree to a diagnosis of automatism.

The defence team would not receive the damning evidence for a further two days, on the eve of the trial. Even on an initial scan of the sheet, they knew the information torpedoed any chance of the insanity plea. Here was evidence, in black and white, of a plot to murder his own mother. It detailed everything from the method, to the funeral arrangements, to the flowers. It was open for the defence to challenge its admissibility but that would be another risk in an already high-stakes case.

Without the note, the prosecution already had enough evidence to make a convincing argument that Macarthur planned to rob, and perhaps kill, again. There was the intercepted driver who had run the errand for Macarthur, picking up Perrier water and two hacksaw blades to deliver to the penthouse apartment. A twelve-person jury, deciding the case on facts, would have to be given a very compelling argument that there was an innocent explanation behind the hacksaw, besides shortening a gun.

However, whatever chance they had of swinging the jury about the hacksaw, no argument was ever going to wash away the damning intention behind Macarthur's memo coldly listing a set of instructions on how to kill Irene Macarthur.

The defence team had no choice but to revert to another of its strategies, painstakingly worked on over previous months. This called for Macarthur to plead guilty to just one murder; to obtain a *nolle prosequi* for the other, meaning the DPP would not be pursuing prosecution; and get the trial over quickly. The plan was that, over time – a decade perhaps – the public outrage over what Macarthur had done would have faded sufficiently, and when it had, Macarthur could put in an application to the parole board for release.

The process of releasing long-term prisoners was more of an art than a science. It was a certainty, however, that a double murderer would be expected to serve a longer sentence before becoming eligible for parole than a person convicted of a single murder. As there were no witnesses to the killing of Dónal Dunne, the defence team argued they might successfully argue a manslaughter plea in that case. But to achieve that, the whole Dunne case would have to be run in court, notwithstanding the plea of guilty to murder in the Gargan case. That would defeat the purpose because it would not make for a speedy trial. Moreover, all the harrowing details would be disclosed in evidence.

Though officially, plea bargains did not exist in Irish law, the reality was the converse: deals were done every day by lawyers in criminal cases. Paddy McEntee's client was a man who had killed two young people in the most horrific circumstances and was as sympathetic a figure to the Irish public as a latter-day Cromwell.

The upside for the prosecution of such a deal was that it would secure a murder conviction without having to run the gauntlet of a trial. The advantage to Macarthur would be that he'd have only one murder conviction against his name, increasing the likelihood he would be released as a relatively young man.

McEntee informed Macarthur that his best option was to plead guilty to the murder of Bridie Gargan. He had no choice but to accept.

*

Tuesday, 11 January 1983 arrived, the first day of the trial. It was cold and overcast with a hard overnight frost on the ground. TV cameras captured detectives arriving at the Four Courts hauling sacks of exhibits and breathing out clouds of vapour into the chilly air.

The state's most serious criminal trials were held in the neo-classical 19th century Four Courts building, designed by James Gandon, also the designer of Haughey's mansion, Abbeville.

The main feature of the building is its large Round Hall, topped by an impressive dome. Around it are the four main courts. For those leaning over the rails of the balcony above, the scene unfolding in the Round Hall below might have been from the 1800s, with the mill of black robes, wigs, tipstaffs, judges, lawyers, clients and criminals. Even the trial judge, James McMahon, looked like an antique curio from another age, arriving into the court buildings wearing a top hat and tails.

The Round Hall had rarely been so busy, with hundreds of curious onlookers amassed, hoping to catch a sight of the exotic defendant, and even make their way into the court.

The witness list, though still a vast number, had by now been whittled down from 300 to 241. The first batch of witnesses had been told to arrive at the Four Courts that morning, including the main prosecution witness, gardener Paddy Byrne, who arrived just before 10am, a little nervous but determined to play his part. Macarthur arrived seconds behind him in a prison van and was accompanied to the court escorted by eight prison officers, with crowds pressing in on either side.

The trial was being held in one of the four courts off the main hall, a traditional room with dark drapes, high ceilings, wooden pews, and a high bench where the judge sat. The room had been full since an hour beforehand with court officials turning people away. Every available pew and standing space in the oak-panelled room was occupied, including the crowded media bench. A large contingent of gardaí were also in court.

Macarthur was brought into the court buildings. The twelve-person jury, who had been sworn in the week before, were gathered in an ante room waiting for the trial to begin. Every eye in the jammed courtroom was fixed on Macarthur as he entered and walked directly to the dock, flanked by two guards.

He was wearing his by-now signature outfit of fawn corduroy jacket, white shirt and claret bow tie. A silk handkerchief protruded from the breast pocket of his jacket. The *Evening Herald* observed that his "dark curly hair" was neatly combed.

Members of the Dunne and Gargan families were in attendance. Macarthur's partner Brenda Little was nowhere to be seen. In the *Evening Herald*, gardaí were quoted as saying she had not been at the house where she had been staying in Daleview Road, Swords, north Dublin, for several days. She was also to be a witness in the case. They were not aware of her whereabouts.

Senior Counsel Paddy McEntee rose to his feet as soon as Judge McMahon settled into the bench. He told him that certain documents relating to the trial came into the possession of the defence only on the previous evening. He was referring, of course, to the matricidal murder plot, in addition to the revised psychiatric reports.

McEntee said he required expert advice to examine the documents and reports. He asked for the trial to be adjourned until the following morning. The judge agreed and adjourned the hearing until then. There was a palpable sense of anti-climax in the courtroom.

Later that afternoon, the bartering between the two legal teams began in earnest as they tried to strike a deal. With the defence team's horizons considerably narrowed, the prosecution would not accept a plea of manslaughter. The insanity plea was out, given the amended psychiatrist reports. But while the emergence of the 'memo' document suggesting a plan to kill his mother posed a formidable barrier for the defence, it was also understood by the prosecution that if the opposing team fought its admissibility tooth and nail, it could delay the trial by weeks.

McEntee's offer was one plea of murder for Bridie Gargan, with the Dónal Dunne plea being dropped. The advantage from the defence's point of view was that Macarthur's prospects of an earlier release would be increased if he was convicted of one rather than two murders. It would mean he could arguably be in a position to apply to the parole board after seven years.

McEntee's whole strategy was to get the case disposed of quickly. It had, after all, been less than six months since the crimes had been committed. Ending it now would help quell some of the public hype. A guilty plea would mean there would be no hearing, no witnesses, no evidence, no grieving relatives following the proceedings over many weeks. More than anything else, it meant the jury – and the public – would be spared from the gory details of the extreme violence used. It was as neat a solution as he could hope for.

But what was in that deal for the prosecution? It had a nailed-on case if it proceeded and a guilty verdict for murder was a certainty in one case, and a very high probability in the other. The DPP agreed in the end to what McEntee was looking for. The accused would plead guilty to the murder of Bridie Gargan, in exchange for a *nolle prosequi* in the Dunne case. During his many years as DPP, Eamonn Barnes never spoke publicly about any of his decisions and the reasoning behind them. He never wavered from that policy. The reason he agreed to that course of action has never been explained. All one can rely on is the strongest supposition, that a guilty plea to one murder gave the prosecution the certain outcome that they wished for and also saved the state the expense of a very costly trial.

But in the cut and thrust of their bartering, there was one crucial issue that did not seem to have been considered by either of the legal teams: the impact that a *nolle prosequi* – the effective quashing of the Dunne case – would have on Dónal Dunne's family and on wider public perception.

Nor did they foresee that there would be widespread belief among the public that the trial was shut down because powerful people in the state had *something* to hide.

As Macarthur was led into the Four Courts for day two of the trial, the Round Hall was again jammed with gardaí, reporters and the public. Again, the accused looked straight ahead, locking eyes with no one, his countenance detached.

Gardener Paddy Byrne watched from his place on the public bench, again waiting to be called. The previous day, Paddy had recognised the killer as soon as he was led in, flanked by two guards. Despite the bow ties and the clean-shaven appearance, it was unmistakably the same man who had stared at Byrne while they grappled with the replica gun, and who shouted, "Get fucking back or I'll put a bullet through your head."

Byrne was nervous, despite having prepped for this moment. "I just did not know how it would go," he said. As it would transpire, his nerves were misplaced, as neither he nor anyone else would get called to the stand.

Prosecuting counsel Harry Hill stood up and informed the court that only the Bridie Gargan murder would be dealt with for the time being.

Macarthur was asked, "How say you to the charge?" He replied "guilty" in a firm voice.

Hill asked that the Dónal Dunne charge, and other charges, be adjourned until July. He added: "On this I do not anticipate that these will be proceeded with."

The deal had been done. The Dunne charges were going to be dropped. Yet this was the first moment that his brother Christy Dunne, his father, and his siblings learned of it. As the court proceedings continued, they grappled with this devastating news.

McEntee told the court that he appreciated that the sentence for murder was mandatory, but he would like to call psychiatrist Dr Ivor Browne to give expert evidence.

Though McEntee did not state it openly, the purpose of this gambit was to put it on the record that the savagery displayed by Macarthur the previous summer was an aberration, the result of an irrational mindset, driven by his obsessive worry about losing his fortune. The psychiatrist would say that Macarthur was no longer in that state of mind, and was unlikely to reoffend. The report would be available to the authorities in the future when they came to consider releasing him.

Judge McMahon would not allow it, but granted an application by McEntee to have the report included in the record of the trial. Therefore, it would help Macarthur's case in future.

Prosecuting lawyer Harry Hill stood up to ask permission to set out the background to the case. He wanted to call the head of the murder squad, Det Supt John Courtney, to describe the gist of the case. The purpose of the set-piece was to outline to the public what Macarthur had done and to extol the lives of the two innocent people who died at his hands. It would also help to knock some of the conspiracy theories on the head, that suggested the innocent victims were embroiled in any of the gay conspiracy myths that had huge currency among the public.

Judge McMahon peremptorily refused the request, saying such a summary would only be necessary if the court had a discretion in imposing sentence. "In this case the sentence is mandatory," he said curtly. By the strict letter of the law he was correct, but his decision showed a tin ear to the court of public opinion.

The judge then asked Macarthur to stand. He told him: "The offence to which you have pleaded guilty involves, in law, only one sentence which I must now impose on you: penal servitude for life."

The sentence was imposed, and with that, the most prominent murder trial in the history of the Irish state was over and done with, in eight short minutes.

That should have been the end of it, the moment when Macarthur began his long wait for the headlines to fade, for the mentions to dwindle, and for him to return partially to the obscurity from which he came.

It was never going to play out like that, though. The *nolle prosequi* – designed to save him – would turn out to be a curse.

# 42

## HAUGHEY GETS BUG-BITTEN

"HAUGHEY ON BRINK OF RESIGNATION" *Irish Press* headline

Meanwhile, in Haughey's camp, the implications of the garda investigation into the phone-tapping incident were explosive. There were no national security considerations to justify the taps. This was Stasi-type eavesdropping to collect dirt on perceived enemies of the state. It was a scandal and there was a huge political price to pay. Minister for Justice Michael Noonan told Garda Commissioner Patrick McLaughlin, and the officer who authorised the taps, Deputy Commissioner Joe Ainsworth, that they had no choice but to resign.

On 20 January 1983, only eight days after Macarthur's murder conviction, Noonan held a press conference in which he disclosed the details of the investigation into the illegal tapping.

A former English teacher with a passion for Shakespeare, Noonan knew the value of drama. He employed a slow and deadpan delivery that imbued his statements with gravity and menace. No one was left in any doubt that the villains of the piece were former justice minister Seán Doherty and, by extension, Charles Haughey.

As a grace note, Noonan also said that Doherty had arranged for garda recording equipment to be given to the outgoing Minister for Finance Ray MacSharry, to surreptitiously record a conversation with anti-Haughey Fianna Fáil colleague Martin O'Donoghue.

The revelations threw Fianna Fáil into further chaos. The situation presented an immediate and significant threat to Haughey's continued leadership of the party. For his part, Doherty willingly insisted it had been a freelance operation. But whatever the truth, few believed this was the case.

It was well known that the leaks from the cabinet all year had infuriated Haughey and he was determined to find out who was responsible. Haughey's government press secretary Frank Dunlop argued that Doherty was so blinded by his uber-loyalty that he made the decision alone, in an effort to second-guess the thinking of Haughey.

"The fact of the matter is that Charlie Haughey was bedevilled by the activities and actions of some of the people he appointed as government ministers," said Dunlop. "Whether those ministers thought they were acting in a fashion that they thought would please Charlie, or whether they thought they were acting in a way that was in the best interest of the country, is impossible to know."

The media and public consensus, however, was that Haughey

likely knew from the start and this was yet another example of a cover-up, of him ducking while using Doherty – an inexperienced politician whose reputation for crooked dealings went before him – as a patsy.

Haughey announced an internal inquiry into the bugging, chaired by an ally within the party. Both Doherty and Ray MacSharry resigned from the front bench. Haughey continued to maintain his ignorance of the scheme but the Nixonian comparisons were nonetheless drawn by the media and his opponents. This was, after all, less than a decade after similar subterfuge in Watergate had led to the impeachment of a US president.

Every day there were more revelations about the phone-tapping, and there was open scepticism about Haughey's claim he knew nothing of it. "Haughey To Be Quizzed on Taps" ran the main headline in the *Evening Herald* on 22 January, placing Haughey very much in the frame.

Within party ranks, rumblings were afoot and a de facto leadership race had already started. Haughey and his supporters knew he was about to face his third heave in 12 months.

Haughey's bitter rival, Des O'Malley, began openly canvassing, as did a number of Haughey supporters, including Michael O'Kennedy and Gerard Collins. There was a growing sense among his TD colleagues that Haughey was on the verge of resigning as head of Fianna Fáil and would do so on that Thursday, 27 January.

Such was the certainty that this would come to pass that day, the *Irish Press*, which was seen as Fianna Fáil's in-house newspaper, ran a two-page political obituary of Haughey that very morning. It ran profiles, analysis and reports on his career, as if it were over.

As a point of fact, the reverse was true. In his book *The Haughey File*, political journalist Stephen Collins wrote that in Leinster House that Thursday morning, Haughey read the morning's papers, including the offending *Irish Press* 'obituary', in the presence of his closest advisers. When he finished, he turned to them and said: "I think we'll fight the c***s."

Haughey met with his TDs later that day and was able to use the *Irish Press* stunt as a weapon against his detractors, whom he said wished to hound him out of office. "I am not going to resign on the basis of media speculation," he said defiantly, adding that he would decide his own future in his own time.

While many of his colleagues believed he would still resign, Haughey mounted an intensive rear-guard action. He mobilised the party's grass roots through the extensive network of *cumainn,* or local branches. Fianna Fáil's foot soldiers remained fervently loyal to Haughey, notwithstanding all that had happened during GUBU.

There were a number of factors that played to Haughey's advantage. The disclosure that his closest ally, Ray MacSharry, had used garda equipment to secretly record a conversation he had with Martin O'Donoghue, who was in the anti-Haughey faction of the party, was embarrassing. But MacSharry argued he had done so to protect his reputation, as O'Donoghue was effectively offering him a financial inducement to switch allegiance from Haughey. O'Donoghue denied it but many Fianna Fáil TDs sided with MacSharry's version of events.

Haughey supporters were also able to report back that those TDs who were no longer supporting him were pledging support not to O'Malley, but to Michael O'Kennedy and Gerard Collins. Haughey reckoned there was a chance of wooing some of them back.

In an interview with RTÉ, he struck a note of obstinacy: "[My supporters] want me to stay and they want me to fight on and it's for them I'm staying on ... I don't believe any small rump in the party, combined with friends in the media, should be in a position to dictate who is the leader of Fianna Fáil."

Fate intervened, however, on 1 February. Clem Coughlan, a young Fianna Fáil TD, was killed in a car crash when travelling to Dublin from his County Donegal home. A critical party meeting was due to be held that night to decide Haughey's fate. However, party chairman Jim Tunney, a key ally, peremptorily suspended the meeting until after the funeral, but did not specify a date. It looked like the funeral would allow Haughey to buy time, or indeed to put the challenge on the long finger.

His opponents were having none of it. The gambit seemed to have backfired when a petition was organised to demand the meeting be rescheduled within a few days. Forty-one TDs signed the petition, a clear majority of the party's elected representatives. The fateful meeting took place on Monday, 7 February and lasted all day.

It had been an incredibly tense week. It did not relent. The atmosphere at the meeting was fraught if never openly acrimonious.

In what was seen as a major tactical coup for Haughey's

opponents, the parliamentary party voted that the ballot would be secret. That was important as it would allow those who secretly disliked Haughey to vote against him without having to admit it publicly. For the rebels, all the signs were pointing to a change at the top.

Party chairman Jim Tunney returned to the party room at 11.15pm to announce the results. To astonished gasps, he stated that the motion to oust Haughey had been defeated by 40 votes to 33 votes. Somehow – in spite of all the odds and all the predictions – Haughey had survived. The news filtered quickly through Leinster House to the waiting politicians, officials and media, and to the large crowd of Haughey supporters who had assembled outside the gates of the complex.

Haughey emerged through the front door of Leinster House followed by supporters and members of the media. It was a cold night and light snow was just beginning to fall. "Take me to my people," he proclaimed, walking over towards the cheering crowds outside on the street, before shaking their hands through the rails. He was wearing a light suit but seemed oblivious to the cold or the snow.

It was a moment of triumph. Little did Haughey realise at the time, it was also a stay of execution.

# 43

## SEEN AND NOT HEARD

"My first reaction when I heard about this murder in the [Phoenix] Park was that I would not even waste any money on a trial." Irene Macarthur

On 16 January 1983, the Sunday after Malcolm Macarthur's trial, an interview with Irene Macarthur was broadcast on RTÉ. Well-known broadcaster David Hanly had written her a polite letter, in an elegant cursive hand, seeking an interview, which he dropped through her letterbox. Unexpectedly, she agreed.

It made for compelling listening, with several arresting moments. Irene came across as brutally honest, spontaneous and with no compunction in sharing her forthright opinions, or the messy details of her marriage break-up. But there was something unfiltered about her responses, a detachment suggestive of someone more in a commentator role than that of a close family member. This came across forcibly in an astonishing moment when Hanly asked her did she believe in capital punishment for murder.

Mrs Macarthur: I'm afraid I do. And I have always done so. Malcolm has always known that I believed in capital punishment.

Hanly: When a murder is committed, you feel that whoever committed it should be hanged?

Mrs Macarthur: Well, I have the old-fashioned belief, what I was taught as a child in terms of my religious upbringing, that I was taught a life for a life, that comes into the Bible does it not?

Hanly: So you believe that your own son should be hanged?

Mrs Macarthur: Well, of course, it's very difficult to say that now but I remember my first reaction when I heard about this murder in the [Phoenix] Park that I would not even waste any money on a trial.

Irene spoke extensively about her son's childhood, his gentle nature, his love of books and academia. But she also cemented a trope that had come to be commonly held: that Malcolm had been a lonely and neglected child. It was her comment to Hanly in that interview that children should be seen and not heard, that her time with him each day was limited as she focused on her gardening and horses, while a "girl" came in to teach and look after him.

She also divulged that Macarthur only told her about Brenda Little, and their son, in late 1975, several months after Colin was born. She did not meet Brenda until the following

Easter. It was, by any yardstick, an unusual relationship with her only son.

Hanly broached the widespread rumour that her son was gay, and she responded in her forthright way that he might be bisexual. It's not thought that she had any evidence for this. In her detached style, she appears to be reflecting on changing societal mores rather than knowledge of her son's personal life.

She also spoke at length about the break-up of her marriage, saying that it occurred when Malcolm was a teenager and also coincided with growing tension between himself and his father. But she dismissed the possibility that this had a bearing on what he had done.

"No doubt about it, he saw violence at an early age. I'm sure there are other children that have been brought up in very violent atmospheres and this sort of thing hasn't happened," she said.

Irene Macarthur told Hanly that during her weekly visits to Malcolm in prison, they had never discussed his crimes. When asked why he had committed them, she could not hazard a guess. It was beyond her comprehension.

Hanly also asked her about the plot to kill her with a faulty electric kettle [it was actually an electric fire]. In a roundabout way she acknowledged it might be true.

"I tried to put two and two together about a lot of things," she mused, "but I didn't come out with any concrete proof. Like other things in life, everything is possible."

Widespread media coverage and commentary was generated on the back of the extraordinary interview. Irene's comments that she unconditionally believed in a "life for a life" in murder, in the knowledge that her own son had been convicted of murder, was one of those compelling radio moments where people stopped everything else they were doing to listen to what was being said.

Irene turned out not to be media shy. Ten days later, she was interviewed in *The Irish Press*. She said that her son was, as an adult, a deep person, and admitted that she sometimes struggled to understand him.

"He keeps himself very much to himself. He once told me that when he died he wanted to be cremated and his ashes scattered over the Greek Archipelago. That's straight out of Oscar Wilde."

Irene, in a manner worthy of Wilde's infamous character Lady Bracknell, said her main concern now was how her son would cope in prison. Again, she did not hold back. "Honestly I often think it would have been better for him if he had jumped from the balcony of that flat in Dalkey when he was arrested," she said. "If he needed money I could have let him have thirty thousand at any time."

Her final comments were piteous: "I will never know why he did such a dreadful thing. And yet I will always love him as a mother loves any son. I must stick by him in these lonely years and accept that he will never be free again in my lifetime."

# 44

# MACARTHUR'S
# LOST DECADES

"He realises he can't undo anything and he doesn't believe he
can do anything for the Dunne family." Fellow Mountjoy
Prison inmate of Macarthur's

As Charles Haughey survived to see another day, for Malcolm
Macarthur, life as he knew it was well and truly over. The
silk cravats and bespoke jackets were exchanged for standard
prison clothing of shirts and ill-fitting trousers, as he settled
into Basement B of Mountjoy Prison to serve a sentence of
indeterminate length.

In his first months there, reports were leaked to the media
from prison sources and from friends describing how he
was coping with the new regime. Several alluded to him
planning to write a book and a memoir on his life that would
disclose everything. He would then set up a trust for Brenda
Little and Colin, who would be financially secure from the

proceeds. If what those sources were saying was true, they were based on hot air.

Brenda was a regular visitor then, and for many years afterwards. She would continue to visit Macarthur during all his years of incarceration, along with their son. She also continued her close friendship with Paddy Connolly.

Macarthur would spend a year in Mountjoy before being transferred to Arbour Hill Prison in Dublin 7, located on a smallish site near the River Liffey. Until 1973, Arbour Hill was a military prison attached to Collins Barracks, but was opened as a civilian prison that year. It was more modern than Mountjoy, with a three-wing cell block and a large yard. Many of its inmates were older, serving long-term sentences. Most of the state's convicted sex offenders were imprisoned there.

Paddy McEntee's strategy of a single murder conviction – in addition to Dr Ivor Browne's report stating the danger of reoffending was very low – had been designed to minimise the term of Macarthur's "life" sentence to nine or ten years' imprisonment.

Macarthur fulfilled his part of it. During his time in jail, he was a model prisoner and never got into trouble. He was unfailingly polite to all he encountered, be they officers or fellow inmates.

Arbour Hill had printing works which produced many government papers. It acquired an elaborate new computerised system, which nobody knew how to operate. Macarthur studied the manuals and mastered the printer and ended up running the printing operations there for many years.

Despite his exemplary prison behaviour and his legal team's

strategy, by 1992, on the tenth anniversary of the murders, Macarthur remained in prison. At that time, I spoke to his solicitor, who stated that Macarthur had been rehabilitated and was no longer a danger to society. However, the notoriety of the case had not faded in the public memory.

Dónal Dunne's brother Christy, who had mounted a campaign for justice in the aftermath of the quashing of the case, was regularly interviewed by the media. He vented his frustration at how the whole legal process had been shrouded in secrecy, without any reference to the Dunne family. He persevered with a long, painful and ultimately unsuccessful campaign to get the *nolle prosequi* overturned and achieve justice for his brother.

The profile of the case remained high. The media would mark every important anniversary – five years, ten years – with extensive reports and interviews. It meant there was no prospect of Macarthur being released within the timeframe set out by McEntee as part of his trial strategy.

In any instance, a parole board recommending release was only the first step to freedom for a convicted killer. The decision ultimately rested with the minister for justice of the day. And ministers were elected politicians, after all. They would have been fully aware of the public reaction to an infamous killer being released after only a decade. Successive ministers rejected successive applications.

In later years in Arbour Hill, a new printer came into the prison. Macarthur "retired" and spent the rest of his time there in the library reading science books and watching educational videos on maths, physics, biology and astronomy. He was to spend 18 years in Arbour Hill before being transferred back to nearby Mountjoy Prison around the turn of the millennium.

Macarthur's new residence was the training unit at Mountjoy, where prisoners were sent to prepare for release. Now in his mid-50s, with almost 20 years in jail served, he had well exceeded the tariff of most convicted murderers. Even then, there was no indication he would be released any time soon.

In 2002, to coincide with the 20th anniversary of the "GUBU murders", journalist Paul Cullen of *The Irish Times* spoke to several former prisoners to get a sense of what Macarthur was like. The ensuing article gave fascinating insight into a man whose outward demeanour divided opinion: aloof, arrogant, disdainful to some; shy and reticent to others.

One prisoner who knew him said Macarthur was "constantly filled with a sense of horror" at what he did. "He is absolutely unrelenting in refusing to allow anyone to suggest there was anything excusable in what he did. But he realises he can't undo anything, and he doesn't believe he can do anything for the Dunne family."

Macarthur's fellow inmate was also adamant the killer was never mad. "Malcolm figured out what he had done long before he was sentenced. He snapped out of it [his murderous intentions] on the night he was arrested. Ever since, he has known that he's not entitled to his life."

In general, Macarthur did not socialise with many prisoners, but would write letters on their behalf, or help them fill out application forms. He had his own cell and had use of a laptop computer. As he'd done in Arbour Hill, he spent a lot of time in the library studying science, mostly astronomy and astrophysics.

One colourful detail was that he liked to watch the TV show *Who Wants To Be A Millionaire?*, and was good at answering the more difficult questions. His main visitors were Brenda and Colin, by now an adult in his mid-20s, as well as his elderly mother.

In 2002, Macarthur was transferred to Shelton Abbey, an open prison in County Wicklow with extensive lands. Ironically, in very different circumstances, he had visited Shelton Abbey as a child with his parents as guests of its then owner Lord Wicklow, who was hosting a "country house cricket" game.

For the Dunne family, time had not healed the sense of injustice they felt. In a 2005 TG4 documentary, *Scannal*, Christy Dunne recalled the trauma of the January 1983 *nolle prosequi,* and how the sense of grievance had lingered for him, for his siblings and for his late father.

"For my father to have to go in [to court] and observe it, I think he took it to his grave. It was a huge disappointment to him. He had lost his son and the state did not even have the decency to explain to him why that had happened."

Even 23 years later, Dunne did not think it was over. "It's probably unfinished business and will remain unfinished business until such time as he is charged, or he stays in prison for the rest of his days. In terms of him being released, that would be a very dramatic event."

At the end of August 2008, Macarthur's mother Irene died at the age of 86. Her family had once been "Castle Catholics", living in a large house with vast tracts of land. Her final home was a modest bungalow in Mullingar but she was happy there and had good neighbours.

Her only son was released from Shelton Abbey for the weekend to attend the funeral in Mullingar and the burial in Trim, only two miles from his childhood home of Breemount. He laid twelve red roses on her grave.

In terms of length, the sentence was now creeping towards *Shawshank Redemption* territory, despite mounting recommendations from the parole board in the previous decade that he be released, all rejected by politicians. The Fianna Fáil Minister for Defence, Willie O'Dea, substituting for the Minister for Justice, Michael McDowell, had been asked to consider one such recommendation in 2004. (Given that McDowell had acted as one of the defence barristers with Paddy McEntee in the 1982 trial, he had to excuse himself from the decision.)

O'Dea refused to release Macarthur. After Irene Macarthur's death four years later, O'Dea told the *Irish Independent* why he had not followed the parole board's recommendation in 2004. "[Irene] was an amazing woman whose life was turned upside down by the events surrounding her son," O'Dea said. "She believed it was not safe to release him and I was told she feared for her own safety. I took that into account when I had to decide on his release, although it was not the only factor." O'Dea said he had also spoken to the families of Macarthur's victims.

In subsequent years, Macarthur was given increased periods of temporary release ahead of a more permanent liberation. The difficulty was whether any minister for justice would grasp the nettle and grant permanent release to one of the state's most infamous killers.

As a new decade turned in 2010, Macarthur was coming

up to the 30th anniversary of his incarceration, and was now one of the longest-serving prisoners in Ireland. In early 2011, there was a change of government and a new Minister for Justice, Alan Shatter, was appointed.

Shatter was not a typical politician. A solicitor by training, he was one of the few Irish politicians whose decisions were not swayed by public opinion. Soon after his appointment, Shatter approved a structured programme of temporary release for Macarthur.

Then, in the autumn of 2012, he approved Macarthur to be released from prison on licence.

"I have been at all times conscious of the dreadful events of 1982 and of their impact on family members," he said in a Department of Justice statement, which also stated that the families of the victims had been contacted and informed of the release.

On Monday morning, 17 September 2012, Malcolm Macarthur packed his sparse belongings into a bag and was taken by prison van out of Shelton Abbey to Arklow, where he got public transport to Dublin.

Thirty years and one month after being taken into custody in 6 Carnsore, Pilot View, Dalkey, Malcolm Macarthur was a free man again. He was now 66 years of age and had spent almost half of his life in prison.

# 45

# AFTERMATH

"Have you ever met a murderer?" Malcolm Macarthur

Charles Haughey would never fully shake off the events of 1982, a year that would long be remembered for its turbulence and horror. But he had survived GUBU and its attendant scandals, two heaves and a general election defeat. His mood was one of defiance. He was still leader, he said in February 1983, "despite everything that a largely hostile media and political opponents at home and abroad could do to damage not only me but the great party and traditions of Fianna Fáil".

After five years in opposition, Haughey would return to government in 1987. Over two successive terms as taoiseach, during that time he took the kind of tough economic decisions he had vacillated on between 1980 and 1982. It was his most successful spell as a politician. He unveiled ambitious projects like the creation of the International Financial Services Centre in the Dublin docklands, which became an engine for the state's recovery. The economy rapidly moved from recession to strong growth.

But in 1992, the curse of GUBU again hovered into view.

After falling from grace after the phone-tapping admissions in January 1983, former justice minister Seán Doherty was himself on a comeback trail. He was now a senator and also an ally of Albert Reynolds, a senior minister in Haughey's government who had ambitions of replacing Haughey as leader.

Doherty decided to act as a stalking horse for Reynold in his efforts to oust Haughey. He decided to deploy damaging allegations against Haughey he had stored in secret for a decade that could destabilise the taoiseach. The vehicle he chose to communicate his message was unusual. He appeared as a guest on a popular late-night light entertainment show on RTÉ called *Nighthawks*, which never featured politics. It was recorded on 10 January 1992.

Within seconds of being introduced by the presenter, Doherty turned to the phone-tapping revelations from a decade before, and made an observation that on the face of it seemed very opaque: "There was a decision taken in cabinet that the prevention of leaking of matters in cabinet must be stopped and as minister for justice I had a direct responsibility to do that."

The presenter of *Nighthawks* had no understanding of the weight of what was said. If truth be told, it was said in such a roundabout way that the impact also seems to have been lost on political journalists. But it wasn't lost on Haughey's opponents among the Fianna Fáil ranks. The following day, political journalists began receiving calls from Albert Reynolds' supporters saying that Doherty had said something significant the previous evening on *Nighthawks*.

Haughey had survived as leader in 1983 by denying any knowledge of the phone-tapping, and Doherty supported his version of events at the time. What Doherty had said the previous night on national television suggested the opposite was true: that throughout 1982, Haughey knew *from the start* that the phones of the two journalists, Geraldine Kennedy and Bruce Arnold, were tapped.

It took two weeks for him to say it out bluntly. At a press conference in Dublin on 25 January 1992, Doherty claimed he had taken the full rap back in January 1983 out of a sense of misguided loyalty to his leader.

All hell broke loose. Haughey denied the allegation categorically and claimed Doherty had been put up to making the allegation by Reynolds as part of his campaign to oust him from the leadership.

He accused the former justice minister of lacking in credibility and of flip-flopping from one version of events to another.

Despite the robustness of Haughey's denials, the very fact the allegation was made was politically damaging. The truth of the matter has never been definitively resolved.

"This was the great cause célèbre in many ways of Haughey, which sums up his entire career," said Haughey biographer Gary Murphy. "Did he know that his minister for justice was tapping the phones of two esteemed journalists critical of him? Some of those who knew him said he was completely shocked that such an activity could happen under his watch.

But there are others who think he knew everything that was going on."

Doherty's accusation alone, however, was enough to precipitate the end of Haughey's career. On 11 February 1992, at the age of 66, Haughey stepped down as taoiseach. He quoted *Othello* in his short valedictory speech: "I have done the state some service, they know't." In the Dáil, he got a standing ovation from his Fianna Fáil colleagues. He ended his short speech by saying he would focus on his "books and bucolic pursuits".

That he did, but not for as long as he envisaged. Haughey all but disappeared from view for five years, but scandal would eventually come back to dog him when, in April 1997, journalist Sam Smyth broke a story in the *Irish Independent*. He revealed that, in the early 1990s, led to the stunning revelation that businessman Ben Dunne had handed Haughey over £1 million to help him out of financial debt.

Smyth had been following the battle for control of the Dunnes Stores empire between Ben Dunne and some of his siblings. During the course of this battle, Ben Dunne's family learned that he had decided, without reference to others, to give Haughey a dig-out of over £1 million, paid for by cheques drawn on Dunnes Stores accounts. The secret payments to Haughey were disclosed in an internal report, drawn up by international accounting firm PricewaterhouseCoopers, which was reported on by Sam Smyth and Matt Cooper of the *Irish Independent*, and Cliff Taylor of *The Irish Times*. It was another of those rare moments, so characteristic of Haughey's career, when people were stopped in their tracks by the news.

Meanwhile, at the end of 1996, a tribunal of inquiry had

begun investigating the former taoiseach's personal finances. A picture emerged of a politician whose whole career and high-spending lifestyle had been bankrolled by wealthy businessmen and sympathisers, to the tune of tens of millions of punts. Haughey's standing collapsed and he was disowned by Fianna Fáil, and excoriated by the media, his political opponents and the public, which turned against him. For a while, there was a possibility he would face a criminal trial. The Moriarty Tribunal eventually reported that the payments he received were corrupt. His disgrace was final.

"His life had been ruined. He lived the last few years of his life as a relative recluse in his Gandon mansion, Abbeville," said Gary Murphy.

Haughey died in 2006 at the age of 80 from prostate cancer. He left behind a mixed legacy, with opinion sharply divided on whether his influence on Irish society had been positive or baleful.

"There is a part of me that agrees with the view that he was inclined to end up corrupting so much of what he touched," said journalist Olivia O'Leary. "Those who were his close followers took their lead from that. That is a dreadful, dreadful, legacy to leave behind in terms of politics."

His political achievements included the peace process; stoking economic recovery; the International Financial Services Centre in Dublin; free travel for pensioners and the disabled; the Succession Act (which gave women equal standing for the first time in relation to inheritances); the abolition of the death penalty; and support for arts and culture. Against that there were many negatives and personal failings. These tended to dominate public discourse about

Haughey in the decade after his death; but that perhaps is changing a little, with some commentators taking a long view on his political legacy.

"He is complex," said biographer Gary Murphy. "He is fascinating. He is deeply flawed. Over everything else, his pursuit of power probably damned him in the end."

After stepping down as attorney general in 1982, Paddy Connolly returned to the Bar, and the semi-anonymous work of a litigation barrister. There was a tradition that former attorneys general were given the option of becoming judges of the superior courts. That invitation was never extended to Paddy Connolly.

In public, he was phlegmatic about the events which led to his resignation and the ensuing fallout, but his nephew Stephen believed it had a deep impact on him. "It lingered for a long time, possibly for the rest of his life," Stephen said. "I do remember talking to him in subsequent years, there was an understanding that the door to a Supreme Court appointment was not being closed when he resigned. But clearly it was closed."

The Macarthur affair also affected Connolly's personal relationship with Haughey. Once the closest of friends, for 20 years afterwards they rarely spoke or socialised.

"The nature of that relationship changed substantially," said Stephen. "Paddy would have still had high regard for Haughey's intellectual abilities. But on the politics side of it, no."

There was a reconciliation of sorts when Haughey was diagnosed with cancer in 1996. He sent Paddy Connolly a

Christmas card and Connolly responded. They again began corresponding on a semi-regular basis.

Paddy Connolly practised at the Bar until he was 82, and died in 2016, aged 88. He had maintained a lifetime friendship with Brenda Little. Generous and open to the end, when Paddy died, Brenda was included amongst the beneficiaries of his will. He left her €100,000 in cash, and his full interest in an apartment in Ranelagh, a well-to-do suburb of Dublin. He also left her son Colin a sum of €75,000 in cash and a valuable collection of cigarette cards that the barrister had been collecting since he was a child.

Stephen Connolly says of the friendship that prevailed up to Connolly's death, "He would have helped Brenda and she would have helped him. They remained very close. He was an intensely loyal person and a man of principle. He was an extraordinary human being and a real Christian. His friendship was always with Brenda, it wasn't with Malcolm."

Stephen said that Paddy had also known their son, Colin, since he was a child, and remained friendly with him as an adult.

Indubitably, said Stephen, the impacts of GUBU have lingered to this day within the Connolly family.

"The whole thing was handled badly from a political point of view. The political masters should have been dictating more clearly to Paddy what they expected him to do. The taoiseach should have been clearer on it [when both men spoke by telephone]. It took a long time [for him to be ordered back from his holiday].

"The reality is that he should never have gone to New

York. He should have come home from London. Paddy was oblivious to that type of thing. The politics of it wasn't on his radar. It should have been on other people's radars."

Paddy Byrne, the gardener who witnessed the brutal murder of Bridie Gargan, is now 85 years old and still lives near the Phoenix Park. He said for some time after the murder, he found it hard to sleep.

"It affected me for a good year, a year and a half. It did not affect me mentally, but I was always thinking about it, could not get it out of my mind. Eventually as time went on, I stopped thinking about it. I was delighted that he was caught."

The two garda detectives centrally involved in the investigation, Tony Hickey and John O'Mahony, went on to have distinguished careers in An Garda Síochána, both retiring with the rank of assistant commissioner.

One of the other detectives involved in the investigation was John O'Mahony's young colleague, Frank Hand. In many of the photographs taken after Macarthur's arrest, Hand can be seen among the colleagues taking the suspect to and from court. The pictures show a young man of stocky build with fair curly hair.

Two years later, on 10 August 1984, Hand and Detective Garda Michael Dowd were escorting a cash delivery to Drumree Post Office in County Meath. They were attacked by Provisional IRA bank robbers, who opened fire on the two gardaí. Detective Hand was badly injured and subsequently died of his wounds. He was 26 years of age.

And what of Malcolm Macarthur?

In one sense, Christy Dunne's long and fruitless campaign to overturn the *nolle prosequi* for his brother Dónal achieved its aim by keeping the case, and the notorious killer, in the public domain, thus ensuring that successive ministers for justice would refuse to order Macarthur's release.

When Alan Shatter went where others refused to go, Macarthur emerged after three decades of incarceration, having obtained the dubious status of being one of the state's longest-serving prisoners. After his release in 2012, he lived for some time in a small house in a working-class suburb of south Dublin. People encountered him out walking along Dún Laoghaire pier, not far from where he'd stayed over three decades before. His son Colin, an academic, was now living in London. Macarthur and Brenda Little never lived together after his release from prison, but still met regularly.

After some time, he moved into a modest apartment in Dublin city centre. Macarthur received a small inheritance from his mother but relies wholly on the state old age pension.

Today, Malcolm Macarthur is 77 years of age. His hair, still wavy and thick, is now silver. He is to be regularly spotted around the city, mostly in bookshops or on the campus of Trinity, which he frequented as a man-about-town in the 1970s. Still a dapper dresser, he no longer wears bow ties, although he sometimes wears cravats. He is always well-groomed, wearing a jacket, a tie and well-polished shoes.

Given his notoriety, one might think Macarthur would keep a low profile, but the opaque sense of disconnect so evident in his nature during the events of 1982 still reveals itself from time to time.

In 2017, he caused consternation when he appeared at the

launch of a book written by Alan Shatter, the former minister who had ordered his release, at Hodges Figgis bookshop on Dublin's Dawson Street. Buttonholed by *Irish Independent* journalist Liam Collins, Macarthur said he had come because of Shatter's decision to release him. "I have an absolute regard for him, he knows the law," he said. "I introduced myself to him. He did not know who I was."

It was not the only time Macarthur turned up to an unwelcome space. After Paddy Connolly's death in 2016, he arrived at the removal for the late attorney general. Stephen Connolly was horrified to see him there and told him he was not welcome. Macarthur left without demurring.

Journalist Peter Murtagh was at a cultural event organised by *The Irish Times* in Dublin when he was approached by a distinguished-looking silver-haired gentleman.

The stranger addressed him with a question: "Peter Murtagh?"

"Yes," replied Murtagh.

"Malcolm Macarthur," he said in a grand accent. Murtagh and Macarthur ended up having a strange conversation about the events of 1982.

Then there was the time in 2019 when Macarthur approached a pair of crime novelists at a literary festival in a rural Irish town. Liz Nugent was with fellow crime writer Jane Casey when they were stopped on the street by an elderly man. Nugent first thought it was former Anglo Irish Bank chairman Seán FitzPatrick, but as they spoke, the man's true identity dawned. Then came a startling question.

"Have you ever met a murderer?" Macarthur asked.

When the authors replied that they hadn't, his response was direct and chilling. "You have met one now," he said.

Nugent tweeted after the encounter: "I recognised him. And called him a murderer to his face during the course of a very polite conversation. Bizarre."

In 2022, Haughey's former government press secretary Frank Dunlop and his wife Sheila were standing on the banks of the Liffey in Dublin city centre watching a display by the Air Corps overhead. A man who had been standing nearby came over. He addressed Dunlop by saying: "A friend of mine was once a very good friend of your boss."

Dunlop had never met or seen Macarthur in person before but immediately cottoned on to who he was. Slightly taken aback by the strange approach, Dunlop didn't linger beyond a politely awkward exchange before returning to view the jets flying low overhead.

Periodically over the years, Macarthur's name has been dragged into other investigations, or he has been accused of being involved in other iniquitous activity. In the weeks following their discovery of the plot to kill his mother, detectives also reviewed the circumstances surrounding the death of Macarthur's father more than a decade before that, but there was no evidence uncovered to suggest Daniel had died from anything other than natural causes.

Over the decades, Macarthur's name has also frequently been mentioned in relation to the murder of Charles Self, the Scottish man cravenly stabbed to death in January 1982, whose killer was never found.

In 2009, a garda cold case investigator presented a paper on the Self murder that suggested that the original investigation team had been wrong to focus all its attention on a male prostitute as the killer. The possibility was also raised that the killer might not have been the man with collar-length fair hair in the taxi but a second man, who gained entry to the mews house sometime during the course of the night.

As I described in Chapter 33, on the night of Self's murder, the house guest Bertie Tyrer heard voices downstairs, and was then awoken after 2am by a man opening his bedroom door.

"Sorry, wrong room," the man said in a posh Anglo accent.

Like Self, Tyrer was a designer working for RTÉ and a skilful artist. He drew a sketch for gardaí of the man he had momentarily seen at the door. The sketch was never released to the public, but Bill Maher, a good friend of Self's, was shown it by gardaí in 1982. He said Tyrer's pen-and-ink sketch showed a man with dark curly hair.

When Macarthur was arrested later that year, comparisons were invariably made, including by gardaí who repeatedly asked one of Macarthur's potential victims, Harry Bieling, if he knew Charles Self. But within days of his arrest, the garda leading the Self investigation, DSI Hubert Reynolds, categorically ruled out Macarthur as a suspect.

Macarthur was not ruled out by others, however, including Self's friends. The sketch bore an uncanny likeness to him. This was buttressed by Tyrer's observation that the man at the bedroom door had a West-Brit accent.

As against that, Tyrer had got no more than a glance of the man at the doorway of the bedroom, with the light of the hallway behind him. He had only heard him utter a single sentence. By contrast, the taxi driver who drove Self to Monkstown gave a detailed description of the young fair-haired man with whom he shared his taxi. Moreover, Macarthur was not gay and had not socialised in Bartley Dunne's since the mid-1970s.

Still, the theory has persisted over the years, notwithstanding any probative evidence. Such accusations became an occupational hazard for Macarthur, given his status as a life prisoner and convicted murderer. The ongoing accusations that Macarthur has found himself subject to also partly derive from the conscious decision he made back in 1982 not to make any attempt to explain, or to apologise. All that has made him something of an enigma. It has left many unanswered questions hanging in the air, none more central and baffling than this one: Why on earth did he do what he did?

# 46

# A MARK ON
# WESTERN EUROPE

"They thought an awful mistake was being made, that we had caught the wrong man for these awful crimes." Tony Hickey, murder squad detective

Human memory is fallible. More than 40 years have passed since the brutal events of the summer of 1982. Different people whom I spoke to over my research remembered events in different ways. Sometimes it was hard to reconcile those differing narratives. It was in keeping. Since the very beginning of events being made public in 1982, there were unreliable commentators who created myths, or large suppositions that hung on thread-like events or facts. Seemingly trivial anecdotes from Macarthur's childhood were telescoped into vast character judgements. His mother, prone to saying the first thing that came into her head, could be unreliable. The passage of time, the gaps, the conspiracies, the myths, his many years of silence, have all conspired to make explanations as to why Malcolm Macarthur did what he did elusive.

But it is human instinct nonetheless to grapple with the motives of one who commits that most extreme of crimes from which there is no way back – the ending of human life.

The Macarthur murders were marked by a ruthlessness that did not abate even after two callous acts in quick succession, as Macarthur immediately set about planning further violent crimes, intent on satisfying his need for money. His methods were as shambolic and baffling as his approach was barbaric. Bridie Gargan was not resisting him stealing her vehicle. If Macarthur had driven off and ditched Bridie's car after it had got him to his Edenderry destination, it was unlikely he would ever have been caught. What made him force her to get into it? What gave rise to his vicious attack with a lump hammer?

Similarly, with Dónal Dunne. Once he had the gun, Macarthur could have threatened the young man, stolen his car and driven off with a high degree of confidence he would not face any consequences. What was the need to shoot him?

On a cool day in February 2022, some forty years on from that fateful summer, I met former detectives Tony Hickey and John O'Mahony in the Phoenix Park to consider the events and those unsettled questions.

We sat outside a café near an artificial lake, well populated by mallards and moorhens. It is a spot not far from where Bridie Gargan was brutally attacked by Malcolm Macarthur on that tragic summer's day in 1982. The two detectives, now retired, spoke for over three hours about a case that was career-defining for both of them.

They are natural storytellers: Hickey with his mellifluous Kerry accent and prodigious memory for detail; O'Mahony with his wry reflections on the challenges the case presented for a young and inexperienced detective.

Towards the end of the interview, we turned to the subject of the killer, his motive and his personality. Hickey began by describing Macarthur as a suspect who was "well outside the rules of the game that you would normally encounter. Criminals do things that normally make sense. In your wildest dreams, you wouldn't imagine that somebody in an attempt to acquire a car – which fellows on the street could hot-wire in minutes – would kill to do it."

Hickey paused for what seemed like a long time, the calls of waterfowl in the nearby lake ringing out in the background. "You know," he finally said, with incredulity in his tone, "he would have come across as an absolute gentleman. We interviewed people who had known him. They could not believe it. They thought an awful mistake was being made, that we had caught the wrong man for these awful crimes."

It is this paradox which makes the case so fascinating to this day. Why did this shy, bookish aristocrat who had until then showed no violent disposition go on such a brutal rampage? Malcolm Macarthur had led an exemplary life. He had never had any brush with the law, not even a parking fine to his name.

Many people who knew Macarthur were utterly baffled by what he did. Soon after his conviction, a relative in California where he had stayed as a student in the 1960s spoke in public about his shock on finding out he had murdered two people. Norman MacLeod was Macarthur's first cousin, a son of his aunt. He was one of his two relatives living in the US; the other was his father's older brother Jack, then 79, who Macarthur had moved to California to live with when he was 17, after he had left Breemount, having had a serious physical fight with his father. Macarthur and his cousin Norman had gotten to know each other while Malcolm was studying at University of California, Davis between 1966 and 1967.

Norman MacLeod remembered the young Malcolm as "most cultivated and educated. He was very quiet, somewhat withdrawn, even. My view is shared by other members of the family: that the crimes themselves were so bizarre and so totally out of character that he was obviously insane at the time he did them."

However, the experts had said otherwise. The legal test for insanity – known as the M'Naghten rule – states that the defendant must either not have known what they were doing, or must not have known that it was wrong at the time the act was committed. This had never been the case for Malcolm Macarthur.

The question of why has confounded people for over four decades and has spawned much speculation. Some of the nexus narratives point to his childhood and the trope of a silent, lonely and neglected child, a helpless witness to the disintegration of his parents' marriage. All of those who knew Malcolm as a boy related a variation of an anecdote that put him walking along the tree-lined avenue at Breemount, ignored by both parents as they separately sped past him in their cars after a heated argument.

It was certainly not a seamless childhood and his parents – at times – were selfish and self-preoccupied. His mother made no secret of the violence between his parents that he witnessed from an early age, or of the physical altercations he had with his father as a teenager, including the one where his father viciously bit his hand, leaving a gash that required five stitches.

In her extraordinary interview with David Hanly, Irene Macarthur had also recounted another freakish incident, this one from the year Malcolm was born, as she cast around to understand what caused her son to do what he did.

"His uncle, his father's brother-in-law, was murdered in England in 1946," Irene told Hanly. "He was a psychiatrist. There was a soldier who looked at the film *Spellbound*, with Ingrid Bergman. He copied the pattern of what happened in the film."

Directed by Alfred Hitchcock, *Spellbound* was released in 1945, the year the Second World War ended, and it was a global hit. The plot revolved around a young doctor in Vermont who suffered from amnesia and believed he had murdered a psychiatrist by shooting him dead, and had now taken his place.

Macarthur's uncle-in-law Neil MacLeod was a 52-year-old consultant psychiatrist who worked in Yorkshire. As he left his clinic one afternoon, he was accosted by a 21-year-old soldier. He made him drive to a nearby disused colliery in his own car and then shot him three times at close range, before dragging his body into bushes. He was arrested shortly afterwards and sentenced to death for the murder. The Yorkshire newspapers reported that the soldier was a fantasist "prone to romancing about his affairs". He made a death-bed confession in his prison cell that two other men had conspired in the murder. In his prison cell, he also said that he had followed the plot of *Spellbound* when killing MacLeod.

Irene Macarthur told Hanly: "I really began to wonder had Malcolm read something, seen something, heard something and decided on a pattern of attack."

It was true that the way the young soldier summarily shot Macarthur's uncle in 1946 was similar to his execution-style killing of Dónal Dunne in 1982. But there was nothing to suggest it was beyond a coincidence, as was another shared trait, that of Macarthur also being "prone to romancing about his affairs".

Irene also alluded to an untrustworthy aspect in her son's nature, suggesting an inherited trait. "In Malcolm's case, I would say that he might have been a dreamer," she said. "When you're dealing with that sort of a person, then it's just very difficult because when they tell you the truth, you just don't know what to believe . . . How you catch these people out is that they forget what they've told you and then the next time they tell you something different . . .

"I think he probably inherited this trait from his father. And that was that they got something into their minds. And when they thought about it long enough, they literally believed it themselves. His father fabricated stories to everybody. I mean, that was quite standard," she said.

When pressed by Hanly, she referred to her son frequently lying to her when asking her for money, telling her his own inheritance funds were in a bank account in France that was temporarily frozen, because a socialist government was in power.

It is interesting to note that the detectives involved in the case and Paddy Connolly's nephew, Stephen, all described him as a "Walter Mitty" type, a person with a faulty relationship with reality. That, in itself, is not a full explanation. Indeed, the character in William Thurber's short story, "The Secret Life of Walter Mitty", is harmless.

A lawyer familiar with the case, to whom I spoke in 1992, told me of Macarthur's state of mind at the time of the murders. He said he had adopted a Nietzschean view of the world and saw himself as an "*Übermensch*", or "superman". An *Übermensch*, as defined by Friedrich Nietzsche, was a person of intellectual superiority, one of the minority who did not follow the herd; an exalted, elevated being who could overcome human weaknesses and limitations, as well as social expectations and Christian morals.

"Macarthur placed himself above the moral and societal orders," said the lawyer. "He also concluded in his own mind that acts which he had committed could be undone simply by wishing them away."

Inspired by Nietzsche's writings, Macarthur could use his intellectual superiority to achieve his aim coldly, with neither remorse nor thought for the consequences of his actions. He himself rejected the notion of a "psychotic interlude" to his lawyers, and later to friends. One of those to whom he spoke said Macarthur described what happened in these terms: "It was a departure from ethics." That is chilling because it rationalised, and justified, awful crimes in a premeditated way.

It brings to mind something the notorious Irish National Liberation Army (INLA) and IRA gunman Dominic McGlinchey told me in an interview in early 1994, weeks before he himself met a violent end. Thought to be responsible for the deaths of 30 people, I asked McGlinchey what it was like to kill somebody.

"You have to desensitise yourself in order to do it," he explained, saying his mindset was focused on hitting a legitimate target. In those moments, human emotion did not come into it.

Macarthur admitted to gardaí when caught that he wanted to carry out a "cold-hearted operation" and was prepared to kill anyone who got in his way. That included some strange self-tests. The most bizarre was when he walked in and out of hotel lobbies carrying a brick to test if he had a criminal mindset. Macarthur considered himself to be generally calm but also thought himself capable of being cold in terms of emotion or sympathy to other human beings. That might have explained how he could coolly ring Dónal Dunne's house only hours after his barbaric attack on Bridie Gargan and rearrange the appointment, or that he could begin shortening the barrel of the shotgun he stole within a day of shooting Dónal Dunne dead. Killing had been built into his plan.

There were two books found in Macarthur's suitcase in the spare room of Paddy Connolly's flat which may tie in with this view, that Macarthur saw himself as Nietzschean *Übermensch* entitled to behave beyond the constraints of morality and the law. One book was *A Materialist Theory of the Mind* by celebrated Australian philosopher David Armstrong. The other was a book on forensic medicine, which suggested he was plotting to kill people. In his book on well-known Irish murders in Ireland, *Killers*, author Stephen Rae wrote that Macarthur had "noted passages [in the book on forensic medicine] relating to disguising guns and the use of rubber gloves in committing crime".

Macarthur notably wore vinyl gloves when visiting the house of an elderly man he intended to rob on Fitzwilliam Square on Wednesday, 28 July. He also referred to the need to wear them in the notes which contained the plan to kill his mother.

If criminal intent was there, however, the criminal actions remained staggeringly inept. But despite it being a preposterous plan, at some remove from reality, Macarthur clearly invested in this plan as concrete and feasible. Events were marked by a ruthlessness that did not abate even after two callous murders in quick succession, as Macarthur immediately set about planning further violent crimes, intent on satisfying his need for money.

A psychiatrist, speaking privately, told me there were certainly indications of sociopathic behaviour, or perhaps a dissociative disorder. Macarthur had a distant personality to begin with and those who knew him socially described him variously as an eccentric, a loner and an oddball.

In Macarthur's confession to police, detailed in Chapter 27, it is hard not to be struck by a sense of dissociation, the almost nonchalant way he sets out his "cold-hearted operation". "I wanted this hammer to injure somebody," he said. "I wanted this venture to succeed and if, by chance, I did kill anybody in this venture, I would use the shovel to dispose of the body."

Through the long-term prism of detectives John O'Mahony and Tony Hickey, who spent most of their subsequent careers in the force dealing with serious crime and paramilitarism, explanations as to what compelled Macarthur are more prosaic than the ones associated with automatism or a violent childhood.

O'Mahony said he had experienced similar cases elsewhere in his career, where greed could get otherwise rational people to rationalise irrational deeds. For him, the clear motive was money, with the lack of empathy in Macarthur's makeup acting as a further barrier to conscience. O'Mahony referred back to Macarthur's confession, when he told gardaí that robbing banks would give him a "way out of my obsessive financial situation".

"He ran out of money, it was as simple as that," said O'Mahony. "He had a playboy lifestyle, going to the Riviera and Italy and places like that. Then the money had run out. He said 'I need money. Where am I going to get money?' There were a lot of armed robberies at the time. He reckoned he could solve his problems by doing robberies. So the next question he asked is where do I get a gun?

"He was saying, 'I want a lifestyle. I'm not willing to work for the money to pay for that lifestyle. So I'll just rob, and kill anybody who might get in my way.'"

In other words, Macarthur's obsessive need for money had metastasised like a cancer in him, obliterating conscience, or morals, or even consideration for other human life. Could it have been as simple as that in the end? Was it all to do with the money?

As for the question of remorse, Macarthur has never apologised publicly. Nor has he ever given any indication that he considers what he did as unforgivable, or shown any sign that it has caused him – or others – anguish or hurt.

He intimated to his fellow-inmate in 2002 that for him to express remorse publicly would seem callow, but is that really a satisfactory reason for not apologising for the appalling deaths of two young people? His friend in prison is not alone. One other who knows Macarthur well, but does not wish to be named, says he feels remorse, especially in relation to the families of the bereaved. Is that remorse sincere, or merely gestural, because it is what is expected of him? In any instance, after 40 years, would the families of Bridie Gargan and Dónal Dunne accept an apology?

For a man whose life was based on a self-created fiction, it is perhaps fitting that the most rounded explanations of Malcolm Macarthur's stoic silence on the killings might arguably be found in the pages of a work of fiction inspired by the events of the summer of 1982, John Banville's *The Book of Evidence*. The book's anti-hero Freddie Montgomery explains why he showed no remorse for killing a young servant girl. "Remorse implies the expectation of forgiveness and I knew that what I had done was unforgivable. I could have feigned regret and sorrow, guilt, all that but to what end? Even if I had felt such things, truly, in the deepest depths of my heart, would it have altered anything? The deed was done and would not be cancelled by cries of anguish and repentance."

# 47

# MEETING A MURDERER

I meet Malcolm Macarthur in the lobby of a Dublin city centre hotel. It has come about through a colleague of mine at *The Irish Times*, Enda O'Dowd, who had spotted him around his local area and engaged him in conversation. At the time, Enda was editing a podcast I was making about the Macarthur case, *GUBU*, and he asked Macarthur if he would meet with me. He duly agreed, emphasising that he could say nothing about the case. Understandable, given that the terms of his release strenuously forbid him from doing so. Breaking them could risk a return behind bars.

Macarthur arrives looking typically dapper, instantly recognisable from images taken all those decades ago. He's dressed in a light-coloured suit, neatly ironed shirt and well-polished shoes. His wavy black hair has silvered, and these days the ostentatious bow ties have been replaced with more conventional ties.

We sit in the hotel lobby. I order coffee, he declines to have anything. His manner is slightly detached and stand-offish to begin. He tells me the only reason he has agreed to speak to me was because I work for *The Irish Times*.

For the first while, I do most of the talking, aware of his reputation for being aloof or diffident. As Stephen Connolly described it, starting a conversation with him was like casting a fly hoping to get a bite. Eventually, when he does speak, it is at length.

His voice is deep. His accent, though unmistakably Irish, is what is colloquially recognised as "West Brit". Macarthur's way of speaking is measured, reminding you a little of a retired judge: formal in manner, as if reading a deposition.

As we talk over the course of two hours, it is quickly clear that Malcolm Macarthur is a man who likes the sound of his own voice. He speaks on a diverse range of subjects, from his family history to education and literature. He talks of his long years in prison and the grind of his battles to convince successive ministers for justice that he be released after the parole board's recommendation in 2004.

It is clear he is not happy with how the media has treated him over the years. He believes the impunity afforded to publications on the back of his murder conviction led to them writing anything they wanted, even if it had no basis in truth, or was exaggerated or distorted. Two examples that particularly irk him are suggestions of a connection between him and the Charles Self murder and descriptions of him as an "astrologer".

When the conversation strays anywhere near the events of 1982, the shutters come down. It is obvious that he is highly concerned that he might breach the terms of his licence. He repeatedly emphasises how strict the conditions are. He will not speak publicly about the case. He will not speak publicly about his state of mind. He will not speak publicly about the victims. Full stop. As a journalist, I am obliged to respect those boundaries.

Perhaps the most telling signs of his interior life come when he speaks of his family background. The Macarthurs had moved up in the world since John Macarthur had arrived in Glasgow as a penniless stonemason in the 1820s. By the time Malcolm was born, governesses, boarding schools and finishing schools were the norm for the family. However, his own childhood coincided with the family's dramatic decline in fortunes. Instead of Ampleforth in York, it was St Michael's Christian Brothers' School in Trim; instead of Stanford, it was Davis.

As we talk, Macarthur expresses more than a hint of regret and bitterness that he was not in a position to attend the great educational institutions that must from a young age have seemed like his birthright. Like his mother before him, he was proud of his elevated social class. It's clear that his fall from it is not something he has come to terms with, even to this day.

He himself recognises the irony stemming from where he lived out the last years of his prison sentence. The estate of Lord Wicklow, Shelton Abbey, was somewhere he had regularly visited as a young child with his parents. Little could he have guessed then that one day he would live there courtesy of the Irish state, after the once vast house and grounds were sold on and entered their next incarnation as an open prison.

These days, Macarthur lives alone in an apartment. He says he is still in contact with Brenda Little, who lives just a few kilometres away. She has remained as inaccessible to public and media scrutiny as she was 40 years ago when the events occurred.

As his reputation has long suggested, in person Malcolm Macarthur imparts a sense of one who presides above the world of ordinary things, preoccupied by class, status, the exhibition of a high level of intelligence. And while there is clearly nothing down to earth about him, nonetheless what he imparts and what comes across are not necessarily one and the same thing. There is something obtuse, disconnected in how he talks at length, in lofty tones, often about matters of interest to him and him alone.

When we part ways, my lasting impression is not so much of a man above the world of ordinary things as at odds with it, someone perhaps as confused by its mechanisms and inept in its everyday dealings as most of us would be by the precepts of astrophysics.

The only communication that Charles Haughey and Malcolm Macarthur ever had was that extraordinary letter Macarthur sent to the taoiseach from his prison cell. But there are some comparison points in the lives of these two notorious men.

Both shared a fear of poverty and an insatiable desire for money. Status, too, was a premium, as were image and wardrobe. Each had attachments to a grand estate with a Georgian mansion and a beech-lined avenue. Given that both were friends of Paddy Connolly, it is more than a remote possibility, in other circumstances, that they might have met.

But they were on different paths. Their lives crossed when

Haughey was still in the up elevator and Macarthur was plunging rapidly in the opposite direction.

Haughey was a self-made man, who had risen to life in the big house because he was gifted, hard-working, and driven by ego and greed. Macarthur had come from the big house but had frittered away his wealth by leading a vain and feckless life.

Both desperately needed money to maintain their lifestyles. For Haughey, this was brazenly borrowed with no intention of payback. Both were acutely class- and status-conscious. Haughey regarded himself as a chieftain to whom his subjects should give tribute.

Both were corrupt, but there a further comparison can't be drawn out. Whatever moral bankruptcy prevailed at Haughey's core, his misdeeds were in a different league to those of Malcolm Macarthur. For Haughey, a "departure from ethics" might have been an acceptable description for some of his unorthodox methods of wealth accumulation, which a tribunal of inquiry found were corrupt. For Malcolm Macarthur, it was of a different order: he deemed the term fitting to describe murder in cold blood.

Bridie Gargan would have turned 68 in 2023. Her family is very private and has shied away from media interviews over the years. Both the Gargan and the Dunne families were approached for interviews for this book but declined.

In comments soon after Macarthur's release in 2012, Bridie's brother Christopher described to the *Irish Independent* how Bridie was still very much in the hearts of her five sisters and five brothers. Christopher was 14 when his sister died, and he said it had a particular impact on his late parents, Vincent and Bridget. He noted that Macarthur had never apologised but he did not wish him to spend further time in jail.

"He's in his 60s now. I've heard people on the radio saying that he was no longer a threat. I hope so," he said.

Dónal Dunne's brother Christy stopped doing media interviews several years ago. His campaign to have his brother's case reopened took a toll on him and on his family.

"The families have been forgotten, maybe to a large extent," former detective Tony Hickey reflects. "They got life sentences on the Sunday when Dónal Dunne died, and on Monday when Bridie Gargan died of her injuries."

It is over 40 years since the sweltering summer of 1982, unforgettably characterised by murder, mayhem and political scandal. Four decades later, niggling, unsettling questions persist. The brittle yellowed pages of old newspapers provide no complete explanations for the conspiracies, the scandals, the motives.

Macarthur, through his strange reserve, has remained an enigma. His boast to the family cook in the early 1970s, that he was going to leave his mark on western Europe, was never forgotten by his mother.

In 1983, she added a plaintive endnote: "He has certainly done that. I will wake up to what he has done for the rest of my life."

Malcolm Macarthur and Charles Haughey never met in person but in that long, parched summer of 1982 their fates became inextricably linked. For ever after, GUBU would define both men, the murderer and the taoiseach.

# APPENDIX

Transcript of Malcolm Macarthur's confession,
14 August 1982

I affirm that I am responsible for the deaths of nurse Bridie Gargan and farmer Donal Dunne.

I would first like to tell you about the Miss Gargan incident in the Phoenix Park on 22nd of July of this year.

A little while before that day – it may have been a week – I bought a heavy builder's hammer in Lenihan's [hardware shop] of Capel Street.

The reason why I bought this all goes back to money. For the past two years my finances have been diminishing. This was something I could not cope with because during the years 1974 to 1976 I inherited the sum of roughly £70,000, part of the proceeds of the sale of my father's estate at Breemount, Trim, Co Meath. All this I spent because of mismanagement and unwise use. I now realise that I should have invested this money in a profitable manner.

I wanted this hammer to injure somebody [in order to] get a car, to travel down the country to get a gun, because I had no transport. In turn I had planned ahead to stick somebody up and the object was to get money. I had read in the newspapers about all the [IRA] robberies, and this seemed a way out of my obsessive financial situation.

Part of that plan also involved a shovel, because my attitude was that I wanted this venture to succeed, and if by chance I did kill anybody in this venture, I would use the shovel to dispose of the body.

I thought this over when I came back from Tenerife. This was on 8th of July 1982. I was there on 23rd of May with my common-law wife Brenda Little, and our son Colin, who will be seven in October.

I had to return to Ireland on the 8th of July because my finances were bad. I left my wife enough to help her for about two months. I told her I would return to her in between two weeks and three weeks with some money, but my wife Brenda did not know where this money was going to come from or any of my plans.

As soon as I got back to Ireland on the 8th of July I started to consider means of getting money. The first thing was to get a weapon.

I went to two clay pigeon shoots: one in Balheary near Swords on 17th July, and the other in Ashbourne on the following day, a Sunday. At first I want to mention an imitation firearm which I made for myself out of a pistol crossbow, which I purchased at Garnet and Regan [fishing tackle shop] after 8th July in Parliament Street. This thing cost me £22 or £23. I did not have much faith in this weapon so I cut part of the barrel off to make it look more like a pistol.

I built up the top of the barrel with plastic car fillers. I sanded it down to put a fine finish on it and I painted it black. I did this alteration on the pistol while I was staying at a guesthouse which is owned by Mrs Alice Hughes at Upper George's Street Dun Laoghaire. I stayed in this guesthouse because I did not wish anybody to know that I was in Ireland.

After I came back from Tenerife on the 8th of July I started to grow a beard and I purchased a fisherman's hat with an organ or brown feather on the side.

Complete with hammer, shovel (which I wrapped in plastic), pistol, fisherman's hat and a dark-blue holdall bag, which I had brought from Tenerife, I went to these shoots that I mentioned in Balheary and Ashbourne solely for the purpose of getting a weapon; but I did not succeed.

The fisherman's hat, beard, glasses and holdall were used by me solely for the purpose of disguise. The shovel I was carrying was very sharp at the edge and I put tape on it to make it more blunt to prevent it from cutting the plastic bag.

On the 8th of July when I returned to Dublin, I went to the Phoenix Park just to walk around. I did not have any of my disguise outfit on that date.

I remember Thursday, 22nd of July. I left Mrs Hughes's guesthouse some time after 2 o'clock, complete with fisherman's hat, ordinary reading glasses, beard, blue hold-all bag, the hammer – which was in a white plastic bag, a shovel – which was wrapped in the black plastic bag – and also the made-up pistol.

I got a bus into town and I got off the bus in the quays at the terminus. I stood there at the wall for about 15 minutes admiring a sort of floating wooden house which was on the river. I was particularly admiring two lads who were sitting on two chairs on this barge.

It was in the back of my mind that I was back [in Ireland] two weeks and I hadn't got a weapon to get money.

The previous day there was an advert in the Evening Press in relation to the sale of a gun in Edenderry, Co Offaly. I rang this number.

I spoke to a girl after getting through, and she put me on to a fellow called Donal, whom I later learned to be Donal Dunne. I remember this lady saying, "It's for you Donal" when I rang.

I made an arrangement to go to Mr Dunne's house on the Thursday evening, 22nd of July, and he gave me directions as to how to get there. With this in mind, I knew I would need a car for that very evening, 22nd of July, so I left the bus terminus and walked along the quays and up to the Phoenix Park.

I entered the park through the Conyngham Road entrance at approximately 4pm that evening. Before I entered the park,

I bought an orange in a small sweetshop on the quays. I stayed there for a couple of minutes.

From there I walked along by the cricket grounds. I walked parallel to the main road, along the joggers' track, carrying the items which included the blue holdall bag. I carried the shovel wrapped in plastic in the other hand.

I was wearing the fisherman's hat, beard, a fawn coloured crew-necked jumper, army type, with patches on the elbows and shoulder. I wore a white shirt, a grey pants and orange shoes.

I crossed the road in front of the American Ambassador's again as I was going towards Castleknock.

When I crossed the road I walked between two straight lines of trees. Before I got to the American Ambassador's residence I looked at a few cars but they did not seem easy prey and I walked on.

As I walked along the row of trees I saw somebody lying in the long grass to the left of these trees. I saw a car parked beside this person and I think the driver's door was open.

The car, which was silver in colour, was facing out towards the main road.

I walked past the car and I decided to make an approach. I did not know at this stage whether it was a man or a woman who was lying beside this car.

I then put my shovel, which was wrapped in black plastic, on the ground beside a tree, and I approached this vehicle.

As I walked towards the car I had this imitation gun in my right hand and the holdall bag in my left. When I came within a few feet I saw that it was a lady who was sunbathing topless. I pointed the gun at her and told her to get in to the car.

She was very calm and she said: "Is this for real?" and I said: "Yes, it is."

She then calmly said: "May I put back on my clothes?" and I said: "Yes."

She put on a blousy top and she did not appear to have any bra on.

She then got in to the back seat of the car. I assured her that I wanted her car. I told her to lie on the back seat and that I would tie her up.

She then began to panic, and I panicked because she would not lie on the seat. I was afraid that she was going to draw attention to us, so I took out the hammer from the bag and I hit her a couple of times, because the first blow did not do what I expected it to do.

There was blood all over her, and some on the window and more on the seats. I used a newspaper to wipe some of the blood off the left side window.

When I was cleaning this window, I saw a gentleman walking towards the car.

He walked around the front of the car and he said: "Is this serious?" or something like that.

I got out of the car and produced the pistol. I pointed the weapon at him. He stood there for a while and then he ran at me and grabbed the gun.

We wrestled for about ten seconds and this man who was bigger and stronger than me, eventually let me go. If it had been a real gun, and he had made a more successful attempt to block my escape, I may have shot him.

I then jumped into this car (a Renault 5) and drove off along the dirt track. As I did so, I saw this man out on the main road trying to hail down a car.

When I reached the end of the dirt track, I turned right in front of the Embassy and along a road which I know fairly well. I was travelling fast in a low gear, because I was not used to the car.

The girl was moving around in the back seat.

Before I got out on the main road by way of the gate at Islandbridge, I passed an ambulance. I arrived at the gate first, and the ambulance drove up on my outside. I drove out the gate and turned left and the ambulance again pulled up beside me.

The passenger put out his head and said: "Follow us" or something to that effect.

I followed the ambulance. It turned right at Islandbridge and I followed him until the ambulance went into a hospital.

During the time while I was following the ambulance I was less desperate, but when I turned into the hospital I felt that my need to escape reasserted itself and I wheeled around the driveway and back out the same way.

I think I turned to my left after going out that gate and drove in towards town.

I then got the feeling that I should leave the car and run away. I took a left turn into a narrow laneway and I abandoned the car there.

I ran back out the same way and ran left along the South Circular Road. I was still wearing the hat and the fawn crew neck pullover and I was still carrying the bag. I left the builder's hammer in the Renault 5 and I left the shovel beside where I first saw the girl sunbathing.

As I ran along the South Circular Road, I noticed some blood on the front of my crew neck pullover so I took it off along with the hat. I went in to a laneway to the left and I left the jumper on some waste ground somewhere near Players Wills factory. I think I put the hat under the wire somewhere.

I was getting concerned that the police might catch me and I tried to get a bus at the bus stop but it did not stop.

I then saw the front door of a house open. I walked in. It had the name 'Odyssey' on it. I saw a big pile of leaflets on the floor referring to holidays. I took it then that this was some type of travel agency.

I asked the lady if it was an agent for the Magic Bus. I used this talk to explain and to delay my presence.

I was panting from the running, and she offered me some water. I drank two or three glasses. I then asked her if she could call me a taxi and that I wanted to go to Blackrock.

I explained my breathlessness by running on too hot a day in the Phoenix Park and forgetting my salt tablets. I remained in this premises for three to four minutes and when I left I got a bus just outside the door. This would have been after 5.30pm.

The bus stopped outside a row of three shops and a pub called the Fingal House. I went in to a general shop that sold a few chemist items and I bought three disposable razors in a plastic bag.

I went to the gents' toilet in the Fingal House. I used all three blades and shaved off my beard there. I left two of these razors after me on the floor beside the toilet. I shaved myself over the cistern in the toilet and I brought one of them with me.

I did not use any soap while shaving and it took a long time.

When I was in the toilet, a number of gentlemen came in and out and one of them spoke to me.

When I had finished shaving I went to the lounge and I had a soda water.

I then rang a taxi and this taxi came pretty quickly. I was waiting at the pub door for him. This would have been around seven o'clock in the evening.

The taxi man was youngish – either mid or late twenties. I asked him to take me to town and when I got to town, I extended the run to Dun Laoghaire. The taxi dropped me off near where you go into the Mail Boat. I had the holdall bag with me all this time.

When I got back to Mrs Hughes' I noticed that there was some blood on the back of my shirt, so I changed out of the shirt and trousers and later on that evening I walked down to the sea near the East Pier and threw both items of clothing into the sea.

Some days later I threw the plastic gun that I used into the sea at Bulloch Harbour. I would imagine that it may still be there as it was a bit heavy. I will point out the spot to you.

I had an appointment to see Donal Dunne in Edenderry on Thursday. As far as I remember, I rang Dunne's home on Friday the 23rd, the day after I attacked Nurse Gargan in the Phoenix Park. I was talking to a lady and I made some excuse that my brother had been involved in a car accident and I apologised for not going down to Edenderry. I told her that I would try and get down there on Saturday or Sunday of the same week.

The following evening Saturday 24th, I got a country bus from Busaras to Edenderry at approximately 6.30pm. The fare was two or three pounds. I got off the bus in a big square where the bus stops at approximately 7.30pm to 8pm.

I walked up the long main street and I thought of going to Mr Dunne's. I forgot about what I was down there for, for the time being, and I just enjoyed a walk along the canal bank.

Later on that evening I got a lift from a man in a car – I cannot describe it. The man gave me an idea where Dunne's house was but he wasn't sure.

I went to a new bungalow. I asked directions to the Dunne homestead from a man in his 20s who lived in the bungalow at the end of a boreen that led to Dunne's house. It was getting dark and he pointed at the lights and said: "That the house down there, where those lights were." It was now approximately 10pm.

I then went halfway to Dunne's house but I got cold feet. The determination was not there and I turned back. I walked back through the town and back again to the canal bank. I stayed there that night. I did not sleep. I was carrying a black plastic bag with a toothbrush and razor in it.

On Sunday morning, July 25th, I spoke to two men who were near the canal. One was out for an early morning walk and the other was out checking his cattle.

I also met two lads who were in their early 20s who were camping by the canal. They also had a motorcycle. One of these lads asked me for the time and I told him that it was 8am.

About 9am the shops opened and I bought a Sunday paper. I thought it was The Sunday Press. I also bought a pint of milk and some fruit which I brought back to the canal along with the paper.

I took my time there and read the paper. When I was finished with the paper I threw it into a waste paper bin somewhere near the canal. I think I threw the milk carton and orange skins in with it.

I then spent about a half an hour watching people – about three people in all – taking out a barge on the canal.

At approximately 11.30am I walked form the canal into town to the telephone box and I rang up Mr Dunne who answered the phone. I told him that I was in Edenderry and that if it was suitable that I would like to see the gun. We agreed to meet at the phone box. He said he would drive in.

He arrived in a silver-coloured Ford car some time after – I'd say it was around 12 noon. He told me that he had the gun with him in the boot. He passed a remark like, "We won't look at it here in the middle of the street", so he drove some distance outside town, at the edge of a bog, in a flattish area. He told me that this was their gun club grounds.

We got out of the car and Mr Dunne took the gun from the boot. It was in a case. He told me that he did not really have to sell the gun but that if he got what he paid for it, he would sell it. He told me that it cost him £1,100 but that he would not sell it at a loss. I wanted a gun badly but I did not want to buy it or I could not buy it.

Mr Dunne put two cartridges in the gun and I shot at a target which was a white post. I don't know if I hit it or not.

I was trying to think of a way of getting this gun without paying for it and I was playing for time. Mr Dunne then got a bit angry and reached out and put his hand on some part of the gun to take it.

I pulled back and pulled the trigger and I shot him in the head. He fell down. I ran towards Mr Dunne's silver car and I left the gun beside it.

I then went back to Mr Dunne and I saw that his head was in a mess. I pulled his body into some bushes and I broke some branches to cover him up.

I then went back to his car and I put the gun inside lying between the two front seats. I drove off in this car towards Dublin, through Rathangan, Prosperous, Clane, Maynooth, Lucan and into Dublin. I turned right at Chapelizod Bridge and went up through Ballyfermot.

I came up as far as the canal and I crossed it and I drove along the south side of it, I think it was at Portobello Bridge that I took a left turn and headed towards Camden Street. I left the car beside the Central Bank.

I took the gun, a few cartridges and my bag from the car. I put the gun into my raincoat and locked the car. I think I took a No 8 bus to Dun Laoghaire. This would have been around 3pm.

I brought the gun with me to my digs at Mrs Hughes' house. A couple of days after that I cut about 12 inches off the barrels of this gun.

On Wednesday 4th of July I left my digs at approximately 4pm and I got a bus to Killiney.

I walked to a house called Camelot on top of Killiney Hill. This house is like a small castle and is owned by Mr Harry Bieling.

I thought that he would have money. I was in his house eight or nine times in all, around 1975, and we were friends then.

I pretended that I wanted to take some photographs from his window but instead produced the gun that came from Edenderry and I pointed it at him and I demanded £1,000.

He told me that he did not have that kind of money. I then suggested to him that he could give me a cheque for £1,000 and that a fictitious accomplice, who I said was working with me, could go to the bank and cash this cheque.

I had earlier opened an account in the Allied Irish Bank opposite the shopping centre in Dun Laoghaire village for the amount of £10. I opened this account in the name of John Eustace, using a false address at Oak Road, Dun Laoghaire. I later withdrew £7 from this account to give the bank staff the impression that the account was being used.

Harry Bieling made good his escape by running out the front door. I don't know whether I would have shot him or not.

After Harry Bieling had run away from his house, I ran over Killiney Hill. After that I called to another house on the same road and a lady answered the door. I had the gun with me and I wanted her to ring a taxi for me. She told me that her phone was out of order and she did not open the door for me.

I then left and a car came along with some people in it who were going fishing. They gave me a lift to Dalkey. I think the man who was driving this car was American but he said that he lived in Killiney.

I then went to a friend of mine in Pilot View and I have been living there ever since.

The next morning I brought the gun away and left it under a bush in Merrion Square. I only brought the gun to this address again on Friday 13th of August. That is the same gun that I handed over to gardaí yesterday.

This statement has been read over to me and it is correct.

Signed: Malcolm Edward Daniel Macarthur.

# Acknowledgements

Writing a book about events that occurred over four decades ago was always an undertaking that would involve some uncertainty. Some of the main protagonists had died and others were no longer contactable. Luckily, there were plenty who were only too willing to help.

First and foremost, I would like to thank Enda O'Dowd. Without the unstinting collaboration of my talented *Irish Times* colleague, the project would not have been possible. He was the editor of the podcast series *GUBU*, which provided the impetus for the book.

I wish to thank former garda assistant commissioners Tony Hickey and John O'Mahony, and former garda detective inspector Brian Sherry. Their granular recollection of this unique investigation from 40 years ago provided the spine of the narrative.

Peter Murtagh of *The Irish Times* was the journalist closest to the events that occurred during the extraordinary year of 1982. He was most generous in giving his time to recount his memories, including media events in which he was a central player.

I deeply appreciate the kind assistance of other journalists who shared their personal observations of those events: Olivia O'Leary, Emily O'Reilly, Brenda Power and Henry Bauress.

On the political side of things, I am extremely grateful to both Bertie Ahern and Frank Dunlop who gave great insider perspectives on what happened during that crucial period. Stephen Connolly, who was only 18 in 1982, recalled the events with great acuity and insight.

I wish to thank two other *Irish Times* colleagues who were centrally involved in the project: senior audio producer Declan Conlon and sound engineer JJ Vernon.

I wish to acknowledge *Irish Times* editor Ruadhán Mac Cormaic, news editor Mark Hennessy, and political editor Pat Leahy, all of whom have given such strong support and accommodated all my unreasonable requests for more time. I wish to thank *The Irish Times* for the use of photographs used in the book.

This book would not have been what it is without the trojan work of my publisher and editor, Ciara Considine of Hachette Ireland, who brought a great editorial eye, was an astute judge of what worked and what did not and injected great energy into the process. I am also extremely grateful to the wonderful Faith O'Grady of the Lisa Richards Agency. Thanks also to the whole team at Hachette Ireland, especially Joanna Smyth, Elaine Egan and Stephen Riordan.

On a personal level, I would like to acknowledge my late

# Acknowledgements

mother, Dr Eithne Conway McGee, whose dedication to others throughout her life inspired me and many others. Also my late father, Michael McGee, and my siblings, Isbéal, Dara and Micheál Óg. During my research, it was a great moment to reach for a book, *Meath: Towards a History*, written by my grandmother Margaret Conway from Ballivor: teacher, local historian and archaeologist.

Thanks to my friends, including the late John H Bourke, for their ongoing advice.

I am grateful beyond words to Fiona Breslin for her continuous love and for being a tower of strength. She was a very perceptive reader of the text. A special thanks too to our daughter Sadhbh who is the apple of our eye. Also to Fiona's parents, John Breslin and the late Ann Breslin, who gave great support.

Two young people, by a terrible quirk of fate, died at the hands of Malcolm Macarthur. We remember them by their names: Bridie Gargan and Dónal Dunne.